AT RANDOM

AT
RANDOM

The Reminiscences
of
BENNETT CERF

Random House New York

Library of Congress Cataloging in Publication Data
Cerf, Bennett Alfred, 1898–1971.
At Random.
1. Cerf, Bennett Alfred, 1898–1971. 2. Publishers
and publishing—United States—Biography. I. Title.
Z473.C45A36 1977   070.5′092′4 [B] 75–10254
ISBN 0-394-47877-0

Manufactured in the United States of America
24689753
First Edition

Design by Bernard Klein

LIST OF ILLUSTRATIONS

EDITORS' NOTE

Between September, 1967, and February, 1968, Mary R. Hawkins of the Columbia Oral History program held twenty-one lengthy question-and-answer interviews with Bennett Cerf. These were tape-recorded and transcribed, and after his preliminary corrections, they were retyped. In March, 1971, he wrote additional notes to bring the History up to that date.

It was his intention to write *At Random* (his title), working from that typescript of over a thousand pages, cutting out the questions, rearranging, correcting and embellishing the text and adding things that had not come to his mind during the interviews. Before his sudden death in August, 1971, he had already started, and during the last months of his life he talked frequently with us and others about his plans for the book. If he had lived to write it, we would certainly have been involved with him in the process, instead of sadly trying in his absence to carry out his intentions.

Though the Oral History is the principal source of *At Random,* it is by no means the only one. We were greatly aided by the fact that probably few people have ever documented their lives as methodically as Bennett did: daily diaries that began during his student days at Columbia and longer ones for trips abroad; elaborate and massive scrapbooks that are a reference library in themselves, containing clippings of news stories about Random House and later about himself, as well as the hundreds of pieces he wrote for publication; numerous bulky files of correspondence which he kept neatly in order (he threw away very little, apparently).

All of these have been invaluable in straightening out dates and facts when Bennett's memory occasionally faltered. More important, they have contributed materially to the contents of this book. When we found pieces that he wrote long ago to be superior to his treatment of the same subjects in the Oral History, we included them instead. Several sequences from his trip diaries, written on the spot, were more interesting and circumstantial than what, many years later, he remembered in the interviews, and they have therefore been substituted. Finally, in selecting from the great bulk of the Oral History, we have been guided by his own title for the book and by what we think he would himself have done, so that the result is primarily about publishing and his preeminent role in it.

PHYLLIS CERF WAGNER
ALBERT ERSKINE

AT RANDOM

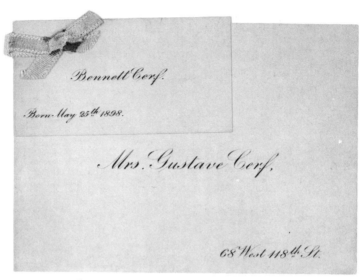

Birth announcement. Annotated in Bennett's scrapbook:
"and that's how the trouble started"

I am a rather unusual specimen in that not only I but all four of my grandparents and both of my parents were born on the island of Manhattan. My father's family were of Alsatian extraction and my mother's family were Germans named Wise. My father's father, Marcel Cerf, was a jeweler. The Cerf family was loaded with charm but little money, while the Wise family had very little charm but a lot of money. My grandfather, Nathan Wise, owned a tobacco-distributing business called the Metropolitan Tobacco Company and in his very conservative way amassed a fortune of over a million dollars. The way that money was eventually divided was very important in the beginning of my career.

Everybody kowtowed to my Grandfather Wise, a rather stern man with a beard—he looked like one of the Smith Brothers then pictured on cough-drop boxes. I saw him mainly on Sundays, the day reserved for having dinner with him and the rest of the family. My mother was one of six children, three boys and three girls. Grandfather had a private house and lived in some elegance, and he had the first automobile I ever saw. He also had a great backhand. At the dinner table he'd reach across and wallop you so fast, you couldn't see it coming. So the object was to sit as far as possible from Grandpa at Sunday dinners. In the afternoon when he would take a nap, the house had to be silent as a church. I never was quiet in my life, and I was usually the one who woke him up and got the back of his hand.

My father, Gustave Cerf, was a very handsome, charming, wonderful man—I absolutely adored him and so did everyone else. He was a lithographer by profession, gave elocution lessons on the side, and at one time even contemplated being a professional ballplayer. He had been a semi-pro catcher on weekends, and in 1892 he even got a tryout with the Brooklyn Dodgers. For the rest of his life we teased him about not being able to hit Big League pitching, and no matter how many times we kidded him, he'd always give a long explanation as to why he hadn't made it.

My father and mother met each other in a rather curious way. Not too many girls went to college then, not in the circles my family moved in, anyway. But when my parents were young, it was considered quite the thing for respectable young ladies to take elocution lessons and recite things like "The Boy Stood on the Burning Deck." So a teacher was hired for my mother, Frederika Wise, and the gentleman who gave her those elocution lessons was my father. The teacher and pupil fell madly in love, and eloped—to the outrage of my grandfather, who looked upon my father as a

Bennett with father, October 1, 1899

charming fly-by-night. And these two people were gloriously in love for their entire life together. So I was born into a very happy family.

The house I was born in is now in one of the most run-down sections of New York—118th Street, just off Seventh Avenue—but at the time it was mostly a prosperous Jewish neighborhood. Then, very early in my life, we moved to a nearby apartment house called the Douglas, which was at 201 West 121st Street.

My father was a very proud man and we lived only on what he made himself. I was brought up as a city child, playing stickball in the streets with a bunch of tough little kids, a lot of whom became very famous. Playing in the streets wasn't as dangerous then as it is today; automobiles were just beginning to appear. We used to roller-skate all over the town, hitching onto ice wagons. It was great to reach in and grab little pieces of ice. And you could also play "punch the ball" out in the middle of the street and not have to run to the sidewalk too often.

We kids were great baseball fans. (I was initiated by my father, who started taking me to games when I was five years old.) In those days the *New York Herald* had a branch office at 125th Street and Seventh Avenue, and out front was a baseball scoreboard. A boy used to come out every once in a while with a rubber pad and stamp the scores on that board. Since there

At about age four

At about age six

was no radio then and, of course, no television, we would stand there after school and wait for that boy to post the scores. When he'd come out, we'd yell, "What happened?" But he always played God and wouldn't answer us; he just stamped those numbers up. We were great N.Y. Giant fans and always hated the Brooklyn Dodgers, even though Pop had once come close to playing with them. They were the enemy.

I went to Public School 10, which was at 117th Street and St. Nicholas Avenue. On my first day my mother dressed me in a Buster Brown outfit, and when I appeared with that big collar and flowing bow, I became the center of attention of the Irish kids from down around Manhattan Avenue and Eighth Avenue. I came home with the collar ripped and my nose bleeding, screaming with rage. I wasn't angry at the boys who jumped me; I was furious with my mother for dressing me in such a manner. I was her pride and joy, her only child, and I am told that though I wasn't exactly spoiled, on suitable occasions I sometimes resorted to holding my breath to get my own way. I have no memory of whether this was one of those times or not, but I do know that I never wore a Buster Brown collar and tie to school again. P.S. 10 was a great school. We considered it a privilege to be students there. We were proud of it, and there were a lot of smart kids in P.S. 10. Some of them became my lifelong friends. One of the boys was Howard Dietz, who became a well-known playwright. He wrote *The Bandwagon*. When he was head of the MGM publicity department, he changed the name of a little actress from Lucille Le Sueur to Joan Crawford.

One of the other graduates of that school was Morty Rodgers, who became a great gynecologist and delivered my two sons. His kid brother, whom we used to kick around the house and tell to "get out of here," became reasonably well known, too. His name is Richard Rodgers, whose hit shows—*Pal Joey, Oklahoma!, South Pacific, The Sound of Music*—have enriched him and the world of music. The principal of P.S. 10 was a man named Dr. Birkens, whom everybody adored. One of the teachers, Abe Greenberg, was also the coach of the athletic teams, and he was so good that P.S. 10 won the interscholastic championship year after year after year. I have always been near-sighted, but I could run, so I was on the relay team.

A love of reading came when I was very young. At first it was magazines, and those that I remember with particular affection were called *Popular* and *Top-notch*. They had baseball stories and football stories and adventure stories—very tame by present-day standards, but I liked them. The *Saturday Evening Post* was a popular magazine then, and all of us used to peddle it. We'd put a white bag filled with copies of the magazine over our shoulders, then park ourselves at the entrance of a subway station or some other busy location. A copy of the magazine cost five cents, and we got prizes according to the number we sold.

The first books I remember were the Rover Boys and the Motor Boys and the Putnam Hall Cadets. And then I found there was a branch of the public library at 123rd Street and Lenox Avenue; my friends and I joined it and discovered together an author named Ralph Henry Barbour. I still recall the titles of some of his books: *The Crimson Sweater, For the Honor of the School* and *Four in Camp* and *Four Afloat*. This was a step up from *Top-notch*—a first step. My mother always liked books. She saw to it that I

At about age twelve

read the children's stories of the day, like *Black Beauty* and *Rebecca of Sunnybrook Farm*. But as to the really good books, my parents didn't know much about them. My Uncle Herbert was the greatest influence on my young life. He was my mother's brother—only five years older than I was and never terribly strong. He was one of the most brilliant people I have ever met—absolutely brilliant. I felt he knew everything.

In 1911 we moved up to Riverside Drive and 157th Street, just about the time I graduated from P.S. 10, salutatorian of my class. Our new home was in an apartment house called the Riviera, and I remember we were on the twelfth floor. We looked right out over Audubon Park on the Hudson River.

Back then, Washington Heights was not yet built up. Just south of where the George Washington Bridge is, the first of the big apartment

With mother and father

buildings were beginning to go up, like the Riviera, which is still standing. You could look out our windows and see the trains go by on the West Side tracks of the New York Central, and another great pleasure was watching the river traffic, especially the night boat to Albany, with the searchlights playing from one side of the Hudson to the other. A lot of people took it to go to the Adirondacks. They'd go by boat to Albany, and then take a train. I remember going to camp that way, and the thrill of actually being on the boat instead of watching it from a window. From the time I was twelve till about fifteen, I went to camp every summer with Morty Rodgers, and when his brother Dick started to grow up, with Dick and his future collaborator, Larry Hart.

I was almost thirteen at the time we moved to Washington Heights. Though both my mother and father were Jewish, I had never even been inside a temple. A lot of the kids my age in the neighborhood started announcing they were going to be bar-mitzvahed. When they all got bicycles after going through the ceremony, I demanded to be bar-mitzvahed too, to the absolute amazement of my parents. I got my bicycle, all right, but I wasn't allowed to ride it in the city streets because my mother thought it was too dangerous.

There were three high schools that most of the uptown kids went to—Commerce, Clinton and Townsend Harris. Commerce and Clinton were downtown, relatively, in the Sixties. Townsend Harris was part of City College of New York, and the remarkable thing about it was that it provided a full curriculum which could be completed in three years, whereas in the other high schools you had to go for four. But to get into Townsend Harris you had to have superior marks in public school, and when you got there, you had to work like hell. I worked harder there than I ever did in college, which was a breeze after Townsend Harris. The dropouts were fantastic. In the first year over half the class would flunk out.

It was in high school that I began to read better books: *Ivanhoe, Silas Marner, The Oregon Trail.* I loved *Ivanhoe,* and that started me on Walter Scott. But I was still reading popular magazines. Also around this time I published my first piece in the *St. Nicholas* magazine; it was titled "How I Spent My Vacation" and I got a silver badge for it.

As I look back, it was when we lived at the Riviera that I started my real life, because in that building there was Howard Dietz, who had also moved uptown, and another friend, Merryle Rukeyser, who later became financial editor for all the Hearst newspapers. And across the street lived a boy named Elliot Sanger, of the Sanger family that owned one of the great stores in Dallas. Elliot would later be one of the founders of the radio station WQXR. We were a group of kids who in later life became quite successful—and we all went to Townsend Harris.

None of us boys were given much money to spend. I had an allowance, as I remember, of a dollar a week. We couldn't really indulge ourselves too much. But there was a vaudeville house on Seventh Avenue between 125th and 126th, the Alhambra. This was big-time vaudeville, and we were regular patrons. We'd sit up in the balcony, where a seat cost twenty-five cents. There was a candy store called Simonette's right next to the theater. We'd get a half pound of caramels in a light-blue box, and a whole bunch of kids would divide them up; that meant about three for each of us. I remember it with pleasure—I can still taste those caramels, chocolate and vanilla. They were great. Movies were just starting, and we began to go to those, too—we'd see three or four one-reelers for a nickel. These were shown in old abandoned stores; one was called the Nickelette, another the Nickelodeon.

Howard Dietz and I later found out about the cut-rate Leblang's ticket agency at 43rd Street and Broadway, where you could get an orchestra seat for a play for about a dollar, way in the back, of course; we didn't know there was anything in front of the fourteenth row. So we began to haunt Broadway on Saturdays because we both loved the theater, something I've never gotten out of my system. To this day, walking backstage gives me a thrill.

I think the first big show we saw was called something like *Top o' the World,* a musical. Then Dietz entered a contest that was given by the Strauss

Theater Program Company, which printed the programs for all the theaters. You were given three lines of a poem and had to write the fourth, some kind of little jingle. Dietz won one of the prizes. And the prize was two seats in the sixth row of the orchestra for the Astor Theatre Saturday matinée. I don't remember the name of the show but I remember the theater. Dietz invited me—and *I* treated *him* to lunch. We both recall to this day that we ate at a place called Lauber's on 39th Street, where we got an eight-course luncheon for sixty-five cents. We had to show the cash before they would feed us—we didn't look like regular patrons. We were kids, a couple of kids in short pants. Then we went to the theater and sat in the sixth-row center of the orchestra. That to me was such a thrill, I still remember walking in and being ushered to those seats and the pride we had sitting there.

On the day before my sixteenth birthday my childhood ended abruptly. My mother died. She had always been desperately anxious to have another child. She'd had several miscarriages, but she persisted, and when I was fifteen a little girl was born who lived only about two weeks. The pregnancy and birth weakened my mother and she never really recovered.

From the day of my mother's death I became the financial head of the family. My grandfather, a very shrewd man, had loved my father, but he didn't trust him with money because he feared Pop would lose it in no time. Pop was the soft touch of the world, and anybody who asked him for anything got it. So my grandfather had left money to my mother in trust for me, and after she died I came into just about $125,000. One of the six children who inherited my grandfather's estate was my Uncle Herbert, Herbert Wise—and when my mother died he came to live with my father and me, and all three of us adored each other.

With father at Pikes Peak, September 6, 1914

At the age of sixteen I decided I was going to learn to be a businessman, and that meant I'd have to go to another kind of school. My handwriting was very bad and I didn't know anything about bookkeeping, but I was determined to become a tycoon. I hated to leave Townsend

• 11 •

Harris for many reasons. By this time I was writing stories for the school magazine and was one of the top students there. Also, I was on the soccer team—even I could see a soccer ball! But I had made up my mind that I was going to make money, so I quit and went to the Packard Commercial School. This enraged Uncle Herbert, but I did it anyway. It was a mighty stupid move in some ways, but luckily it worked out well for me. For one thing, my handwriting improved: they taught the Palmer method in those days. I also learned double-entry bookkeeping and began to know something about the business world. After school I worked for a certified accountant and went around with him to check his clients' books. In this way I got backstage of a big restaurant and learned that all the money's in liquor, not in food. I saw how department stores and various other businesses operated, and I became interested in all of them. Thus I had a lot of experience while I was still in the business school.

During my year at Packard and my job with the accountant, Uncle Herbert continued to talk to me about going to college; and if I hadn't taken his advice, God knows what would have happened to me.

I didn't have enough credits, since I hadn't graduated from high school. I decided in January that I was going to college if I could, so I had until September to get all my entrance requirements. I went to Columbia and took several extension courses, and my uncle coached me in a couple of other subjects.

I quickly decided, after looking at the required courses, that I could never learn Latin or Greek; I had no aptitude at all in that direction. I discovered that at the School of Journalism you didn't need those languages, so then and there I decided that was the place for me. (It was then an undergraduate school. It became a graduate school some years later.) But I still didn't have enough credits. Although I never was good at algebra, I had counted on being able to pass the exam—for the last two points I needed. But I flunked. I simply couldn't do it. So I took an exam in free-hand drawing, which almost anyone could do, and I passed that. That was one point. Then I took advanced French. This was a desperate gamble, because if I didn't get that last extra point, I was dead. But I passed and got into the School of Journalism.

That summer Morty Rodgers had the next locker to me in gym class, and we continued our friendship. Morty's father, Dr. William A. Rodgers, was a very important man in my opinion because one of his patients was my dream girl, Norma Talmadge, the beautiful movie star, and the idea that she was one of his patients dazzled me. I remember pleading with him to let me carry his bag when he went to see her. It was Morty Rodgers who introduced me to the fraternity I joined: Pi Lambda Phi. The head of the fraternity was young Oscar Hammerstein II. A boy named Horace

Manges—who became the lawyer not only for Random House but for a half-dozen other big publishers—was also a member. Richard Rodgers soon joined it, and Rodgers and Hammerstein got me more and more interested in the theater.

The School of Journalism in those days was very famous, and while I was there it attracted such young men as my friend Howard Dietz, and George Sokolsky, Morrie Ryskind, Corey Ford and Max Schuster. Richard Simon, the other half of the future Simon and Schuster, was also there, but in the College.

In my freshman year I became pretty well set. First of all, I was already in a fraternity. I didn't have to worry about that, as most freshmen did. Second, I went out for the college newspaper, the *Spectator*. The fellow who had written a column had just graduated, so they had the problem of who was going to take his place. I submitted several samples, and suddenly, and only a freshman, I was the columnist for the Columbia paper! Well, this was an open sesame to everybody and everything. I was elected vice-president of the class.

The freshman

• 13 •

The *Spectator* column I wrote was called "The Stroller." It was not a gossip column, though there were little pieces about personalities on the campus. I also tried to start controversies about the city government and the dismal subway service, demanding that 116th Street be made an express station—that kind of stuff. "The Stroller" was lively—and it was read! Soon I began sending in little things to *Jester*, the humor magazine, and I became even better known.

Not the least important thing that happened to me was that one of my freshman classes was with a professor named Harrison Steeves, and I will never forget Professor Steeves, because in his course we had to study contemporary authors. In those days the English authors were the popular ones. (This was around 1917. There have been great changes in the publishing business since then, and I like to believe I contributed to them.) There were very few popular Americans. There was one, Henry Sydnor Harrison, two of whose books I remember—a best seller called *Queed* and one called *V. V.'s Eyes.* They're forgotten today, but were then considered outstanding literature. And of course, many Americans were reading books like *Pollyanna.* The professor also introduced me to H. G. Wells and Galsworthy; to Kipling's *Jungle Stories* and *Kim;* and Arnold Bennett's *Old Wives' Tale.* I discovered for myself that there were authors like Anatole France, Theodore Dreiser and James Branch Cabell, and I began to appreciate good writing.

Steeves suddenly popped back into my life many years later. He had written a detective story, *Good Night, Sheriff*, not a very good one, but he brought it down to me, and I was so grateful for what he had done for me that I published it in 1941. It didn't sell very well; it didn't deserve to. But it pleased me to do it. I was making him very happy—this austere English professor who had written a mystery novel.

I soon discovered that if I played my cards right at Columbia, I could get two degrees at the same time—a B.Lit. at Journalism, and a B.A. at the College—without doing too much work. This required manipulating, but I thought that added to the fun. In 1917, right at the beginning of my college career, we got into the war. At that time there was something comparable to the ROTC: it was called the SATC, the Student Army Training Corps. We all became members and wore uniforms. One of my first exploits in the SATC was the day I was commander of the company and I had them in company rank marching across South Field (which is now all covered with buildings). As they were walking toward the grandstand I panicked, and couldn't think of how to stop them. So to their intense delight, they went marching up into the stand, the whole company, while the real officers howled with laughter. I was not cut out for an army career. But anyway, I made a good story of all this in the column.

When the call came for officers' training school, I applied for and was accepted by the infantry training school down in Camp Lee, Virginia, bucking for second lieutenant. Since I was the night editor of *Spectator* when the rule came through that anybody going off to the war would get full credit for any course he had signed up for, without even having to take it, I saw the notice the day before it appeared in the paper. So I rushed over to sign up for all the courses I could and then went to the dean for an okay. He looked at my program and said, "This is an interesting course you've planned out. I figure it would take about sixteen hours of homework a day to really do it right."

I said, "Really, sir?"

He said, "You haven't by any chance seen the rule that you're going to get credit for everything you've signed up for before you go away to camp?"

I said, "I don't know what you're talking about, Dean."

He said, "I didn't think so," and he stamped his approval.

So off I went. I was at Camp Lee until the war ended. I got credit for advanced geometry, something I could never do, and a couple of other science courses where you have to be exact—and I was terrible at those things. In history, economics and literature I was great. I'm very good at adding figures, too, but when it comes to algebra or quadratics or geometry, I'm absolutely hopeless.

Just as I returned to college, Morrie Ryskind, the editor of *Jester*, left Columbia, and in my sophomore year I was made editor in chief of the magazine—that was heady stuff!

Being editor of the *Jester* was a great experience for me, so I was delighted that both my boys worked on a college humor magazine. Chris was the vice-president of the *Harvard Lampoon*, of which Jon later became president. Chris's first book, *The World's Largest Cheese*, was published by

Illustration for Jester *cover, December, 1917*

Doubleday in 1968; it has all the things he wrote for the *Lampoon* and other pieces done since. He's a great boy. They're both great boys.

To improve the *Jester,* I quickly started both a book-review column and a drama column—the drama column, of course, got us free theater tickets. Then I thought that this could finally be my chance to meet Norma Talmadge, my dream girl. So I wrote a letter asking if I could interview her for the Columbia *Jester,* and a reply came setting up a date. Soon the whole campus knew I was going to meet Norma Talmadge. I was so darn excited about it, but when the day came, I lost my nerve; I was afraid to face her, and I never went. I wrote a glowing interview, anyway—faked the whole thing, ran it in *Jester* and sent copies to Norma Talmadge. I got a warm letter from her in return, saying she had enjoyed meeting me so much and that the interview was masterful and she hoped we'd meet someday again soon. The letter was framed and put up in the *Jester* office.

There was a course at Columbia called Comparative Literature, which was one of those cinches where you got two points for doing practically nothing. The whole football team and the entire staff of *Jester,* including me—all the finaglers—were taking it. The professor who gave the course was Henry Wadsworth Longfellow Dana. He was a great-nephew, or maybe just a nephew, of the poet Longfellow. We had out first class with him, and the next day Dr. Butler kicked him out of Columbia because he was a pacifist. We were just being thrown into a war, and here was Dana making very pacifist statements and joining I-didn't-raise-my-boy-to-be-a-soldier groups. If his name had been Smith or Jones, I don't think Butler or anybody else would have given a darn. He was only an obscure English teacher up at Columbia, but since he was named Henry Wadsworth Longfellow Dana, the papers quoted at length everything he said. It took two lines just to print his name. And Butler was infuriated, so Dana got the heave-ho.

Now all we dedicated students rejoiced: "It will take them a month to get another professor." We went to the next class expecting to see a little white notice on the door saying there would be no class until they got a new teacher. But overnight they did dig one up, and to our disgust, he was standing there, ready for action, when we came in. His name was Raymond Weaver. He had a very deep, mellifluous voice. He wore one of those long, stiff Arrow collars that met in the front, and he was a very formidable gentleman. We resented his turning up so quickly, and when he started talking, I'm sure we all thought, especially the football team, My God, what are we in for! But this class turned out to be one of the greatest things that ever happened to me, because Raymond Weaver's course in Comparative Literature was extraordinary. Inside of three weeks this man had even the athletes reading Dante and Cervantes and Melville (on whom Weaver was an authority), and discussing them with deep interest. He was a persuasive teacher and a wonderfully nice man.

There were only about thirty people in the class, and I decided I was going to make Weaver one of the most popular teachers at Columbia. I started writing stories about him in my *Spectator* column. There was a baseball player on the Chicago White Sox, Buck Weaver, who was a wonderful player, except that he later became one of the Black Sox in the great baseball scandal. But at the time he was still a great hero, and of course I kept referring to Raymond Weaver as "Buck" Weaver. The dignified Mr. Weaver was not amused. And then I made up stories from whole cloth about him—anything to keep his name in the paper. He used to fuss at me, but I could tell that he was not really displeased. The following spring over a hundred people registered for his course. What at first seemed theatrical about him soon became very attractive to us.

Another thing happened through Weaver. He had rooms in one of the Columbia dormitories, and students would drop in after class once in a while to see him and talk. I met Richard Simon there. Dick was always something of a dreamer. He loved music and played the piano beautifully. He was also one of the most self-centered men who ever lived; he did what he wanted, and what didn't interest him simply didn't exist so far as he was concerned. He read only the assignments he liked, and if we were discussing a book he hadn't read, he'd just get up and play the piano.

My education at Columbia was not only getting a background in literature and history; I also learned at the School of Journalism—mainly through my experience on *Jester* and *Spectator*—how to write a quick story, how to put it down in as few words as possible. Something else that I think is invaluable: I learned not to clutter up my mind with a lot of useless information, because an intelligent man doesn't have to carry all that stuff in his head; he has only to know where to find what he needs when he needs it. I learned where to look for the things I needed and just how to go about getting them. Of course, there was another thing. Those were the years when I was becoming a man, and good teachers like Raymond Weaver and Benjamin Kendrick in the history department were an inspiration to me. I learned a lot just by knowing them.

I made Phi Beta Kappa in my junior year. I earned it because the courses I took were the ones that interested me and I worked on them—English, economics, history.

Editor of Jester, *surrounded by some members of the staff*

It was during my senior year at Columbia that one of the most important encounters of my life took place. One of the courses I was taking was called Appreciation of Music, and the teacher who gave it was Daniel Gregory Mason, a well-known man in his field. His was another of those courses in which you got a two-point credit almost automatically. Mason would play classical music on the piano, and I used to sit in class and write *Jester* jokes and never bother to listen to him.

Many orchestras used to send two free tickets to members of Mason's class, but you couldn't bribe these brilliant music lovers to go to one of the concerts. The tickets went begging. There was one big exception, however: the Philadelphia Orchestra, with the great Leopold Stokowski conducting. It wasn't that we could tell the difference between it and the orchestra at the Roxy, but for Stokowski, everybody wanted that pass because this was the thing to do. We used to put our names in a hat, and the two who drew the lucky numbers got the passes for the afternoon concert.

One day I drew one of the winning numbers, and the other was picked by a boy I had never paid any attention to before—he was a freshman and I was a big-shot upperclassman. His name was Donald Klopfer, and we went together to hear the concert. I liked Donald immediately. He was as tall as I was, had an interest in literature, and most important of all, had a good sense of humor. When we came out of the hall he told me that he had to pick up some theater tickets; he was going to take his girl to see the Portmanteau Players perform Lord Dunsany's *The Gods of the Mountain*. He asked me to go to the ticket office with him, and as we walked along together, Donald went on and on about the troubles he was having with his girl, sixteen years old, very rich and spoiled within an inch of her life. I couldn't have cared less, and since I didn't respond, Donald probably thought I hadn't heard a word he said. I have a habit to this day of listening with one ear. This quirk of mine astounds my friends, because they often think I'm not paying attention, but I know everything that's going on. What Donald was saying about his girl registered somehow or other. After that occasion we'd say hello to each other around the campus, but he transferred to Williams the second semester and I didn't see much of him for a while. Certainly I never guessed that he would become my best friend and lifelong partner in business.

In June, 1919, I found I needed only a few more points to finish up, so I spent that summer at school and graduated, according to plan, with two degrees—bachelor of arts from Columbia College and bachelor of literature from the School of Journalism. I didn't have much general education, but I had gained valuable experience writing and editing for *Jester* and *Spectator*. From commercial school and by working for a certified accountant, I had learned a little bit about business. Everything worked out beautifully. I've just been lucky all my life.

I didn't have to be much concerned about money; I could rely on the income that came to me after my mother's death, and I had saved a little bit in the year I had worked. But I began meeting people who had far more money than I had, and I suddenly found myself in a world that I hadn't known existed, where belonging to country clubs was taken for granted and girls were having big coming-out parties at the Ritz. It was very easy for me to get accustomed to this kind of life. I learned there was such a game as golf and that young men actually owned their own automobiles. I bought a dreadful second-hand car, and once when I drove it up to the White Mountains, it broke down six times.

Bennett

Uncle Herbert

At the beginning of the 1920's a graduate of the Columbia School of Journalism could almost automatically have a job down at the *Tribune*—it was still the *New York Tribune,* not the *Herald-Tribune* yet. On the other hand, my Uncle Herbert had become enamored of the stock market, and one of his best friends was a young stockbroker named Irving Sartorius. My uncle took to going down to Wall Street, and he was fascinated by the ticker, the old-style big ticker with a glass dome over it. In those days the board boys had their fraction tabs in a belt around their waists and would slap up the price changes on the board. By the time I had graduated, my uncle had made a lot of money in the market and was a very valued customer at the office of Sartorius, Smith and Loewi. Now, here I was in a quandary: Was I going to go into journalism? Or was I going down to Wall Street, where the job would be handed to me on a platter? I decided to try both.

By this time Merryle Stanley Rukeyser, the boy who had lived in our apartment house up on 157th Street, had become assistant financial editor on the *Tribune.* So when I went to call on the newspaper for a job, instead of just applying routinely, I went directly to Rukeyser and told him I was about to go to work in a brokerage office. The result was that I had two jobs at the same time: one at Sartorius and one on the financial page of the *Tribune.* This seemed to me a wonderfully winning combination for learning things fast.

Rukeyser knew I had been one of the honor students up at the School of Journalism and was a reasonably smart kid. I was assigned to write a column called "Advice to Investors." A lot of letters asking about investments, and so forth, came in from little old ladies and the like. All I had to do was run the ones I thought had the greatest general appeal, and my advice unerringly was to be, under strict instructions, "Buy Liberty Bonds," the popular government bonds in those days. "Don't you try being fancy," I was warned. "What do you know about the market? You just tell people to invest in Liberty Bonds and print the letters that will lend themselves to that kind of answer. If it's a specific stock they're asking about, turn the letter over to somebody who knows what he's talking about." It was considered patriotic in those days to buy Liberty Bonds. The war was over, but it still had to be paid for.

I started the column and did just what I was told to, but after a couple of weeks that became rather boring, and I suddenly discovered that nobody on the paper was even looking at the darned column. So I began expanding a little bit, and when I'd write my answers I'd get in a few touches of my own ideas of finance. One day a little old lady wrote to say that she had ten thousand dollars to invest, and she had noticed a stock that had gone down from 76 to 2, so she thought this would be a very good time to buy five thousand shares at two dollars a share. This gave great financier Cerf—drunk with power—a chance to say, "Why do you think this stock went from 76 to 2? The fact that a stock has gone down to nothing or near nothing sometimes means that the company is completely kaput. As a matter of fact, this company happens to be bankrupt, so you'd be insane to buy the stock."

When I got in the next day the financial editor was grimly waiting for me. As a matter of fact, the company in question was *not* bankrupt. It was busted higher than a kite, but it didn't actually go bankrupt until about a week later. I almost saved it from bankruptcy! The editor said, "They're going to sue us for a million dollars." Then he added, "This will teach you two lessons, sir: one, when you're given an explicit order, obey it; two, check your facts before you print a story. You're fired."

I bravely made my way to the men's room and burst into tears. I'll never forget my humiliation and downfall at the *Tribune*. Of course, I still had the job at the brokerage office.

That summer I went to a Fourth of July dance at a country club I belonged to in Woodmere, Long Island, and there I met an absolutely beautiful young girl named Marian Ansbacher, who was with some klunk. I started dancing with her, and finally persuaded her to drop her sad sack and let me take her home. Of course, I tried to kiss her the minute we got there, but she said she thought it wouldn't be right because she was in love with a boy who was a counselor at an upstate camp. She began describing him, and for some reason or other (I'll never know why), I said, "I bet I know him." She said, "That's ridiculous." I said, "His name is Donald Klopfer." I was right! There was something about her imperious manner that jibed with the way Donald had described her to me months before. She, of course, thought this was incredible. We laughed and talked a little bit about Donald, and as I left I said, "Well, that's that, goodbye." She said, "Wait! If I *wasn't* in love with Donald, this is the way I would kiss you." All the rest of that summer she was my girl while Donald was up in that camp. She was writing him every day, but she neglected to mention that she was seeing me.

When Donald came home he soon found out about me, and raised hell. She went off to Vassar, a freshman, with Donald and me both crazy about her. This suited her just fine, but for a while Donald refused to see me and I didn't want to see him either.

Then Thanksgiving came along, and Marian brought down a Chicago girl she had met at Vassar. By this time she had such a complete hold on both of us and was so sure of herself that she demanded we take her and her roommate out for the Thanksgiving weekend. We were suckers enough to say yes. We went to a football game together, the four of us, and then we went dancing at the Plaza Grill, which was the place to go in those days. We ended up at the theater, and although Donald and I had started out glaring at each other, we found that we still liked each other very much. I suggested that it might be fun when he was in New York someday that we *pay* to go to an evening performance of the Philadelphia Orchestra. Marian was delighted she had brought us together; she now had her two flames right under her thumb, and she went happily back to Vassar. Donald came down from Williams one Tuesday and we went to the concert, as we had planned. When we left Carnegie Hall we decided to take a walk. Donald and I went all the way around Central Park—over to Fifth Avenue up to 110th Street, over to Central Park West and down to 59th Street, just talking. And when we finished that walk, we were friends for life, even though I was four years older than Donald, out of college and down in Wall Street.

When Donald left Williams he took a job at the brokerage office where I was. Sartorius, Smith and Loewi was at 20 Broad Street, right next to the Stock Exchange. I was working there in 1921 when the Wall Street explosion took place—across the street in front of the Morgan Building and the Subtreasury. I learned every job in the office, even worked on the floor of the Exchange for a while, taking the orders and giving them to brokers.

Donald soon left to join his family's diamond business, but by that time we had become inseparable. Our friendship was stronger than our rivalry, and later on, when Donald and Marian were married, I was his best man. Before that marriage ended, they had a daughter, Lois, to whom Donald has always been devoted. A few years after the divorce he married Florence Selwyn, who is known to everyone as Pat, and this time it was for good.

Someone who played a big part in my later life was Charles Allen, who was with me in the brokerage office. We were the two mavericks, because both of us had as much interest in what was going on outside the office as within, and we used to sneak down to the Battery, which was only three or four blocks away, and sit there watching the boats go in and out. And we'd go over to the Statue of Liberty on a little steamer and wander around or climb up to the top, or explore the wharves on South Street up to the fish market. This was during office hours, of course.

There was a German member of the firm, Mr. Heimerdinger, whom I can still remember yelling, "Where's that veesil Bennett?" He called me "veesil" because he often couldn't find me, since I was out prowling half the time. But I was also studying the history of listed stocks, and both Charlie and I did our work. There was no question that we were somewhat favored; after all, my uncle was the firm's best customer, and Charlie Allen was a charming young man—and we were in. We were paid somewhere around twenty to thirty dollars a week. That was the usual starting salary, but we soon got quite a bit more.

Charlie Allen is today one of the most successful men in the United States. In those days, if anybody down there had asked, "Which two members around here are least likely to get very rich?" I'm sure they would have nominated Charlie and me, because we were less interested in details or "meetings" than we were in the world around us. There's a moral in this. I think even the most ambitious young man should not be so engrossed in the particular thing he's doing that he doesn't know what else is going on. The two of us had a wide interest in everything.

Since I was working in Wall Street, I began to speculate a little bit on my own. The market was pretty good; it was starting to head up. The war was behind us, things had gotten settled and the country was beginning to expand at a great clip. There was no great art to making money in the market when you were right down there and could move fast. I got to the point where I was seriously thinking of buying a seat on the Stock Exchange so that I would be made a junior partner. In those days a seat was selling for around a hundred thousand dollars, but I had made quite a little money on the side, and I also had the nest egg that I'd inherited, so I began investing some of it, always in very small amounts, but getting my fingers wet. I was just learning about the market and I made a few terrible mistakes.

At this point, in 1923, my friend from college, Richard Simon, called me. When I had finished Columbia, though I was the one who loved books, I had gone to Wall Street, and Dick Simon, who primarily loved music, had gotten a job with a publisher. I don't know how it came about, but suddenly he was working for Boni and Liveright as a book salesman

Richard Simon

learning the business. Every time I met him I would rage at him and say, "You, you dumb cluck, you don't open three books a year, and *you're* working for a publisher! That is *my* dream. And what am I doing? I'm working in Wall Street." Of course, it had been my own choice.

Then, on that memorable day, Dick said, "You're always moaning about wanting to go into the publishing business. If you want to, I'm handing it to you on a silver platter. I've decided to go in business for myself with Max Schuster. When I told my boss, Horace Liveright, I was leaving, he said it was a terrible time to walk out on him, with the fall season coming up. He asked if I could suggest anybody to replace me." Dick said he told Liveright I would be perfect—editor of the college paper, Phi Beta Kappa, columnist on the *Tribune*. He didn't tell Liveright how I had ended my career there, of course, and Liveright said he'd certainly like to meet me.

Dick said, "When can you come up?"

I said, "Anytime."

Meeting Horace Liveright, a publisher! I'd never met one in my life. So the very next day I went uptown for lunch with Dick and Liveright—and never went back to Wall Street.

We went to the Algonquin, and Liveright pointed out the famous Round Table—the table where a group of bright young literary people met for lunch—and for the first time I cast my eyes on a lot of people who were going to be very closely associated with my life: Dorothy Parker, Robert Sherwood, Marc Connelly, Franklin P. Adams, Robert Benchley. I was delighted! Liveright looked like John Barrymore and was quite vain, but he had a flair, and when he wanted to be, he was a very charming man. He sure charmed the hell out of me. He said, "We're a small, very individual firm. I have my own ideas of publishing." And added, "You can go up very quickly if you've got the stuff. I hear you've got some money, and I need money very much. If you'd like to start with style, you could put a little money into the business."

So I asked how much, and he said that if I would lend him twenty-five thousand dollars, which he needed very badly (I found out why later), I could come in as vice-president.

That was very interesting to me, so I said, "Let me give it some thought."

He said, "No, I've got to know pretty quickly. I have to get back to the office now, because I promised to take Theodore Dreiser to the baseball game this afternoon. I'm bored to death by baseball. Bennett, if you want to get in good with me quick, how about taking Dreiser up to the ball game?"

I'd never met an important author, and at this time Theodore Dreiser was a giant. He hadn't written *An American Tragedy* yet, but he had long ago published *Sister Carrie* and *Jennie Gerhardt*.

Well, that's when I went to the telephone and called downtown and said, "I won't be back this afternoon. As a matter of fact, I might not be back at all. I'm thinking of going into the publishing business. Goodbye, everybody."

The Liveright offices were in a private house, and I can still remember walking into that building at 61 West 48th Street, the exact spot where later the Twelve Caesars restaurant opened. It's part of Radio City now, but then it was all brownstones. On the ground floor of the house there were little windows with books behind them, and as I went inside with Horace Liveright, I knew this was where I wanted to be.

I didn't give Liveright a final answer right away because I had to think about that twenty-five thousand dollars. My money was invested and I wanted to talk the deal over with my uncle, and just to please him, with my father too. They were fascinated by the idea of publishing. They said, "Twenty-five thousand dollars—you'll probably end up losing it, but it will be good experience for you."

Before I left him, Liveright had said, "I've got to check up on you. Whom do we know in common I can talk to about you?" We exchanged a few names, and suddenly he said, "I have a friend down in Wall Street." He mentioned a Mr. Lowenstein, who was a prominent broker. I said, "I happen to know him." So Liveright said, "Fine, I'll speak to him about you."

Horace was naïve. I immediately called up Mr. Lowenstein and said, "Horace Liveright is going to call and ask you about me, and this is what I'd like you to tell him." He was a friend of mine and knew I was an honest, decent boy, and he told Liveright just what I wanted him to hear: that I'd be perfect for the publishing business.

We went to the baseball game, Dreiser and I. He was a dour, sulky, unpleasant man. He got bored about the fifth or sixth inning and said, "Come on, let's get out of here," so I had to leave. I remember it was a close game and I was outraged, but I had to go with him.

When I want back to see Liveright the following day, I told him I had made my mind up, and he said, "You sound great. What Lowenstein told me about you was very impressive." I said, "Well, I hope it was, because I told him just what to say." Liveright said, "Wasn't I a fool to tell you I was going to call him?"

We both laughed. We started off right, and I became sort of a protégé of Horace's. He always needed an audience, and suddenly here was a young man who thought everything he did was glamorous and exciting. So he would show off for me because I was a perfect stooge for him. He would sort of bounce things off me. Of course, starting off as a vice-president was ridiculous, but there I was. Later I realized that some people resented my coming in at that high level. They knew why.

The first thing I had to learn was how to sell books in New York City, Boston, Springfield, New Haven, Hartford, Washington, Philadelphia and Baltimore—the most lucrative territory in the country. Dick Simon agreed to stay on for a month and break me in. He was a superb salesman, and the very fact that he hadn't read the books made him able to sell them that much better. Some of the best Hollywood agents, for instance, are the same. They can sell movie rights for much more when they haven't read a book than if they have.

After I had toured the New York stores with him, Dick took me to New England. We drove up in my car and planned everything to coincide with the Harvard-Yale football game up in Boston. That first trip was very instructive. Liveright had just published Hendrik Van Loon's *The Story of the Bible*. Because of the success of *The Story of Mankind*, Liveright thought this new one was going to be a great best seller, and Dick had loaded all his accounts with huge piles of *The Story of the Bible*. But when the book came out, it was clobbered. The religious people were especially outraged that Van Loon had written a sort of jazz Bible. Today books are sold on a fully returnable basis, but then a bookseller had to get permission to turn them back. So everywhere we went, the first cry was: "Hey, what are we going to do about this disaster?"

That was my introduction to the publishing business, finding out what to do with a flop. Most of the time the stores had the upper hand, because if books weren't taken back, they wouldn't pay for them anyhow. They'd say, "Well, we want to send these books back. You stuck us with them." In those days a salesman tried to sell as many copies as possible; the trick was to oversell. That was what made a good salesman—if a bookseller wanted to take ten copies and he could make him take twenty-five, he was a hero. Today this would be ridiculous, since the books would come bouncing back.

On that trip all I did was watch Dick, and it was a great lesson. The way he had gotten people to order extra copies of *The Story of the Bible!* Those who took a hundred copies had been given a little platform with wheels under it on which they could pile books and then roll the whole display from one side of the store to the other, so a lot of fools who should have bought ten copies had taken a hundred to get this thing that cost about three dollars. And of course, when we got there, they were wheeling whole piles back and forth. Nobody was buying it. Eventually, Liveright had to take back thousands of copies, and these were stored in our basement. One day a fire broke out in the storage room. There were screams of joy, but they didn't last long. The fire burned up a lot of good books, but just as it reached the huge pile of *The Story of the Bible,* the firemen came and put it out. Luckily, though, a few thousand copies were destroyed by water.

At the time I went to work for Boni and Liveright, Albert Boni, Horace's original partner, had already left the firm. He and Horace had started it together, but shortly before my arrival they had had a great argument. And this was typical: they tossed a coin to decide which one would buy out the other for a price they had settled in advance. Liveright won, and Boni went away and started his own firm with his brother, Charles.

Horace's staff was outstanding. One of the editorial readers was Beatrice Kaufman—Mrs. George S. Kaufman. She was up on the top floor. The manufacturing man, Manuel Komroff, later became quite a well-known author. One of the assistants downstairs was a girl named Lillian Hellman. What a group! Sitting at a desk next to me was Ted Weeks, who was to become editor of the *Atlantic Monthly.* Liveright's sales manager was Julian Messner, who started his own publishing house in 1933.

The Liveright list was impressive. They'd just had a big, big season. *The Story of Mankind* by Hendrick Van Loon; so Van Loon was hanging around the office—a fascinating fellow—very gregarious. *Upstream* by Ludwig Lewisohn. Ludwig Lewisohn also hung around the office. *Tramping on Life* by Harry Kemp—a tramp, a wonderfully interesting character. Also on the list was one of the biggest best sellers in the United States—Gertrude Atherton's *Black Oxen,* about rejuvenation by monkey glands. It was the talk of the town. Some Viennese doctor had promoted the idea, and presumably a withered old woman could become a sex queen again!

I soon learned that the people I would see around the waiting room weren't all authors. About seventy-five percent of them were bootleggers. It was crazy. But Liveright ran a crazy office, and I loved him for it. There were about eight employees who had unlimited expense accounts. Arthur Pell was the treasurer. He used to run around in circles, trying to make ends meet. Pell would give Liveright false cash statements, because as soon as there was any money available, Liveright would spend it. Pell would have to tell him, "We have no cash," even when there was plenty, to keep him from squandering it immediately.

Horace's editorial assistant was T. R. Smith, who had been editor of the *Century* magazine; he was a very erudite, round-faced, gray-haired cherubic man who wore a pince-nez with a black ribbon. To look at him you'd think he was a Baptist minister, but he was a devil. Every afternoon there would be a cocktail party at the Liveright office, and every afternoon Tom Smith would mix the cocktails—and add a dash of what was virtually ether, plus, I think, a dash of Pernod, then put a little rim of sugar around

Thomas R. Smith

the edge of the cocktail glass. Just two sips were enough to send you reeling. At the time there was a little thing called Prohibition, so this was bootleg liquor and it was absolutely poisonous. Horace Liveright paid for the liquor, of course. That's one reason he needed money all the time.

The office became quite an amusement center. The ground floor of the house had an extension in back which had a flat roof that you could walk out on from the second-floor rear through big casement windows. One of Horace's great ideas was to turn it into a sort of roof garden, with potted plants and a lot of summer furniture, and he went up to Bloomingdale's himself to buy a whole set of rattan couches and chairs. It looked very nice. Then, of course, Liveright had to give a whopping party as soon as it was all set up. This was another of the ways money got used up. The party was organized, and everybody came, including the usual freeloaders who thrive on literary cocktail parties. Ford Madox Ford, author of *The Good Soldier,* was one of the guests. He was terribly fat, and when he sat down on a brand-new rattan couch, he went right through it with a terrible crash. I'll never forget that moment. It was a great day.

One of Liveright's intimates was Herbert Bayard Swope, who was then the young editor of the *New York World*. Dorothy Parker was also a close personal friend. Eugene O'Neill, already famous as a playwright, was part of the ensemble. Sometimes in a single day Swope would come up from the newspaper, and O'Neill and Dorothy Parker and then maybe Marc Connelly. Or Ben Hecht, one of the most amusing of all, and his friend Maxwell Bodenheim. It was heady stuff.

Beatrice Kaufman had a friend named Peggy Leach, who used to be around all the time too. Very soon after I got there, Peggy married young Ralph Pulitzer. One of the most charming convivials was Samuel Hopkins Adams—a wonderful man from upstate New York who had written several best sellers. He became a lifelong friend of mine. All these people were very much alive and very friendly, and the racket that went on in the office was colossal.

At night everyone went to the Swopes'. Swope was then becoming the great host of New York. Anybody you'd see on the front page who had arrived from Europe that day was at his house that night, from the Prince of Wales up and down.

Beatrice Kaufman and I liked each other very much. Between Liveright and Beatrice, I was accepted. I was the wide-eyed boy—just drinking it all in and loving every minute of it—and young people who are enthusiastic and respond with worship are liked. Beatrice started asking me to drop by her house. George Kaufman was frequently out of town with one of his plays, and I would escort Beatrice to the Swopes' and sit there beaming—I was so happy. There around me would be the district attorney of New York, the Prince of Wales, the new playwrights. Everybody was there, everybody.

Swope was a great man. *Swoping* became a word. When anybody went around acting the big shot, they'd say, "He's Swoping." He did throw his weight around quite a bit all his life, and he had a booming voice: "Swope talking!" But I admired him. And he was a great newspaper editor, until he began to get interested in too many other things and then the whole *World* collapsed—I mean the paper, not the world itself.

Eugene O'Neill was too much of a brawler for me in those early days, a real wild man, but I loved him. He spoke very slowly and hesitated several times in a sentence. He'd say, "Let's . . . uh . . . take a walk . . . uh . . . down Broadway tonight." But to Gene, I would listen patiently. He'd already published *The Moon of the Caribbees and Six Other Plays of the Sea* and had won Pulitzer Prizes for *Beyond the Horizon* and *Anna Christie*.

O'Neill's drinking often led to blackouts; in fact, in 1909 his first marriage had resulted from one. He woke up in some flophouse with a girl in bed next to him, and he said, "Who the hell are you?" and she said,

"You married me last night." He actually had. In disgust he signed up on a boat and went on a seven-month trip, and that's where he got the background for his sea plays—all those wonderful one-act plays.

Robert Benchley was a teetotaler next to O'Neill. O'Neill was a drunk. Benchley just played at it. He'd get a little stiff and say things like "Get me out of this dry suit and into a wet martini." He was a playboy, Benchley, a wonderful, wonderful man. But he wasn't a "regular" of the Liveright group. His usual place was the Algonquin Round Table.

Dotty Parker was already known for being devastatingly witty, and many things were being ascribed to her that she'd never said. Great lines were credited to Dotty, just as later on they were to Fred Allen or Bob Hope. She was something of a fraud all her life, a charm girl. "Oh," she'd say to a girl I'd introduced her to, "what a *darling* person you are." And then she'd come up to me ten minutes later and hiss, "If you bring her around me once more, I'll knock your goddamned brains out." Oh, what fangs. George Oppenheimer wrote a play called *Here Today,* which was about Dorothy Parker, and I took her to the opening night. She wriggled in her seat, muttering with rage at the caricature of herself. Backstage after the performance she threw her arms around George and said, "Oh, you caught me so perfectly! It was absolutely wonderful! How did you do it?" She had been threatening to kill him all during the show. That's the way she was throughout her life. She was a very dangerous woman.

Dorothy Parker

I loved Robert Sherwood the day I met him, and that feeling lasted till the day he died, and his wonderful wife, Madeline, is still one of our great friends. He was a great big gangling man about six foot eight. He always looked at you solemnly and spoke very slowly and very seriously, but with a humor that was simply superb. He was a most charming and generous man. I remember with affection that he liked my feeble jokes, even my puns. When I started doing columns, whenever I included some puns, Sherwood would call up and groan, "Bennett, this time you've gone too far." Then I knew I was in.

Theodore Dreiser

The year before I arrived, Liveright had published Theodore Dreiser's *A Book About Myself*, with no success, but Dreiser was hard at work on *An American Tragedy*, which was published shortly after I left. He was one of the most churlish, disagreeable men I ever met in my life, always thinking that everybody was cheating him. He'd come in about every three months to examine the ledger to see whether his royalty statements were correct.

We soon discovered Dreiser didn't know what he was doing. He'd make a great pretense of checking, but he was just trying to scare us into being honest. He'd make little marks against all the items he'd examined and then he'd go out for lunch and we'd rub all the marks off, and when he came back he wouldn't even notice. We had a very pretty telephone operator, and Dreiser was intent upon making her his. It was the joke of the whole office, because his clumsy approaches were so ludicrous. Finally she went out to lunch with him to see what would happen. When she came back she used an expression that became quite popular, but this was the first time I'd ever heard it. She said, "He's just an old garter-snapper."

Editorial meetings at Boni and Liveright were very informal. There'd be a call: "Come down to Horace's office." We never knew whether it was to have a meeting or to listen to him boast about his latest conquest. There would be Komroff and Lillian Hellman and Ted Weeks and Beatrice Kaufman and Tommy Smith, and another promising lad, Louis Kronenberger, later the drama critic of *Time* magazine.

Also at those meetings sometimes was Pauline Kreiswirth, who became extremely important in my life. She was a little rosy-cheeked kid—a darling, darling girl. I nicknamed her Jezebel. She would never allow anyone else to call her that, but to me she was always Jezebel. And later, after Donald and I had started our own business, she came with me and was my secretary for the rest of her life.

Horace taught me something at those haphazard meetings. If an editor felt strongly enough about a book, Horace let him sign it up; and we've always done the same at Random House. If we have an editor we trust, if he's behind a book and the advance isn't too staggering, we don't even always read it, any more than Horace did. He'd say, "Well, if you're that crazy about it, I trust your judgment. Go ahead."

But Horace didn't always approve of what you did after you'd done it. For instance, I asked him to let me do the catalogue. It was the kind of place where anybody who volunteered to do anything, got to do it, because most of the staff were busy drinking. It was a very frivolous place. I had ideas about the catalogue, one of which was to get Ralph Barton, an artist who became very famous in *Vanity Fair* and *The New Yorker,* to do a cover that would have little caricatures of all our authors. Barton agreed to do it for me. I neglected, however, to ask him what he was going to charge, and when I got his bill for three hundred dollars . . . Oh, God, did I get bawled out by Horace, and rightly. Three hundred dollars for a catalogue cover! But it *was* by Barton!

Horace had a compulsion for making a pass at every girl the first time he met her. His office was very fancy and he had a private bathroom, which

Ralph Barton's catalogue cover

Horace Liveright at work

was considered quite unusual in those days in a business office. He also had what is known as a casting couch. And when a pretty young authoress came to see him, Horace would have two things in mind—her manuscript and proving to himself what an irresistible man he was. He was only showing off. And if the girl said no, it didn't break his heart.

With a silk hat on, he would have been a perfect Mississippi River boat gambler. He'd ask the girls, "Do I remind you of anybody?" and if they said John Barrymore, he would be particularly pleased. He was a kind of matinée idol in his own way, very handsome, smoked cigarettes in a long holder. There was a great deal of phoniness in him, but by some kind of intuition he picked people who were going places—people for his office, as well as authors.

One day Horace was reading us a love letter from a girl, a passionate letter indeed, when the door opened and Lucille, his wife, came walking into the room. Horace had a little desk with a shallow drawer at the top. He jammed the letter into the drawer and shut it. She sailed in, ignoring us, and said, "This time I caught you red-handed. What was that letter you were reading—a letter from one of your girls, I'll bet." We sat there terror-stricken. Horace reached his greatest height. In his best Barrymore manner he said, "Lucille, you have insulted me in front of my staff." I particularly remember that "my staff." He said, "I demand that you open that drawer and read aloud to my staff the letter you just saw me put in that drawer." She looked at him for a minute, wilted, and apologized. We were absolutely stunned. A performance by a master mountebank!

One night after seeing a play called *The Racket* (the reason I remember it at all is that Claudette Colbert was in it), I took my girl to show her the Liveright office. It was a good place to do a little necking. We walked into Horace's private office, and there he was with a girl on the couch, absolutely caught in the act. I pulled my girl out of there in a hurry. I said, "Well, that's the end of me. I'll be fired tomorrow morning."

The next day, sure enough, Horace sent for me. I went down all ready for the bad news. Horace closed the door and said, "What must you think of me, Bennett? I know you're a very moral young man." Then he explained, "This girl is a very promising young writer, and the only way I felt I could really get her was to have a little affair with her." I assured him I understood fully. And he said, "I'm ashamed of myself." The girl was a poetess, and we published a book of her poems. It sold about eight copies.

That was Horace Liveright! For him, everything was for the moment, and he never took the trouble to seek solid things that might mean future growth. It didn't interest him. *Flaming Youth* was his kind of baby—a book about the flapper age, the biggest success of its kind until Scott Fitzgerald came along. It was by Warner Fabian, a pseudonym used by Samuel Hopkins Adams, who wrote it more or less as a joke. It was an immediate

Samuel Hopkins Adams (alias Warner Fabian)

· 39 ·

best seller. There was great speculation as to who Warner Fabian really was, but we kept the mystery going for a long, long time. When we published Sam's novel *Siege*, one of New York's leading department stores refused to order a single copy; they were angry at him because they had been the target of one of the many pieces Sam wrote for newspapers and magazines, attacking various forms of quackery and false advertising. But what amused us all, especially Sam, was that that same store was selling *Flaming Youth* in great quantities.

Of course, it was fine to have new books by Eugene O'Neill and Gertrude Atherton and Hendrik Van Loon and Sam Adams, but the backbone of Liveright was The Modern Library, which had been Boni's idea. It was modeled on Everyman's Library in London, but Everyman's was very English and included no American authors at all. Boni's plan had been to start a series with all the classics but to mix them up with works by young American authors and books that were famous in this country. I had always admired The Modern Library and had used it in college, so it was a great thrill to be connected with its publisher.

When I got to Liveright, nobody was really in charge of Modern Library. One editor would say, "Hey, we've got to find a couple of new titles for Modern Library"—and they would be selected in a haphazard way. If I wanted to put in a book, I could always talk Horace into it because he didn't really care; that kind of publishing wasn't exciting enough for him. I very quickly became—by default—the editor of the series, and promised myself I was someday going to get hold of it.

When an author brought a manuscript to the office, Liveright would say, "We'll let you know tomorrow," and he'd have one of us read it overnight. And we'd bring him a précis the next day. He was too busy to read manuscripts. He believed in the personality approach, and spent most of his time out on the town entertaining authors. He was great at drinking in what we'd tell him about a script. He'd listen carefully for about ten minutes, and when the author came in, Horace would give the big build-up—how he'd sat up till three in the morning to read the book. Authors are pretty hard to fool on their own work, but for the most part he got away with it.

Liveright was a great gambler. He published books that the old staid publishers wouldn't touch. And he was doing big ads with black, black type and eye-catching borders—something previously unknown in the industry, which at that time was mostly in the hands of middle-aged or older stuffed shirts who considered publishing a very respectable business, and they didn't approve of flamboyant advertising. Most of them were dignified, conservative members of old, old families. They wore gold watch chains across their fat bellies, and they would sit in their offices and never dream of going out for a book; the author came crawling to them. In those days the book publisher was everything. The movies and the magazines were paying writers pittances—not those huge prices that are tossed about today.

Liveright was deeply resented by the established publishers. They hated him; they even hated Alfred Knopf and B. W. Huebsch, who had started at about the same time. There had never been a Jew before in American publishing, which was a closed corporation to the rising tide of young people described in *Our Crowd*. Suddenly there had burst forth on the scene some bright young Jews who were upsetting all the old tenets of the publishing business—and the flashiest of all was certainly Liveright. Liveright, Ben Huebsch, Alfred Knopf—and later, Simon and Schuster and Harold Guinzburg—changed the course of publishing. Theirs were the young firms, and though they were lumped together by the old-timers, they were not alike. Knopf was already a young publisher with literary taste and dignity, when along came Horace Liveright, who Alfred thought was cheap and flamboyant. Alfred "had the honor to announce the publication of the Such-and-Such Sage," and here was Horace doing books like *Black Oxen*. And when he published *Flaming Youth*, Mr. Knopf disapproved.

Alfred Knopf had the one thing Liveright lacked: he had class. Liveright was a showman. Knopf was—and still is—a great, great publisher, and Liveright was extremely jealous of him. He didn't care about the old fogies he was competing with. It was Knopf he had his sights set on. By the same token, Knopf disliked and resented Liveright, and didn't want to be considered in that class of "fresh young Jews."

The change in Liveright's fortunes came when he decided to become a play producer. He had always been interested in the theater, and he produced his first play in 1924. The author was a young friend named Edwin Justus Mayer—another regular at those famous office parties. The play was *The Firebrand*. It was about Benvenuto Cellini, a very, very good play, and Liveright had the misfortune of having a hit in his first production. It introduced to the American public several people who became extremely well known in later years. Cellini was played by Joseph Schildkraut, and two of the minor characters, by Frank Morgan and Edward G. Robinson. Liveright made too much money on that play and it went to his head. The next thing he did was *Hamlet* in modern dress with Basil Sidney, who was his wife's brother-in-law. *Hamlet* got plenty of attention in the papers but it lost a lot of money.

Then Liveright became interested in a musical show. That was the beginning of the end, because musical shows are murder. Also, about that time he had the bad luck to meet Otto Kahn, the New York banker, who was very amused by Horace and gave him several tips on the market that often turned out terribly. Horace lost a lot of money. Otto Kahn was being honest. He lost a lot of money on those stocks too, but he could afford it; Horace couldn't, and his fortunes began to wane. He was always skating on thin ice.

I had "invested" twenty-five thousand in Boni and Liveright, and later on in a very tough pinch, another twenty-five. So he was "in" me for fifty thousand dollars, and it began to look as though getting that back was going to be quite a problem. But I felt it might be considered a reasonable price for a complete course of instruction in publishing. What an experience! I learned all the things to do, and more important, a lot of the things not to do.

Liveright owed a lot of his friends money, and in particular, he owed another fifty thousand to his father-in-law, who felt this entitled him to come to the office and grumble about the way Horace was conducting himself and the way he was betraying his daughter.

When Horace went into show business, an entrance was cut through the wall into the house next door, where he opened a theatrical office; people could get there only via our waiting room. A bevy of little actresses and actors began coming around, and this made life even more glamorous and exciting. Besides the Dreisers and O'Neills, now, suddenly, theatrical personalities were wandering in. One Friday morning a dazzling little blond Southern girl named Miriam Hopkins appeared, and I immediately invited her to go up to New Haven with me to a Yale-Princeton game the next day. And she accepted. It developed that she had no great gift for silence—she never stopped talking. Those were the days when people used to hang on to the trolleys going out to the Yale Bowl, trolleys which they brought out of the car barns just for the big games. But I walked Miriam out there from the station, which was quite a way, and at some point we passed a pet shop and Miriam fell in love with a little puppy and wanted me to buy it for her. I pointed out that we were going to a football game and she couldn't sit there with a dog in her arms. But I had to promise I'd buy it for her on the way back.

The stadium was jammed. Miriam had never seen a football game, and within eight minutes she had twenty Yale boys explaining football to her—everybody in front of her, everybody behind her, on all sides. She was immediately the center of attention, not because she was a famous girl—nobody had ever heard of her yet—but because she was irresistible.

As we walked back from the game Miriam kept looking for that pet shop, and not finding it. As we got in sight of the station, it suddenly dawned on her that I had brought her back a different route, and we had quite a battle.

I fell—oh, did I fall—for Miriam. She soon got a part in a play called

Excess Baggage, in which she played the lead. One of the things she had to do was partially undress. Her mother came up from Georgia to see her, and when she saw that costume . . . ! But nobody could tell Miriam what to do. She was a determined little girl. When Pat Kearney later made a play of *An American Tragedy,* the lead was played by Miriam Hopkins; by this time she was becoming famous. Then years later it was made into a movie, and Sylvia Sidney starred in it. So *An American Tragedy* just weaves through my life.

In the spring of 1925 I had been at Boni and Liveright for almost two years, and I began getting restless. Dick Simon and Max Schuster had already made a big success on their own. And here I was, still working for Horace Liveright and feeling it was high time I got going for myself, too.

I had never been to Europe, and I decided to make my first trip abroad. With Liveright's approval I booked passage on the *Aquitania* and persuaded Dick Simon to take his vacation at the same time and go with me.

The day I was to leave—the boat was sailing at ten o'clock that night—Horace Liveright took me to a farewell luncheon. My excitement amused him—the great sophisticate! We ate at a speakeasy called Jack and Charlie's, which is now "21." It was then on 49th Street. I remember this all so clearly because it was a very important day in my life. Horace obviously had had one or two drinks before we went out, and this was unusual—he was not a drinker. The minute we sat down he ordered another. I said, "What's the matter? You're a bundle of nerves."

He said, "My father-in-law is driving me crazy. He comes down and gives me the third degree and wants me to account for where all the money is. Well, you know as well as I do that I don't know where it is." He continued, "What's more, I'm not going to tell him about every girl I go out with. He thinks that because I'm married to his daughter, he can demand this sort of thing. Oh, how I'd like to pay him off and get rid of him."

So I blandly said, "One very easy way to pay him off, Horace, is to sell me The Modern Library."

I had suggested it to him four or five times, but each time he had thrown me out of the office. He knew at heart that The Modern Library was the greatest asset of the business. This time, however, instead of saying, "Don't start that again," he looked at me rather feverishly and said, "What will you give me for it?"

The door had been opened, and we started dickering. Horace began figuring out what he needed to pay off his pressing debts and leave himself with some cash to continue operating. For once he had a rough idea of his finances, and we agreed on a price: two hundred thousand dollars. That meant I really was going to get The Modern Library for an additional hundred and fifty thousand in cash, because I figured that the fifty thousand I'd lent him was otherwise down the drain. Liveright cheered up and said, "We'll go right back to the office, and I'll call my lawyer. There's no need for you to postpone your trip. We'll go on with The Modern Library as we're doing. We won't change the usual way we replenish the stock; and we'll make no extra effort to sell stock off to get rid of it, so that when we turn it over to you, there'll be the normal inventory. That's fair, I think. We'll carry on, and when you come back the deal will be signed—two hundred thousand dollars for The Modern Library, and all the inventory on hand goes with it."

We went back to 48th Street, a block away, to the office. I was deliriously happy, but worried. First of all, I didn't *have* a hundred and fifty thousand dollars.

The Liveright lawyer was Arthur Garfield Hayes, very famous for his work in the field of civil rights and a very fine man. Horace also summoned Julian Messner, his adviser and oldest friend. Julian absolutely worshipped Horace, who used him as a sort of office boy, and Messner was too good a man for that. When Hayes and Messner heard that Horace was going to sell me The Modern Library, they had an absolute fit. They said, "You idiot. It's the backbone of Boni and Liveright. It's one of the great properties in the whole publishing business. Why in God's name do you want to sell it?"

Liveright reminded them sharply, "I'm the owner of this business." He said, "This will get me out of the hole I'm in. As a matter of fact, Macmillan is about to start a competing new series, and how can I hold my own against a great big firm like Macmillan? They'll put The Modern Library out of business in two years. I'm selling at the top. Bennett knows this. He's taking a chance. I've warned him about it." (He had, and I had said, "Nonsense. Macmillan's a stuffy old firm. We just have to concentrate on our own series. We've got a big head start on them.") "Anyway," Horace added, "I've given Bennett my word. I don't break my word."

So they started arguing with him that he hadn't really given his word—the deal had just been talked about—and I began to fear my whole great coup was going out the window. Then I had one of those strokes of luck that have occurred from time to time all through my life. There arrived one of the most famous literary agents in the country—Liveright was having an affair with his wife and he had found out about it. Word came up that Mr. So-and-So was downstairs in a rage, waving a pistol, and Horace, shaking with fear, sent Messner to calm the man down. So my most vehement adversary at the moment, Julian Messner, had to leave to soothe the irate agent who was threatening to shoot Horace. This left only Hayes with us, and he was getting tired of the argument. He said, "Well, you're my client. I've given you my advice. If you don't want to listen to it, the hell with you."

Meanwhile, Messner and the agent had been having a few downstairs, and when last seen, the two of them were weaving off, arm in arm, down 48th Street. This was musical comedy—that's exactly what it was—because I doubt the man even knew how to shoot a pistol. I don't even know if it was loaded, but he was brandishing it. It was an incredible break for me. I don't know if Messner would have been able to persuade Liveright not to make the deal, but he might have turned the tide.

Horace and I shook hands and signed the little notes that Hayes wrote out. We had no time to draw up a formal contract, since I was leaving for Europe that night. Mr. Pell, the treasurer, was outraged, of course, when he heard of the deal.

Donald Klopfer had been working for his stepfather's firm, which owned a very big diamond-cutting business in Newark. Donald loathed it, but there he was. I called him up and said, "Remember, Donald, we have always said that someday we would go into business together. On a gold platter, here is the opportunity. I've just agreed to buy The Modern Library from Liveright for two hundred thousand dollars. I'll be back from Europe in about three weeks. I don't have to put up money until then. If you want to come in with me, it'll cost you a hundred thousand dollars. We'd be in fifty-fifty, absolutely alike."

Donald, of course, was excited. He loved books, and we had dreamed of doing things together. He said, "Where the hell am I going to raise a hundred thousand dollars?"

I said, "That's your problem, but it's got to be cash."

So that night when Donald came to see me off for Europe, neither of us knew whether or not we were going to be partners.

On the *Aquitania* going over to England with her husband, there was a young lady who was just finishing a book for Horace Liveright. Her name was Anita Loos and the book was *Gentlemen Prefer Blondes*. The last chapter was written on the ship, and I guess I was the first person in the world to read it. I almost fell off the boat laughing. It was a hilarious book—still is, in fact. Anita's husband was John Emerson, president of Actors Equity and a very big man in the theater.

In my excitement over going to Europe, it had never occurred to me to reserve a hotel room in London. About two days out I began to worry about it. I heard other people were having trouble too, because, it turned out, we were getting to London the night before the Derby. John Emerson said, "We have no reservations, either. Leave it to me." The careful Simon, of course, already had a room reserved in some inexpensive hotel. That wasn't my idea at all. When I travel, I travel in style, and I wanted to go to a big hotel and be a big shot.

Anyway, John Emerson said, "Leave it to me," and he started sending

Anita Loos

telegrams: WIFE AND I AND YOUNG FRIEND WANT SUITE. And we began getting back answers: HAPPY TO TAKE CARE OF YOU TWO DAYS AFTER YOU ARRIVE, BUT UNTIL THE DERBY IS OVER, THERE ARE NO ROOMS.

Then Emerson began to get worried. Here we were within two days of England, with no place to stay. Finally he bethought himself of a man named Rudolph Kommer, the agent for Max Reinhardt, the big German producer, and a man who cut quite a swath in those days. Emerson telegraphed him, saying: WE'VE GOT TO HAVE TWO ROOMS AND AT LEAST ONE BATHROOM, PREFERABLY TWO, AND I DON'T WANT AN ANSWER TO THIS. JUST GET THE ROOMS AND MEET US AT THE STATION.

We got off the boat at Southampton, and when I got my first look at England, I can't describe how excited I was. We rushed to buy a London paper right away, and the first remark Dick made on English soil was, "The bastards." I said, "What's the matter?" He had opened the paper and found an ad for some whiskey that had the same checked border that Simon and Schuster used, and he was outraged. Of course, he was only half serious, but we couldn't help laughing at him—here was a young American over for his first look at England, screaming because the border of a whiskey advertisement was like his firm's.

When we got to London, Kommer met us, wringing his hands. He said, "I couldn't do it. There isn't a room in London." Emerson started berating him, and Kommer said, "I have only one thing to tell you. Lord So-and-So has a beautiful suite at the Savoy Hotel, and he's up in Scotland grouse shooting." He concluded, "I say no more."

John Emerson said, "That's all I have to hear." So we proceeded to the Savoy. We needed an extra cab for Anita's nineteen suitcases. Emerson was in life the character W. C. Fields played, the absolute bluff. He went swaggering up to the desk and said, "I am John Emerson. This is my wife, and this is my young friend Bennett Cerf. We're to occupy Lord So-and-So's suite."

They started looking up records, but of course could find none. Emerson went into a rage and demanded to see the manager. The manager came bustling forward, rubbing his hands on his frock coat, and Emerson bawled the hell out of him. He said, "We've just arrived from America, tired from our journey, and nothing is ready for us. Lord So-and-So will hear about this." It ended up with the manager apologizing abjectly and taking us up to the suite, which consisted of a huge living room, two great big bedrooms and a bath for each. These luxurious quarters overlooked the Thames—you could see part of the Tower of London to one side and Parliament to the other, and Westminster Abbey and the boats going under Waterloo Bridge.

The minute Anita saw the place she said, "We've got to have a party right away." And before she even started unpacking, the Emersons were calling all their friends in England to invite them to a great party that very night. They seemed to know everybody in London.

Dick Simon and I had arranged to meet and have supper together at Simpson's; then we walked on the Strand and Picadilly and nearly got run over about eighteen times because we were looking the wrong way. I hadn't slept the whole night before, and I was very tired. I came back to our suite, and it was bedlam—there were at least a hundred people, most of them in white tie and tail. There were a lot of names that it seemed to me I had heard of, and I was impressed, but so exhausted that I went right to bed. The next thing I knew I was being shaken by a blonde who was saying, "What the hell are you doing in bed? Get up and join the party." I threw her out in a rage.

In the morning I went in to see John and Anita, who were having breakfast in bed. And Anita said, "You're a pretty choosy young man. Wait till people hear you threw Tallulah Bankhead out of your bedroom."

Crestfallen, I mumbled, "My God, is that who it was?" Tallulah, at that time London's reigning young beauty, was starring in a Noel Coward play. So that afternoon I attended a matinée of the play and went backstage to apologize. She didn't remember a thing about it.

I stayed in London for the first week. On the weekend John Emerson proposed that we visit Stratford-on-Avon, and promptly hired a Rolls-

Royce. I had met a young salesman from Scribner's named Gilbert Vail, who decided to come along, so the four of us set forth in the Rolls and drove up to Stratford. We were very irreverent, I'm afraid, making fun of all the guides and souvenirs and tourist traps. Before dinner Anita—I don't know how she did it—got hold of a rubber ball, and we went out in the street at Stratford-on-Avon and started playing catch. John wound up and threw the ball right through a window, and we all ran wildly back to our hotel. I can still hear the crash of that ball going through that window. I can still see Anita Loos, who within six months became one of the most famous women in the United States, running down that street like a little girl. To this day when we meet we recall that time with delight.

Uncle Herbert and "Pop"

I hadn't been in England for three days when Pell went to see my father and uncle, with results that I recorded in a journal of that trip:

LONDON

June 3, 1925

Disgusting news from New York. Mr. Pell, Boni & Liveright's charming treasurer, has evidently been making one of his characteristic gestures, and demanded $25,000 more of the purchase price of the Modern Library, though it isn't due until Sept. 1. I can't understand this move, and neither, evidently, do Herbert, Don, and Ed Falk, for they cabled advising me to chuck the trip and come home at once. I guess they signed all three names to impress me with the gravity of the situation, though, knowing the way things are usually done at Boni & Liveright's, I am not too much concerned—yet I guess they're right though, and I'd better cut the trip short and get back on the scene of action, or possibly regret it the rest of my life. DAMN in many languages ... The Berengaria sails this Saturday; the Mauretania a week later. I cabled tonight to see if I mightn't delay until the latter boat goes, and thus salvage a week in Paris from the wreckage ... I'll bet my cable has already set Herbert gnashing his teeth over my carelessness, lack of dependability, and total void of business acumen! I wonder what Pop is saying about it all ...

Letters from Pop, Don, and Julian Messner arrived on the Berengaria, but with that havoc-wreaking cable in hand, they were as stale as the news in the Times of May 26 that came with them.

June 4, 1925

Another day featured by hectic exchange of cables ... I am absolutely convinced that conditions are O.K. at Boni & Liveright and that my going to Paris is entirely safe, diplomatic, and the saviour of my vacation. I would feel eternally "done" if I went back home without getting to the continent. Herbert and Ed are taking the conservative course in urging my immediate return, and rightly so ... Some of Pell's manoeuvres in the past year would have turned their hair grey. I was jolly well disgusted, too; but I feel I know what they're up to. After all, I assured Horace that an additional $25,000 would be forthcoming ahead of time if absolutely needed; and they've struck for it as early as possible. I know how well they can use it—paying about 12% for money—and in a way don't blame them. Horace has cabled assuring me that they can well wait until June twentieth—and later if necessary—and I've burned my bridges behind me. I'm going to Paris, and return on the Mauretania on June 13. This is distinctly against the advice of Pop, Herbert, Edwin, and Don, and I am setting down these facts in fullest details so that if anything goes wrong, I'll have *nobody* but myself to blame, and swear that I'll not squawk about it. I am *absolutely sure* that if I returned on the Berengaria I'd find things exactly as I've pictured them—and would curse myself for every kind of an idiot for not following my *own* judgment in the matter. After all, I'm the only one in the world who knows the ins and outs of the transaction, and my only fear is not that I've done the wrong thing, but that my best friends, whose advice I'm definitely ignoring, will think I'm a blithering idiot.

I wonder, also, does this prove I'm an irresponsible ass? Somehow, I *cannot* feel dreadfully concerned about the matter. I *know* it's going to turn out *right*.

MY LAST DAY IN LONDON

June 5, 1925

The cables buzzed only once for me today—a terrible slacking-off. The message was from Pop, still advising me to come back on the Berengaria, and adding that I am antagonizing Herbert, Don, and Ed by daring to differ with them . . . Well, I stick by my guns. I'm going to Paris . . . It is inconceivable that they know something they haven't told me in all these cables, which means that things stand exactly as they did when I left home. Liveright *cannot afford* to try any shenanigans on the eve of his biggest publishing season, not to mention his advent as a lone theatrical impresario. So I'll take my chances . . .

Several aspects of this rather ridiculous situation annoy and puzzle me. 1. Pop, Herbert, Don, and Ed seem to have no faith whatever in my judgment. If I had thought it necessary to rush home now, I should never have come over here at all. 2. They all seem to have decided that Liveright is an awful crook who is going to "gyp" me if ever he can. With this estimate I violently disagree. He has always played fair with me, and I am sure, regards me as a very good friend—certainly not a business enemy. Both Julian and Komroff are there too—and more honest men never lived. I conclude that what principally frightened my faithful defenders was Pell's unfortunate manner . . . He has frightened people before with what he fondly believes is a good business technique. 3. Pop says I am "antagonizing everybody." They have given me good advice. I have cut out all but four days of my trip on the strength of it. Where in Christ do they come in to be "antagonized" if, with nothing that is not my own at stake, I choose to deviate from their instructions?

This *ends* all this palaver. I've put it down in greatest detail because I have an idea that it will make very interesting reading in the near future.

June 6, 1925

Packed my trunk, kissed the Emersons (at least, half of the Emersons) a tearful farewell, changed £50 into approximately 1500 francs, and boarded the Imperial Airways motor bus in front of the Hotel Victoria at 10:45 A.M. Dick Simon was already in the bus . . .

The Aerodrome is located at Croydon, forty-five minutes by

bus out of London. There were seven people for two planes, and by hanging back, Dick and I got one of the machines for our exclusive use! We stepped into the plane at 12:20 P.M., the motor roared—and off we went on OUR VERY FIRST TRIP BY AEROPLANE. It seemed to me that we shot up like a rocket, and scarcely before I could realize it, we were almost a mile above the earth, with England stretched out beneath us like a map. I discovered at this point that I hadn't stuffed cotton tightly enough in my ears to miss Dick's "Well, my trip to England wasn't wasted, after all. Pall Malls *are* a shilling there!"

We landed at the old French field that Lindbergh made famous just two years later—Le Bourget.

When we arrived in Paris, I headed for a little pension on the Left Bank; right around the corner from La Ronde and all those famous 1920's saloons at the corner of the Boulevards Montparnasse and Raspail. I knew that Manuel Komroff, the Liveright manufacturing man, was staying there, along with a young salesman, Jack Clapp. We had a happy reunion. Then Dick Simon and Henry Sell, editor of *Town and Country*, called for me, and I got my first look at Paris after dark.

I came home, I remember, in a taxicab by myself, trying out my very sketchy French. When I got to the house the taxi driver tried to tell me that after midnight the fare was doubled. We began having quite an argument, and Manuel Komroff and Jack Clapp leaned out the window and said, "Don't let him get away with it." Finally I gave the man what the meter read and added a ten-percent tip. He promptly threw the money in my face and drove off in a rage. When I got upstairs my two dear friends told me the driver was absolutely right—the fare did double after midnight. I'll never forget it. If only I could have found that taxi driver to apologize, I would have been greatly relieved.

I soon discovered that there was only one bathroom in the place, although there were about fourteen bedrooms. I thought, My God, this is going to be absolutely terrible, only one bathtub. But before long, it became obvious that we three were the only ones in the house who ever took a bath.

The landlady was very fat, and an equally fat lady was her assistant. The two of them looked like the kind of characters who might have sat around knitting when Sidney Carton was executed in *The Tale of Two Cities*. The first morning I wanted to have breakfast somewhere, and in my very best schoolboy French I asked them to recommend a place. They looked at each other in astonishment, burst out laughing, slapped their fat knees and asked me to please repeat my question, which I did very indignantly. Again they went into hysterics. So we struck a quick deal. If I would talk to them in French, they would give me breakfast. The first two days all I got was a croissant and coffee. By the third day I was such a success, I demanded more; I said, "If I'm going to be this funny—eggs!"

I never saw that house again, but it was wonderful living there then. That's when I first learned about French prices. I would go in a store and buy something, and they'd tell me what it cost, but when I'd give my address, they'd say "Oh" and cut the price immediately. When they found out I lived in this little street and wasn't a rich American sucker from the Ritz, I was one of them.

When I returned on the *Mauretania*, Donald had his half of the purchase price of The Modern Library—he came from a well-to-do family, so it wasn't too hard. Donald told me that Pell, despite everything, had sold for cash about half The Modern Library inventory for way below what it should have been priced at. This was absolutely disgraceful, of course, but in his defense I will say that he wasn't doing it for himself—he was doing it for Liveright. But it meant that when Donald and I finally got started, all this stock would be bouncing around the city. It would cut into our New York sale for weeks. Pell had sold a lot of books to Macy's, the biggest account. It was a dirty trick, and Liveright was furious when he heard about it. I want to emphasize that this was the way Horace was. If he and I had had time to draw up a contract, he would have done anything under the sun to trick me once he had signed it. But if you shook hands with Horace, as I did, and said, "I'd trust you with my life," Horace would die before he'd take advantage.

Donald and I had the necessary cash, but then two things happened. At the last minute Horace demanded that we give him a contract as an adviser for five years at five thousand a year. That had to be a last-minute thought, and I think either Messner or Arthur Garfield Hayes put it into his head. Horace said, "You boys are going to need my advice." Well, his advice was the last thing we needed, but he said that if we didn't agree to it, the deal was off. So we had to give in. It put an extra burden on us, so my uncle lent us five hundred shares of Norfolk and Western Railroad, which at that time was selling for about two hundred dollars a share. It didn't cost him a penny, since all he had to do was lend us the stock, and with that collateral we borrowed fifty thousand dollars from the bank. That covered our operating expenses. Of course, we owed my uncle the five hundred shares, but we were able to pay him back a hundred shares at a time.

To show what an incredible purchase The Modern Library was: in two years we had made back not only the fifty thousand we had borrowed, but the entire investment. The minute we gave our full attention to it, the series simply boomed. The only competition was Everyman's Library, and it was languishing. There were no paperback books in those days. We had the only cheap editions of *Moby Dick, The Scarlet Letter, Dorian Gray* and all the modern classics. The Modern Library was used in every college.

Shortly after we took over, I said to Donald, "You know, Horace is such an idiot about money. I'll bet if we offered him a lump sum, we'd cut

Announcing a new partnership: Cerf and Klopfer

down that obligation." So we went to Liveright and said we'd give him fifteen thousand dollars to call off the agreement, and Horace accepted. So overall, The Modern Library cost us $215,000.

Later on, Dick Simon and Max Schuster tried to buy it from us. Schuster was a great promoter, and I still have the elaborate proposal he prepared, proving to his own satisfaction at least that we should sell them The Modern Library, and that since I was a pleasure-loving boy, I would have so much more time to travel and enjoy myself. I never saw such bunk in my life! We could have made a profit of a hundred thousand dollars, but we didn't want it, because this was the beginning of our publishing business. The Modern Library, Inc.

For a while all Modern Library orders still went to Liveright, so the first thing we'd do every day, Donald and I, the two great publishers, was go to 48th Street and collect them. Then we'd rush back and count the number of books ordered. We did this for months. It was lots of fun. When we'd get a big order from Macy's, we'd dance around with glee because it ran the total way up.

One of our very first letters was from Alfred A. Knopf, a man I'd never met but who was one of my heroes in publishing. His Borzoi books were my dream of the way books should look. To me, everything he did represented publishing at its best. So when he invited us to come and see him, we went happily up to his office in the Heckscher Building on 57th Street and Fifth Avenue, and were ushered into the great man's presence.

Alfred A. Knopf

Knopf shook hands in a rather condescending way, and said, "I've heard about you two boys, and I just wanted to find out if you're going to be as bad crooks as the man you bought The Modern Library from."

He thereupon launched into a tirade about Horace Liveright, which came down to the fact that Liveright had put *Green Mansions* into the series. There was no United States copyright on it, but Alfred Knopf considered it his property because he had met the author, W. H. Hudson, and introduced the book in America. Furthermore, it was at the time the biggest-selling book in the whole Modern Library.

I said, "I didn't know about this, Mr. Knopf."

He said, "Well, what are you going to do about it?"

I proposed then that we pay him a royalty on *Green Mansions* of six cents a copy. He acknowledged that he thought it was very fair, since legally he had no case. I left him with my admiration unimpaired and I think he decided we were pretty decent kids. That started a friendship with Alfred Knopf that led to his becoming a part of our organization many, many years later.

We first set up our new venture in a small office on the ninth floor of a loft building at 73 West 45th Street, right across the street from a place called Lewis and Conger, which was very much like Hammacher Schlemmer, and which long ago moved out of Manhattan. We had only about six people working for us. Donald and I sat at desks facing each other. Later on, even when we moved to larger and more elegant quarters on 57th Street, and until Donald went off to the Air Force in World War II, we still had desks facing each other. When something private would come up, one of us, without being asked, would go out of the room. There was a bond between us that I can't describe. And we had only one secretary. To this day I share a secretary with Donald. Even the minor editors in our company have their own secretaries, but the two people who built the business share one. Many people have thought this strange and have kidded us about it, but what they don't realize is that the ones we've had—Pauline Kreiswirth, who was with us until she died, and then Mary Barber, who has been with us ever since—were three times as good as other secretaries. So Donald and I came out ahead.

After Donald and I started our business, I remained Liveright's very good friend because I was sort of his Boswell—I followed him around everywhere. He was so amusing and he knew so many wonderful people. Between Beatrice Kaufman's taking me up to the Swope house and Horace's introducing me to his Greenwich Village characters and the literary and theatrical people, I was still meeting the celebrities of the day. I'd always had those stars in my eyes, and I was having a wonderful time.

In 1925, just after I left, Liveright had published Dreiser's *An American Tragedy*. It was a big hit and almost immediately became a best seller. Horace by this time was casting an envious eye on Hollywood, which was becoming bigger and bigger, and he was made to order for it. He decided he was going out there to look over the terrain. Before he left he said to Dreiser, "I think I can sell *American Tragedy* while I'm there." Dreiser said it was ridiculous to think that anyone could sell Hollywood a story about a young man who gets an office girl pregnant and then meets a society girl and drowns the office girl.

So Horace said, "I'll make a deal with you, Dreiser. The first fifty thousand dollars I get for your book in Hollywood, you get complete. After that, we go fifty-fifty."

Dreiser said, "You won't get a dollar for it. Nobody will make that picture, Horace."

Horace said, "Watch me!"

So they shook hands. In those days fifty thousand dollars was a lot of money for movie rights. But Horace sold *American Tragedy* for eighty-five thousand dollars! When he came back, of course, Horace had to boast about his triumphs, and I was a very good person to tell, because I was always appreciative. So he called me up and said, "What do you think I got for *American Tragedy*? Eighty-five thousand dollars! Wait till I tell Dreiser!"

I said, "Gee, I'd like to be there."

He said, "I'm taking him to lunch next Thursday at the Ritz, and I'd like you to come and watch Dreiser when I tell him."

So the three of us went to the Ritz. The main dining room had a balcony all the way around it, a few steps above the main part of the restaurant, and we had a table on the balcony right next to the railing.

Dreiser said, "What do you want with me, Liveright?"

Horace was very coy. He said, "Now, now, we'll have our lunch."

Dreiser was getting grumpier. "What have you got to tell me?"

Finally after we had finished our meal, before the coffee came, Horace said, "Dreiser, I sold *American Tragedy*."

Dreiser said, "Oh, come on."

Horace said, "I did."

Finally Dreiser said, "Well, what did you get for it?"

Horace said, "Eighty-five thousand dollars."

It took a few moments for this to sink in, and then Dreiser let out a cry of triumph. He exulted, "What I'm going to do with that money!" He took a pencil out of his pocket and began writing on the tablecloth. He said, "I'm going to pay off the mortgage on my place up in Croton and I'm going to get an automobile," and so on.

Horace listened for a minute, then reminded Dreiser, "You know, you're not getting the whole eighty-five thousand. Remember our deal? You get fifty and then we split the thirty-five. You're going to get sixty-seven thousand, five hundred."

Dreiser put down his pencil and looked at Liveright. He said, "Do you mean to tell me you're going to take seventeen thousand, five hundred dollars of *my* money?"

Horace said, "Dreiser, that was the deal we made. You didn't think I'd sell your book at all."

Just at this moment the waiter brought the coffee in. Suddenly Dreiser seized his cup and threw the steaming coffee in Liveright's face. It was shocking. Horace jumped up, coffee streaming down his shirt front. Luckily it didn't hit him in the eyes. Dreiser got up from the table without a word and marched out of the restaurant. Horace, always the showman, always gallant, stood there mopping himself up, and retained enough of his equilibrium to say, "Bennett, let this be a lesson to you. Every author is a son of a bitch."

There were 108 titles in The Modern Library when we took it over. About nine or so were books that Liveright had added because of some whim or to please some author he was trying to sign up or to show off to somebody. If a girl he was trying to win said, "You ought to have this book in Modern Library," and it meant a weekend at Atlantic City, he'd put the book in. We knew what we were going to do with Modern Library when we got our hands on it—throw those out immediately.

Up to this time Modern Library volumes had been bound in imitation leather. It looked like leather, but actually it was cloth treated with some substance that had castor oil in it. The oil had been deodorized, and when the books were new, there was no odor at all. But in hot weather that castor-oil smell would return, and you could smell a warehouse full of books three blocks away. It was awful.

THE MODERN LIBRARY
A DESCRIPTIVE CATALOGUE

HE MODERN LIBRARY is a collection of the most significant, interesting, and thought provoking books in modern literature, hand bound, fully limp, and designed to sell at ninety-five cents a copy. The judicious selection of one new title a month has resulted, after eight years of strict adherence to a definite policy, in the notable list described in this catalogue. Most of the books have been written in the past thirty years, although there are also included a few works of earlier writers whose thought and spirit are so essentially modern, that the publishers feel they are properly embraced in the scope and aim of the series

THE MODERN LIBRARY · INC.
NEW YORK

The first thing we did, after discarding the dubious titles and making a list of books we wanted to add, was get rid of that imitation-leather binding. We went to a man I had heard was a great typographer: Elmer Adler, head of the Pynson Printers. He was so good that he was allowed to have his office on the eighth floor of the *Times* building on West 43rd Street. He turned out beautiful work at only about eight times what it should have cost. He had no more business sense than my father. But Elmer helped us redesign Modern Library. For the imitation leather we substituted an attractive semi-flexible binding covered with balloon cloth.

We wanted a new colophon, too, for The Modern Library. So Elmer Adler introduced us to Lucien Bernhardt, a well-known German designer, who drew our flying girl with the torch. I had met a very famous artist, Rockwell Kent, and Mr. Kent designed new endpapers. So The Modern Library had a new dress that was very stylish.

Instead of the old trashy-looking catalogue, we wanted to put out something with class. In those days publishers' catalogues didn't amount to anything; they were all unimaginative and routine. So Elmer Adler also redesigned our catalogue. His bill was fabulous. Bills and estimates didn't

Cover (opposite) and title page, new Modern Library catalogue

mean anything to Elmer—he'd tell you he'd do something for a thousand dollars, and when it was finished he'd charge three thousand, and when he was reminded that he was supposed to do it for a thousand, he'd say, not the least bit abashed, "Well, I figured wrong."

Donald and I agreed at the outset that I would take care of the editorial side and advertising, publicity and promotion; he would run the office and supervise production. We decided to divide the selling, because Don was a very good salesman too, and everybody has always loved him. He's one of the nicest men that ever lived. In all the years when the business was growing and growing, Donald was always the one that anybody who had trouble came to. I'd be too impatient.

Everything was to be absolutely fifty-fifty. It would have distressed either of us if there had been any difference. I think we each started with the princely salary of about a hundred dollars a week, and after about three years we had gone up to ten thousand a year. We weren't getting a penny back on our investment. We were building our business, and we pulled ourselves up by our own bootstraps. Not one penny above that $215,000— except from its own earnings—was ever put into the firm that was sold ultimately to RCA for approximately forty million.

Donald was always a stabilizing influence. I would blow my top, and Donald always knew how to handle me. He would sit there, chewing the earpiece of his glasses, and listen very calmly. Then after seven or eight minutes, when he saw that I had had my say, he would get up and say, "Oh, shut up," and walk out of the office, leaving me absolutely enraged and finished—I mean, drained. Then a few minutes later I'd burst out laughing. (I've always been that way. My wife and two kids know me so well, they let me blow off. They know that in ten minutes I'll have forgotten all about it.) Donald was always there to say, "Now . . ." when I'd come up with some cockeyed scheme, and he'd let me talk about it, and then he'd say, "That's the most goddamned foolish idea I ever heard in my life." I had to want to do something very much indeed to convince Don!

At first Donald and I did our own selling, and we would take turns going to Boston and Washington and Philadelphia. When we went into a store to sell our books, the bookseller knew he was meeting the actual publishers. They liked that. We'd also take the time to check to see what titles were missing. We weren't just salesmen now, we were in it for ourselves. And we were beginning to be heard about. We got The Modern Library into many stores that Liveright had never bothered with. In fact, nobody had ever bothered *selling* The Modern Library. It was taken for granted by Liveright, but we were giving our entire time to it—except for the time we spent playing bridge and backgammon and golf.

One of the first things Donald and I did—I remember we were up in Lake Placid—was to go through catalogues of all the publishers and pick out books we hoped to get for The Modern Library. We began adding titles that Horace had not been able to get, partly because the publishers didn't like or trust him. They believed the minute they'd give him a good book, Horace would establish contact with the author and steal him for himself. But we were not competition in those days; we were just The Modern Library. We began getting famous books that Liveright probably hadn't even bothered trying to get because it took too much trouble and time to go and woo the publishers. But as I said, there were no paperbacks in those days, and if you offered a five-thousand-dollar guarantee for an old book, that was pretty attractive. When Boni and Liveright started the series in 1917, the retail price was sixty cents a copy, but after World War I prices went soaring, and by the time we took over, it was ninety-five cents, and it stayed there until after World War II.

The first title we bought for Modern Library was a book that was very popular then, but has long since been forgotten, *Jungle Peace* by William Beebe. And as a result of our first meeting with Mr. Knopf, he later let us add such important books as *The Magic Mountain* by Thomas Mann, *Death Comes for the Archbishop* by Willa Cather and *The Counterfeiters* by André Gide.

We devoted ourselves exclusively to The Modern Library from 1925, when we bought it, until 1927. That's the year we started stepping out! Modern Library was a roaring success and the money was rolling in, but there was very little work to do. By noon we had already counted our orders and processed them; so we played bridge or backgammon. Those were days of easy living, but it soon began to pall. I kept thinking of my Liveright days, the excitement of publishing new books, which I was now divorced from, since we were dealing only with reprints of books other people had had fun with.

Furthermore, at that time there was a great craze for fine press books—beautifully made limited editions—and a demand for autographed first editions. Everybody was rolling in the money they were making on Wall Street. Everybody was a financial wizard. And authors that were popular, like Kipling and Galsworthy and Conrad—their first editions were going up the way the stock market was. Collectors were paying two hundred dollars apiece for a first edition of *The Forsyte Saga*, although I think that edition was over twenty-five thousand copies. This was how popular those "firsts" became. I still have some of them.

I loved press books, and the ones that were becoming the most famous were those of the Nonesuch Press, published in England by Francis Meynell, of the famous literary family. These editions were so enormously popular that every time a new one came out, there would be ten times as many orders as there were books, and since a very small number were sent to America, the prices here skyrocketed. If it was a book that came out at twenty-five dollars, a few days later people were offering seventy-five dollars for a copy. Donald and I were among the bidders.

In the latter part of 1926 I made my second visit to England, and I told Donald that while I was there I'd try to get the agency for the Nonesuch Press for America. Of course, they didn't need an agent because of the great demand, but I said, "If we can't get the agency, at least we may each get a copy of every book for ourselves." This time I was going to meet the English publishers. There was nothing I wanted from them, since we were not yet really in original publishing, but I wanted to meet them for the future.

I was a little abashed about calling on Meynell, so it was my last day—I was leaving that afternoon for Southampton to get the boat home—

Francis Meynell

when I went around to the private house where Francis and his wife, Vera Mendel, ran the Nonesuch Press. Francis proved to be one of the most charming gentlemen in the world. He said, "What can I do for you?" I was rather brash, but a little nervous. I said, "My name is Bennett Cerf and I would like to be the American agent for the Nonesuch Press." He burst out laughing. I said, "What's so funny about that?"

He said, "I'll tell you what's so funny about it. At least twenty-five American publishers have been wooing me to become the agents for Nonesuch Press—they take me out to dinner and they take me to the theater, and after about three nights of wild entertainment, they then bring up what they really want, which, of course, I already know." He concluded, "You come marching in here—I've never even heard of you—and announce you want to be my American agent."

I said, "Well, I'm sailing this afternoon, Mr. Meynell, so I don't have time for all that, but I thought if you turned me down, you'd at least let my partner and me put in our personal order for two copies of every book you publish."

Well, he started to laugh again. His wife came in and we had a very pleasant conversation and became friends within an hour. Then they discovered that a great friend of theirs was one of the partners in my old brokerage office in New York—the one who had called me a weasel because he could never find me. So Francis said, "You know, I can find out all about you very quickly from Heimerdinger. If he gives the okay—and I presume he will—you're our agent," and we shook hands on it.

Then I came home, and of course I called up Mr. Heimerdinger, who graciously agreed to write and tell them that I was a very nice boy, certainly honorable in every way. So Donald and I became the agents for the Nonesuch Press.

Rockwell Kent had become a great friend of ours after he did the endpapers for The Modern Library. I would say he was at that time the leading commercial artist in America. One day Rockwell dropped in at our office. He was sitting at my desk facing Donald, and we were talking about doing a few books on the side, when suddenly I got an inspiration and said, "I've got the name for our publishing house. We just said we were going to publish a few books on the side at random. Let's call it Random House."

Donald liked it, and Rockwell Kent said, "That's a great name. I'll draw your trademark." So, sitting at my desk, he took a piece of paper and in five minutes drew Random House, which has been our colophon ever since.

The Random House colophon made its debut in February, 1927, on the cover of a little pamphlet—called "Announcement Number One"—

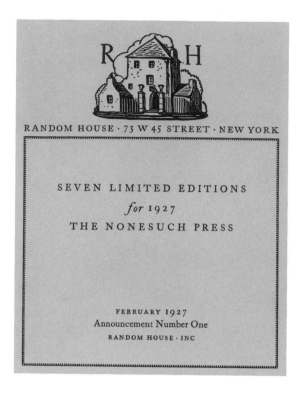

which listed the first seven limited editions that would be published during the year under the joint imprint of Random House and the Nonesuch Press. The first of these to appear was Melville's *Benito Cereno*, illustrated by E. McKnight Kauffer, but the most elaborate and expensive book listed in that first catalogue didn't actually appear until the following year. It was an edition of the *Divine Comedy*, containing both the Italian text and an English translation. It was bound in leather and had about forty double-page collotype reproductions of Botticelli's illustrations. It was priced at forty-six dollars a copy, and though we had only 475 copies, we had orders for about five thousand! So we were in the position of having to cut orders instead of soliciting them.

We got these books at a considerable discount—I've forgotten what it was; it was something like sixty-five percent off—and we sold them for a very small discount. It was not like regular bookselling, and although we had to pay a lot for freight and customs, there was still a good margin. But profit was not what we were looking for; it was the prestige. The entire arrangement was really a gift from Francis, because he could easily have sold all those books direct.

By this time we had outgrown the 45th Street office and needed a bigger place. I had seen Elmer Adler's office, which had been decorated by Lucien Bernhardt, who had done our Modern Library colophon, and I loved it so much that when we moved to 20 East 57th Street, it was Bernhardt who designed our new home.

Since my 1926 trip to London had proved so productive, I decided to go back in the spring of 1928 to renew acquaintances. Then I went down to Naples and spent my thirtieth birthday there. My real objective was Florence, where I had set up dates with two people I was very anxious to meet. One was D.H. Lawrence, the other was Norman Douglas.

Douglas' novel *South Wind* was one of the top sellers in The Modern Library, and he had become famous because of it. He had done a few others, but *South Wind* was his great triumph. When I got to Florence, I found a note at the hotel: Mr. Douglas expected me to have dinner with him. He was a handsome, silver-haired gentleman who couldn't have been more charming. We got along famously. He introduced me to an Italian publisher who was publishing Lawrence's brand-new *Lady Chatterley's Lover* in a special edition in Florence, and I subscribed to a copy. I made my check out to D.H. Lawrence, so that when it came back to me it would be endorsed by Lawrence, and I later pasted it in my copy of the first limited edition of *Lady Chatterley's Lover*.

I'll never forget that evening with Norman Douglas. He started to plan my whole next day for me, and I said, "Now wait a minute. Tomorrow I'm scheduled to meet D.H. Lawrence." Douglas and Lawrence had had a terrible fight a year before over an introduction one of them had written for a book, and they weren't talking to each other. I can still hear Douglas saying, "What do you want to waste your time with Lawrence for?"

But I said, "I'm terribly excited about meeting him."

The next day we had lunch together, and I was supposed to go up to Lawrence's that afternoon. I told Douglas I'd hired a car but that I didn't know any Italian and I had been going crazy trying to tell the driver how to get to Lawrence's, which was up in the hills about ten miles away across the Arno. Douglas began drawing on a napkin and explaining how to get there, but he was not an Automobile Association of America type, and the more he went on, the more confusing he became. Finally I said, "Your directions are incomprehensible. I'll never find him."

Finally Douglas said, "Oh, you're a fool; I'll have to take you myself."

Which, of course, was exactly what I wanted. So we got in the car and off we went to see Lawrence. All the way there Douglas kept telling me not only what a bastard Lawrence was, but how awful Frieda, Lawrence's wife, was. He also continued demanding why he was going with me on this very unpleasant trip. We finally rounded the last curve, and there was Lawrence's villa—an extremely ugly house with a little balcony above the entrance. And standing on the balcony, waving, was Lawrence with his red beard. He was unmistakable—I'd seen all those pictures of him!

Suddenly Lawrence noticed that there were two men in the back seat—and that one of them was Norman Douglas. Lawrence had a very shrill voice. "Norman!" he cried, and came running down the stairs. This frail man died less than two years later of TB, but he literally dashed down those stairs. Douglas jumped out of the car. And the two men, tears of joy in their eyes, wrapped their arms around each other. Lawrence paid no attention to me whatever; I might as well not have been there. The two of them were ecstatic, and Lawrence was calling, "Frieda, Frieda, look who's here!" Out came Frieda, still a very handsome creature, though now quite rotund, and she joined the celebration. The three of them were patting each other on the back and squealing, but finally Douglas said, "This is my young friend Bennett Cerf, whom I know you've been waiting for." They greeted me, and we went inside. The house was a pigpen. Frieda Lawrence was no housekeeper, and I still remember that in the middle of the parlor's marble floor a dirty milk bottle was lying on its side.

We sat and talked—that is, they did, and I sat listening with amazement. Finally Douglas said, "Well, this young publisher has come here to see Lawrence. Frieda, let's you and I take a walk and leave them alone for a little while."

Directly they got out of the house and Lawrence and I were alone, he wheeled on me and said, "How dare you bring that man into my house!" It was so unbelievable, I almost fell over. He said, "Don't you know that we're not talking?"

I said, "Since I couldn't learn the directions, Douglas said he'd bring me here himself. I heard you've been having a feud, but when we arrived I could see right away that basically you're deeply fond of each other."

Lawrence grumbled, "Well, it's an absolute outrage, but never mind." Then *he* started telling me stories about Norman Douglas and what a scoundrel he was. We didn't have much time to talk about literature—he was too busy damning Douglas! Then back came Douglas and Frieda, and the embraces continued as though there'd been no interlude. These two old fakers obviously admired each other. We left finally, and the minute we started down the hill, Douglas, who had been slopping all over Frieda seconds earlier, promptly resumed telling me more scandalous stories about her.

It was an incredible encounter—to meet two literary giants like D.H. Lawrence and Norman Douglas together this way.

The first book we published with *only* the Random House imprint was listed in "Announcement Number Two" in the spring of 1928, along with Nonesuch Press and Golden Cockerel Press books. It was a prize Rockwell Kent production. I had said, "Rockwell, you've got to do our first book." And he said, "I've always wanted to illustrate *Candide.*" That book was one of the most popular in our Modern Library, with no royalty to pay poor old Voltaire; he was in the public domain—the kind of author it's easy to deal with. So we commissioned Kent to do an illustrated *Candide,* and Elmer Adler to print the book at Pynson Printers. As I recall, in early 1928 we did thirteen hundred copies to sell at fifteen dollars each, all signed by Rockwell Kent, and ninety-five copies hand-colored in Mr. Kent's studio, priced at seventy-five dollars. The day it came out, a copy of the fifteen-dollar version sold for as much as forty-five dollars. The limited Kent

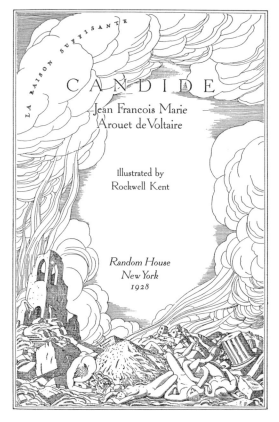

Title page and colophon (opposite), Candide

Candide has of course become almost unobtainable; it's a beautiful book. Because of the great demand, the following year we published a trade edition, which was a Literary Guild selection.

After he produced *Candide,* we asked Elmer Adler to become a partner of Random House, and he agreed, but when the business began to mushroom, Elmer didn't cotton to trade publishing, so we bought him out. He was a very difficult partner anyway—very querulous and dictatorial, had to do everything his own way—and when we wanted to have other printers do books, Elmer was very jealous. He thought he should be in charge of all of it. Very soon we outgrew Elmer, but till the end of his life he was quite indignant with us and was convinced that he should have stayed a partner, that he had been euchred out just at the time that we were beginning to be successful—quite ignoring the fact that he cared nothing about trade publishing. By the time he died Random House was famous.

In 1930 we published a book that also involved Rockwell Kent—one that turned out to be extremely important to us. He had illustrated *Moby Dick* for R.R. Donnelly out in Chicago—the Lakeside Press. Donnelly was doing this as a sort of advertisement. They were huge printers who did telephone books and mail-order catalogues, but they did a few beautiful books for their own private enjoyment. One of them was this handsome *Moby Dick*, which I think sold for a hundred dollars—there were three volumes boxed in an aluminum case—and we persuaded them to let us bring out a one-volume trade edition. We were so excited about it, we forgot to put Herman Melville's name on the cover, so our edition of *Moby Dick*, to the vast amusement of everybody (*The New Yorker* spotted it), said only: "*Moby Dick*, illustrated by Rockwell Kent."

As a result of that book, another big door opened for us. The Book-of-the-Month Club was just getting under way. I had never met Harry Scherman or his partner, Robert Haas. The day they called up to tell us that our *Moby Dick* was a selection, we weren't very excited—we just closed the office and gave everybody the rest of the day off! It was about eleven in the morning and we said, "Go home. This is a holiday."

When a book club makes a selection it agrees to pay, on each copy it distributes, a royalty that is always divided equally between the author and the publisher. It also guarantees to pay an advance against the sale of a specified number of books, and that advance is not returnable even if the club doesn't sell that many. If it sells more, of course, the royalty is paid on each additional copy.

At the time the Book-of-the-Month Club was quite young and small, and the guarantee for a selection was five thousand dollars, which was very little compared to what the club now pays. But when we got that check for the first trade book we published, we were delighted.

About a week later the Book-of-the-Month Club met in executive session, and we received a letter from Harry Scherman telling us that they had decided to raise their guarantee—to double it. And since our book had been selected only a week before, they felt that we shouldn't be short-changed, so they were enclosing a check for an additional five thousand. Well, Donald and I thought about this for a while, and I wrote back: "Dear Mr. Scherman: This is really a fantastic thing to happen, and it renews one's faith in human nature. But I must tell you that if you had cut your guarantee from $5,000 to $2,500, I'm damned if I would have given you back $2,500. We made a deal at $5,000 and I must tell you we were so delighted we closed the office for the day. So with tears streaming down my cheeks, I am returning your check for $5,000."

Well, they were pleased with the letter, and the check came back with an admonition that we shouldn't be damn fools, but should cash it. And again we sent it back, saying, "This is not businesslike at all." So we all decided we'd better meet for lunch—Harry Scherman, Robert Haas, Donald and I. By this time there was great mutual respect, and when that lunch

BENNETT CERF
DONALD KLOPFER
HAVE THE HONOR TO INVITE YOU
TO A SO-CALLED TEA
OR INSPIRATIONAL ORGY
FOR THE SPIRITUAL BENEFIT
OF
ROCKWELL KENT
FRIDAY, JANUARY TWENTY-FOURTH
FROM FIVE O'CLOCK TO ELEVEN
RANDOM HOUSE
20 EAST FIFTY-SEVENTH STREET
R · S · V · P

THIS EDITION, PRIVATELY PRINTED,
LIMITED TO 99 COPIES, OF WHICH THIS IS NO. 1

Rockwell Kent's invitation for a party. All examples are numbered "1."

was over we had become friends for life—all of us—and we finally settled on seventy-five hundred dollars, splitting the difference down the middle, and everybody was very happy about it.

Everybody was being decent, and when people are decent, things work out for everybody. That has been my theory all through life. If you're making money, let the other fellow make it too. If somebody's getting hurt, it's bad, but if you can work a thing out so that everybody profits, that's the ideal business.

Francis Meynell visited America as our guest in the spring of 1929. By that time he was not yet *Sir* Francis Meynell. As the founder and head of the Nonesuch Press, he was in enormous demand by all the bibliophile societies, and everybody wanted him to make speeches. He was an elegant Englishman; he could have walked right onto any stage or into any drawing room—an absolute knockout.

We were now in our new offices on 57th Street. We had plenty of money: The Modern Library was a wild success and the private press books were booming. We were on the fifth floor, and on the second floor there was a brokerage office called De Saint Phalle and Company. It was doing a land-office business because the bull market was nearing its top. Nobody was ever in his office; he was always at the broker's.

A good example was Mr. Womrath, who owned a great chain of bookstores and rental libraries in New York and kept a complete set of The Modern Library in about forty stores. It occurred to me that if I could persuade Mr. Womrath to put *two* copies of each Modern Library book in each store, that would mean orders for forty more complete sets. So I went to see Mr. Womrath and said that if he would put two sets in each store instead of one, I'd give him an extra one-percent discount. And Womrath said very loftily, "My dear boy, don't talk to me about one-percent discounts. I just made ten thousand dollars today in the stock market."

Now, when Francis Meynell came to our office, work stopped—everybody adored him. I took him to lunch one day, and on the way down in the elevator I said, "I want to stop at the brokerage office." He had never seen a brokerage office, and when we walked in, there was wild excitement. The market was surging, the wild bull market. Francis loved everything about this country, and he was completely overwhelmed by all these goings-on—the ticker and the boys rushing around to slap up prices on the board. People were shouting happily—everybody making money hand over fist.

Francis said, "Tell me about this." And I said, "It's the easiest thing in the world. I'll show you how it's done." So I picked out a stock that was moving—they would move in groups—and said, "Before we go to lunch I'll buy you some stock, and show you how easy it is." I bought him three hundred shares of Stone and Webster, and when we came back from lunch the stock was up four points, so I sold for him. He still didn't know what it was, but he got a check for twelve hundred dollars less the commission.

· That was in April, 1929. In November, 1929, Francis, by now an addict of the stock market, got wiped out along with so many others when the crash came. He had only a few months of fun because he'd started near the end, in the most frenetic part of the market, when the averages were going up eight points a day.

The Modern Library was doing nobly for us, and after we established our ties with Nonesuch we became the leading distributor of press books in the United States. We had the Golden Cockerel Press, the Spiral Press, the Fountain Press, the Shakespeare Head Press and many others. All of these private presses came begging us to take them on, since they would then be basking in the reflected glory of the Nonesuch Press, which was the established name in limited editions. By 1929 we had a catalogue of about thirty limited-edition books each season.

Out in San Francisco there was a printer, Edwin Grabhorn, who was becoming famous. I had bought a few of his beautiful, beautiful books—done on handmade paper—and I went out there to get Mr. Grabhorn to do a book for Random House. We settled on Walt Whitman's *Leaves of Grass*—to sell, if you please, for a hundred dollars a copy. When it was announced that Random House was doing a Grabhorn Press edition of the Walt Whitman at that price, we immediately received orders for five times the number to be printed. But just about the time Mr. Grabhorn, who usually did things about a year later than he was supposed to (he was another one of those temperamental geniuses like Elmer Adler), got the book finished, the 1929 stock market crash was on us, and a lot of the people who had ordered copies were now broke, and most of those who had already paid the hundred dollars pleaded with us to give the money back.

Those were fantastic days. People who had been living like millionaires found themselves suddenly penniless, owing their brokers large sums of money. By the time they were sold out, very often not only was their entire equity obliterated, but they had debts that for the rest of their lives they were unable to pay off.

The books that were coming in from Nonesuch proved suddenly difficult to place. Instead of getting orders for ten times our allotment, we were lucky to get rid of what we had. There still remained some solvent collectors, but the whole fever had abated. A first-edition copy of *The Forsyte Saga*, which had sold for two hundred dollars just before the crash, went for twenty dollars at an auction—down ninety percent, just like the stock market.

Though the market for press books collapsed when the crash came, we had The Modern Library—inexpensive books—so even during the Depression we were sitting in clover. In fact, every year we went a little bit ahead, and there was never one when we went backward. Twice a year we'd add five or six new titles. The publishing business has always been rather stable. It doesn't soar when things are going crazy and people with a lot of money are spending it on things like travel, night clubs and expensive theaters. Anyway, book lovers don't usually indulge in speculative excesses. By the same token, when everything goes to hell, books become one of the cheapest forms of pleasure. So The Modern Library rode through the Depression magnificently.

But that was when trouble hit Horace Liveright. It had been mounting for some time. He never did have any business sense, and finally, he couldn't go on any longer. He was forced out of the firm in 1930. (By this time they had changed the name from Boni and Liveright to Horace Liveright, Inc.) The business was more or less taken over by his old bookkeeper, Arthur Pell, who had gotten Horace loans at something like twelve- or thirteen-percent interest.

When Horace was really quite close to the end of his string, he married a wild, beautiful girl who had been married to young Joseph Schildkraut, the actor. Horace was then living in an apartment hotel, the Middletown—148 East 48th Street. There was a reception after the wedding, about six o'clock in the evening at his apartment, which was dotted with famous people who still had an affection for him; actually, as his troubles increased, he became a much nicer person. He thrived on adversity. I had deep love for this man. He played a very important part in my life and I'm very grateful to him.

The wedding party was a wild one because there was a lot of liquor, and on his way there, Arthur Garfield Hayes encountered a German street band on Third Avenue and brought these crazy musicians up with him. The racket in that small apartment—a fellow with a great big bass horn wrapped around his fat belly, and a lot of other brass—was really ridiculous. In the middle of it all, a stranger came in and said, "Which one is Mr. Liveright?" and when Horace was identified, the man went up to him and said, "I have a message for you from Joe Schildkraut," and he hauled off and socked Liveright on the nose, knocked him down and walked out of the apartment. It was very shocking and dramatic—Horace bleeding profusely. It put a damper on the proceedings, but the party went on nonetheless. The marriage didn't last very long; they soon began having terrible fights, and within a short time they broke up. After their divorce Horace was a shadow—a frail, broken man. He took a couple of rooms in one of those converted private houses just around the corner from the scene of his former glory.

Manuel Komroff tells about the last time he went to see Liveright. He walked in—the door was partly open—and Horace was sitting in his shirt sleeves with a blue serge coat on his desk in front of him, and with a bottle of fountain-pen ink and a rag he was trying to cover a threadbare spot in the sleeve of his coat where the white showed through. The great Horace Liveright! A few days later he died, in September, 1933. The man who to me had represented the glamour and glory of the publishing business faded out as a nonentity. It was a very sad story.

I went to see him shortly before he died, and I wrote a piece about him for *Publishers Weekly* that was quite different from their usual run of things and attracted a lot of attention. I'm very proud of it because I took great pains with it:

A straggling handful of people gathered in the Universal Chapel yesterday morning while Upton Sinclair, fearfully embarrassed, mumbled inadequate nothings over the last remains of Horace Liveright, dead at 46. Most of the authors he had started on the road to success, and the friends for whom he had neglected his business when it needed him most, were far too busy to spare the few moments necessary to pay him a last tribute. It was a dismal last curtain to a spectacular career—and to a publisher whose like will never be seen again.

There has been much talk to the effect that Liveright failed in publishing only when he began to neglect it. This is not so. A man who conducted his publishing business at Liveright did was doomed by changes in the book world over which he had no control. Intensified competition, the rise of young men who breathed fresh life into doddering, but financially impregnable, old houses, and, above all, the spectre of diminishing outlets and narrower profit margins, left no chance for a madhouse like Liveright's. His excursions into the theatrical business undoubtedly hastened his downfall, but the foundations were crumbling long before he stepped out. The famous Liveright "flair"—it came through too often to be set down as just a series of incredibly lucky breaks—staved off the inevitable time and again, but it simply could not hold out forever.

Liveright was the worst judge of his employees I have ever known, and the least appreciative of the people who really cared for him. All he wanted around him was people who would inflate his ego and echo his own judgments. The editorial meetings, which he assembled occasionally with much fanfare and ceremony, were one-man shows, with little patience wasted on anyone who dared dispute his edicts. And yet he had an amazing faculty for winning the unquestioning loyalty of a great number of fine men and women. They stood for anything. They love him still. They probably always will. Underneath all his sham and pretense, they saw a rather helpless person, craving affection and admiration, with a rare love of life and a reckless generosity they could not resist.

Other publishers—particularly in London—were continually outraged by Liveright's methods, and amazed that he could continue in the wild, reckless manner that he pursued. Of course, they were right in the end . . . finally there came a day when the whole house of cards began to tumble about his ears. Liveright, always more of a gambler than a publisher, played out his string like a gentleman, and proved infinitely more gallant and more admirable when he was taking it on the chin than he did in his heyday. A poseur to the last, he could be found tapping his long cigarette holder nervously at a table at the Algonquin, a mere shadow of his former jaunty self, announcing ambitious theatrical projects to all the critics, a few weeks before he died, although everybody knew that he was playing through a heartbreaking farce. He told me a lot about his autobiography, but I never read a page of it. It was a magnificent gesture of Simon and Schuster—that old loyalty again!—to buy it sight unseen. Now that he's dead, I hope they will never publish it; at least, not in the original form he planned for it. The really noteworthy events in his life—his dealings with some of the most important literary figures of the generation—he didn't seem to remember. He dwelt on episodes that were far better left unmentioned. He was still obsessed with the quaint idea that the world must know him as the irresistible lover. One of the many successful authors whom Liveright befriended when they didn't have a dime could repay his debt by finishing that manuscript, and telling of some of the genuinely important accomplishments to Horace Liveright's credit—by bringing out the underlying charm of personality that he could turn on at will with such devastating effect; by emphasizing an incredible streak of generosity that piled up over a hundred and fifty thousand dollars of unearned advances before he stepped down from control!

A few months ago Liveright happened into the publishing office he had founded, to visit an old friend. He looked tired and worn. His friend was out. Liveright waited and waited. Then—in the presence of at least three employees—one of the new directors (Liveright had given him his first job there) said gruffly, "Better leave, Horace. I don't think it looks well to have you seen hanging around here!" Liveright didn't even answer. To those of us who knew the old Horace, charlatan and poseur, if you will, but alive, on the move, bursting with vigor and supreme confidence in himself, that is one of the saddest anecdotes we have ever heard.

A few months before Horace's death his old firm had gone into bankruptcy and its assets had been sold for a fraction of their real value. It is ironic to consider that if Pell's advice had been heeded back in 1925 and Horace had not sold The Modern Library to Donald and me, both he and his company might have weathered the Depression. We prospered because of that purchase and built a base for major expansion in the thirties, during which we added some illustrious names to the Random House list. The first two of these became available, also ironically, because of the Liveright difficulties.

After the firm's collapse, it was obvious there was going to be a raid on what few important authors it had left. Everybody was making offers for Eugene O'Neill, and also for one of the leading American poets who was on the Liveright list, Robinson Jeffers. Those were the two I wanted most, and I also wanted Sam Adams—Samuel Hopkins Adams. But O'Neill was the prize. His agent was Richard Madden, and every publisher in New York made a beeline for him when it became known that Liveright was in difficulties. I had a much better idea; I flew down to Sea Island, where Gene and his wife, Carlotta, lived. Gene met me, and I spent two days with the O'Neills. Carl Van Vechten and Fania Marinoff, his wife, were also there at that time.

Eugene O'Neill was the most beautiful man I ever met, and when I say beautiful, I mean in the sense that to look at him was soul-satisfying. He looked just the way a great playwright ought to but practically never does—brooding, piercing eyes, a wonderful smile and a superb figure. He was a great swimmer; he could swim five or six miles at a stretch. As I have said, he talked very slowly, and he would often hesitate in the middle of a sentence. I'm a very impatient man and I keep interrupting everybody all the time. I'm not even aware of it; I even did it with President Roosevelt.

But Eugene O'Neill was the only man I ever knew who without trying could shut me up. I would sit quietly and wait for him to finish his long sentences with the long pauses in the middle. He was one of my heroes, and when anybody asks me to name five or six great men I have met in my life, Eugene O'Neill is always one of them.

At Sea Island, I found him much changed from the wild man I had known at Liveright. He had lived down along the waterfront in those days, among all those men in flophouses, a bunch of drunks who were always in trouble. He was so often at Bellevue to dry out that they knew him there

Eugene O'Neill

by his first name. He had stopped drinking now, partly for health reasons and partly because he had matured; instead of being a young carouser, he had become a dignified gentleman having honors thrust upon him, which at first he avoided. Gene never went to one of his first nights; instead, he'd wander around the city. The night *Strange Interlude* opened he met an old sailor friend, who said, "Gene O'Neill! What the hell are you doing these days?" At that very minute his greatest hit was being played on Broadway!

It was down on Sea Island that I really became Gene's friend. Up until then I was just one of the adoring public that he knew from Liveright, where I was a kid who would hang around him like a faithful little dog. But this time I was becoming somebody, and Gene was the great American playwright. We took long walks on the beach and talked and came to know each other.

Of course, from sixty to eighty percent of the time spent with any playwright or novelist is usually devoted to talking about that author's work. Obviously, a writer loves to talk about himself, and it's a publisher's business to let him. Also, O'Neill fascinated me. This was the life I had chosen for myself, and when he was talking about himself and his plays, I was in heaven; so we got along very well. One thing he talked about at length was a project already in his mind: the Cycle of Seven Plays, which was going to be the story of an American family through many generations, starting back in the Pilgrim days in New England and coming down to the present. The history of this family would be the history of America. The Cycle never came to pass. O'Neill became sicker and sicker, and finally died—leaving only a few of those plays finished, including *A Moon for the Misbegotten;* but none of them was yet ready for production.

When I saw him in Sea Island he had not been married to Carlotta too long, and he was still quite a vigorous man. Carlotta is a story in herself—one of the most beautiful girls in America, brought up in a strict Catholic way out in California, I believe, and then off to New York. When I first met her she was living with Ralph Barton, the famous *New Yorker* illustrator, the one I got to do a catalogue cover for Boni and Liveright. When I went to make that deal with him, the hostess at his place was Carlotta Monterey. But when I got to Sea Island, she pretended she had never seen me before. She knew damn well she had, and I knew damn well she knew she had, too, but the circumstances under which we had met were not permissible for discussion.

When Ralph Barton died years later, he had never forgotten Carlotta, who was not an easy woman to forget. Barton left a suicide note, saying that the only woman he had ever really loved was Carlotta. Someone called her at the Madison Hotel and said, "Mrs. O'Neill, we want you to know that Ralph Barton has died and left a note about you." She snapped, "Why

Bennett and Eugene O'Neill

are you disturbing me while I'm having my lunch? I haven't the faintest interest in Mr. Barton," and slammed down the phone. That's the kind of woman she was.

Gene had met her in 1922, when she was acting in *The Hairy Ape*, his play about a brute stoker down in the hold of a boat and a society girl up on deck who is mesmerized by him. Louis Wolheim, a very wonderful actor who later became famous in *What Price Glory?*, played the hairy ape, and Carlotta Monterey was the society girl. Gene saw her and fell for her. By the time I got down to Sea Island, Carlotta had become a saintlike creature who raised an angry eyebrow when you used the word "damn" in front of her—she was now the great lady. Gene absolutely adored her, but as life went on, theirs came to be more and more of a love-hate relationship.

So while all the other publishers were besieging Richard Madden with offers, I signed up Gene O'Neill personally. We shook hands and the whole deal was made. Madden got his commission, but he was very surprised when O'Neill told him that he was going to come with Random House, since all the big publishers wanted him and we were still beginners.

One of the conditions made by Eugene O'Neill was that I give a job to his old friend Saxe Commins, who had come to Liveright as his editor just about the time I was leaving. We gave Saxe a job, and he turned out to be one of the great men of Random House, a wonderful man, and was our senior editor for many years, until he died.

I came back to New York elated. We had O'Neill, and this gave me a leg up on getting Robinson Jeffers, whom I had never met because he had never visited the Liveright office, but luckily I was the one who had written to him when we were getting his poetry together, so he knew about me. I hustled out to California and signed him up. So we got Liveright's two prizes. Then quite a bit later we signed Sam Adams.

Jeffers was rapidly winning the kind of acclaim that in America is accorded to only two or three so-called popular poets in a decade—like Frost and Edwin Arlington Robinson and Millay, and in later years, Auden

Robinson Jeffers

and Dylan Thomas. There are always a few poets that people think it's smart to have around, and Robinson Jeffers had become a topic of conversation because of his passionate poetry, which at that time was considered pretty far out. Jeffers sold just well enough to make a little money, but there was great prestige in publishing him. Eugene O'Neill was quite different from other playwrights; his books were great best sellers.

Around the middle of 1933 we proudly sent out our notice: "Random House is pleased to announce that it has become the exclusive publisher in America of the books of Eugene O'Neill and Robinson Jeffers." We listed as "available for immediate delivery" eleven volumes of O'Neill plays and five books of poetry by Jeffers—at prices that would not be believed today! Also: we would publish that fall *Give Your Heart to the Hawks* by Jeffers and two new plays by O'Neill.

The first play we did of O'Neill's was absolutely out of his general line. Instead of writing one of those brooding, morbid tragedies he was so famous for, he wrote the comedy *Ah, Wilderness*. It starred George M. Cohan. It was the first time Cohan had ever appeared in a play other than his own. The book was a huge success, and it was a happy start. Our second O'Neill play was *Days Without End*, one that he loved, but it was a complete failure.

I continued to be O'Neill's admirer, publisher and friend for the rest of his life, which became increasingly unhappy and difficult. Toward the end Gene developed Parkinson's disease and his hands started shaking. He became more and more of a recluse because he was ashamed of the fact that when he'd eat, his food would fly all over the place. It is a dreadful disease. During this time Carlotta had become more of a jailer than a wife; she alienated his lawyer and a lot of his best friends, including the Langners of the Theatre Guild. She just threw them out of Gene's life and took possession of him herself. They sold the house on Sea Island. He got tired of it, she said. I don't know what the facts are, but I thought he loved it down there. But he was a restless soul. They bought a house out in California about twenty-five miles from San Francisco, across the bay, in Mill Valley. For some reason or other I was still in Carlotta's favor, and I went out to spend ten days with him in Mill Valley. It was very sad. Here was this great playwright living close to San Francisco but rarely getting into the city, seldom seeing anyone. Carlotta had electric gates installed, and to get onto their property, you had to go through not just one gate, but two; and unless a button was pushed at the top of the hill, those gates didn't open. She could watch over the terrain like an old feudal lord guarding against invading armies.

Gene by this time was quite sickly and very thin. He was still working, but it was getting harder and harder for him. He always wrote standing up. He had a tall desk and he would stand at it and write in longhand in tiny script. In some New Orleans whorehouse he had bought—I don't know how he found it—a player piano which he named "Rosie": it was white, with naked ladies painted all over it. And Carlotta, the great religious girl, thought it was terrible, so Gene had it down in the cellar. He'd sneak down once in a while and drop nickels in the slot, and while it played old ragtime tunes he'd sit there with an ecstatic look on his face. He loved "Rosie."

When I got out there, the first thing Carlotta told me was that Eugene, Jr., and his bride were due shortly after I left. (He was the son who later committed suicide.) Carlotta hated him, as she hated anybody who had anything to do with Gene. She said, "He married a girl who looks like a Minnesota fullback. They think they're going to stay two weeks. Ha, ha, ha! I'll have them out of this house in four days." Those were her words. And she did, too. She also pushed his other children, Oona and Shane, completely out of his life.

But Gene, the afternoon I arrived, beckoned me with his finger, like a mischievous little boy, and we went down to the cellar and I sat there while he played me a couple of rolls on the player piano. He was having a ball. In the middle of it, Carlotta found us and screamed, "You ought to be ashamed of yourself, bringing Bennett down here. You're in pain, remember?" He had forgotten all about his pain, but she reminded him of it and ordered us upstairs. If I'd had a baseball bat, I think I'd have clobbered her over the head. But Gene meekly went upstairs.

At the end of 1945 Gene and Carlotta came to New York, where he worked on the Theatre Guild production of *The Iceman Cometh*. They decided to remain in the East, and in the spring of 1946, took an apartment in the Eighties and began to see old friends. I remember one night Gene and Carlotta were at the Russel Crouses' for dinner. The Irving Berlins were there, too. After dinner Berlin began playing the piano. I can still see Eugene O'Neill standing over him, singing "Alexander's Ragtime Band" in a very bad voice but having the time of his life. And he remembered a song of Irving Berlin's that Berlin himself had forgotten. Gene sang him the song and Irving then recalled it, and the two of them sang it together. It was a great sight.

Another evening Carlotta and Gene came to our house for a dinner party. My wife, Phyllis, and I had invited Burl Ives, who brought along his guitar, and after dinner he sang a few songs. Gene always had to be warmed up, and I knew how to do it. After Burl had entertained us for a while, I said, "Gene, Burl can accompany you on anything. Do you remember some of your old sea chanteys?"

Gene smiled and said, "I guess I could think of a couple of them."

Then he sang a few chanteys, one or two of which Burl knew and the others he picked out. As Gene warmed up, Carlotta got angrier and angrier because Gene was remembering dirtier and dirtier songs. After a little while she said, "I will not be a party to these goings-on. We're going right home, Gene," and Gene stood up, for once in his life, and told her, "I wouldn't dream of it. You go home without me."

I said to Carlotta, "Don't worry, we'll get him home." So she swept out in a rage, and when she was gone, it was as though Gene had been released from prison. He went on singing those obscene sea chanteys, with Burl playing the accompaniment. It was an enchanting evening. Carlotta didn't want him to have a good time; she wanted to own him. They loved each other—but what a way they had of showing it! When Gene would go into one of his Irish furies, he would hurl things at Carlotta. He once threw a wall mirror at her, and if it had hit her, it might have killed her. There were two sides to the story—there always are.

As time went on, Carlotta became more and more irrational. There was no question about the fact that her mind was now affected. She had become obsessive about Gene. He couldn't do anything without her, in her opinion. They finally left New York and moved to Boston. Then Carlotta bought a house in Marblehead, and it was there that things began to be even worse.

By this time Gene really saw nobody. One night he sneaked out for some reason or other. On his way home it started to snow terribly, and just in front of the house Gene, who was now very frail, slipped and fell down and broke his leg. Carlotta came out and stood over him, laughing at him while he lay in the snow with a broken leg. That's when they put her away. Gene stayed in the hospital until his leg mended. Then Russel Crouse brought him down to New York and put him in a hospital. Gene was terrified that Carlotta would find him. "Keep that woman away from me. She almost killed me." He was in the hospital for weeks. Then we all decided together that he was going to stay in New York and never go back to Carlotta.

At the time there was no space to be had in New York; everything was overcrowded. But Phyllis and I found a place for Gene at the Carlyle Hotel on Madison Avenue. Of course, for Eugene O'Neill they moved heaven and earth. And since he was so weak and would continue to need care, we arranged for a male nurse to call for Gene at ten o'clock on the morning he was to leave the hospital and go with him to the Carlyle. But when the man arrived to get him, Gene was gone! Carlotta (they couldn't keep her confined; nobody would certify that she was insane, and at times she could be absolutely normal, very convincing and charming, and meek and beautiful) had found out where he was and had come down to Doctors

Hospital and talked him into going to Boston with her. This was the woman of whom he had said, "Keep her away from me," but he couldn't resist her. He never told Saxe Commins; never told Russel Crouse; never told Phyllis and me. He was ashamed to, and off he went—not a word from him.

Well, of course, we were terribly sorry for him, and furious with him too. He lived for another two years, but we never saw him again. And to finish the saga, when the great Eugene O'Neill died in 1953, this woman allowed not a single friend to come to the funeral. The hearse was driven out to the cemetery, and behind it was one automobile with Carlotta O'Neill and a nurse and a doctor sitting in it—not another soul.

Before Gene died he had delivered to us the manuscript of his long autobiographical play, *Long Day's Journey into Night,* with instructions in writing that it not be published until twenty-five years after his death. We put the manuscript in our safe, fully intending to abide by his wishes; but soon after he died we learned that Carlotta had a different view: she demanded that we ignore Gene's directive and proceed with publishing the play at once. We refused, of course, but then were horrified to learn that legally all the cards were in her hand; what the author wanted, and what he had asked us to do, had no validity if *she* wanted something else—which she did. When we insisted that Random House could not in conscience publish it, she demanded that we give her the manuscript—it was now her legal property—and Yale University Press, apparently caring as little as she did about what O'Neill had wanted, published it promptly. They therefore had a best seller on their hands and a Book-of-the-Month Club selection, but I do not regret that we took the stand we did, because I still think we were right.

Eugene O'Neill was a great man, the great American playwright. He had a streak in him, too, of boyish enthusiasm that didn't seem to fit. He loved talking about the old days and the sea chanteys he had sung. Then that somber, beautiful face of his would light up and you really loved him very, very much indeed.

A man like this comes along maybe once in a generation.

Our great *Ulysses* adventure, which culminated in 1934, had really begun in 1932, when James Joyce's *Ulysses* was contraband in the United States, absolutely forbidden. The only way you could buy it was under-the-counter in an edition published by Miss Sylvia Beach in Paris under the colophon of Shakespeare and Company, the name of her very famous little bookstore on the Left Bank, where many American tourists found their way. Everybody would buy copies of *Ulysses* bound in paper: a light-blue—Columbia-blue—cover. You couldn't come home from Europe without a copy of *Ulysses*, which Sylvia Beach sold for ten dollars. I think Shakespeare and Company really lived on *Ulysses*. The *Little Review* had done some of it in successive issues, but it had even less money than Joyce. A man had pirated some of it and gone to jail, and not only for *Ulysses*; he was also publishing alleged "pornography" of a less literary nature.

I had heard Morris Ernst, the great lawyer, say one night that the banning of *Ulysses* was a disgrace and that he'd like to wage a fight to legalize it. So in March, 1932, I had lunch with Ernst and said, "If I can get Joyce signed up to do an American edition of *Ulysses*, will you fight the case for us in court?" I added, "We haven't got the money to pay your fancy prices"—he was a very high-powered lawyer—"but I'd like to make you a proposition. We'll pay all the court expenses, and if you win the case, you'll get a royalty on *Ulysses* for the rest of your life."

Ernst said, "Great, great." He loves publicity just as much as I do!

So I wrote to Joyce in care of Shakespeare and Company, where I knew he made his headquarters. I said I was coming to Europe and that I'd love to meet him in Paris to see if we could work out a way of publishing *Ulysses* officially in America. I received a letter saying that he'd be delighted to meet me. Why not? He'd never gotten a penny out of America on *Ulysses*. Maybe this was opening a door for him!

On the morning agreed upon I walked into Sylvia Beach's, and there was James Joyce sitting with a bandage around his head, a patch over his eye, his arm in a sling and his foot all bound up and stretched out on a chair. He looked like one of those characters in "The Spirit of '76." I retreated a pace, and Miss Beach, a very lovely gray-haired lady, said, "Oh, Mr. Cerf, don't think he always looks that way. He was so excited about meeting you, on his way here he was run over by a taxicab. But he insisted on seeing you today, because he needs money and he thinks maybe you're going to get some for him."

I said, "Well, I'm certainly ready to give him some."

The eye-patch, I learned later, he always wore, but the other damages were temporary.

I said, "I don't know whether we can win this case or not, but I do think the climate is changing in America, and I'm willing to gamble on it. I'll give you fifteen hundred dollars, with the understanding that if we legalize the book, this is an advance against regular royalties of fifteen percent. If we lose our case, you keep the fifteen hundred."

He was delighted with that; it was a lot more money then than it would be today. He said, "I don't think you'll manage it. And you're not going to get the fifteen hundred back."

I said, "Of course not. That's to make the deal binding." I wanted ours to be the official *Ulysses*—with his full authorization. (Viking Press had published his other books but were afraid to do this one.)

When I met him, Joyce was just over fifty. After he removed those bandages he looked like quite a vigorous fellow. His wife, Nora, was a typical Irish lady—garrulous and friendly. We spent several evenings together, and the last one was the funniest, because this time Joyce, who always had quite a lot to drink, got really potted. Back in his apartment after dinner, he decided he was going to sing me some Irish ballads, but Mrs. Joyce decided he was *not* going to sing me some Irish ballads. And so a

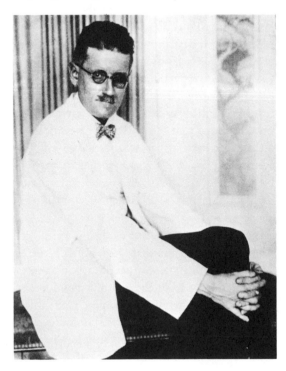

James Joyce

great fight started when Joyce went over to the piano. There was a long bench in front of it, and Nora grabbed one end and Joyce the other—both pulling in opposite directions. Suddenly she deliberately let go, and Joyce went staggering back and landed on his behind on the floor against the wall with the piano bench on top of him. Nora said, "Maybe this will teach you a lesson, you drunken . . ." I thought the time had come to retreat, and so she and I left Joyce still sitting on the floor, quite happy and in no pain. Nora took me downstairs and put me in a taxicab and apologized for the vulgar display, but of course we were both laughing—it was so ridiculous. The last thing I heard from her as I got in the cab was, "Someday I'm going to write a book for you, Bennett, and I'm going to call it "My Twenty Years with a Genius—So-Called.""

I came home and told Mr. Ernst that I had a signed agreement, for whatever it was worth—Joyce's approval that ours was to be the official edition of *Ulysses*. Now several problems had to be solved. We hoped to get a judge who we thought would be favorably disposed to our cause. This was where Ernst's experience was invaluable. He knew that John M. Woolsey was a man of erudition who had already established a reputation for liberal literary opinions, so he timed our case to come up when Woolsey was sitting in New York.

The next big problem was: How were we to get into the court records the pieces that had been written about *Ulysses* by men like Arnold Bennett, Ford Madox Ford, Edmund Wilson, Ezra Pound and other great men of the times. All of these great people and others had written about *Ulysses*, proclaiming it a landmark in literature. We couldn't enter their opinions because the court would not allow outside criticisms to be read in a case of this kind—why, I don't know, but the United States had established that rule. The only way we could do it was to make them part of the book, since anything that was in the book could be used as evidence. So we took one of the Paris paperbound editions of *Ulysses* and pasted in it every opinion we wanted to use—dozens of them in several languages. By the time we finished, the covers were bulging. Since that copy had to be the one that would be used as evidence, we got somebody to take it over to Europe and bring it back on the *Aquitania*, and had our agent down at the dock when it landed. It was one of the hottest days in the history of New York. The temperature on that dock must have been a hundred and twenty degrees, and the customs people wanted only one thing: to get returning passengers off and get the hell out themselves. They were stamping everything without opening it, saying, "Get out; go on out." When our man arrived, the customs inspector started to stamp his suitcase without even looking at it. Our agent, frantic, said, "I insist that you open that bag and search it." The inspector looked at him as though he were an absolute lunatic, and said, "It's too hot."

"I think there's something in there that's contraband," our agent said, "and I insist that it be searched."

So, furiously, the fellow had to open the suitcase. And the agent said "Aha!" as he produced our copy of *Ulysses*. The customs man said, "Oh, for God's sake, everybody brings that in. We don't pay any attention to it." But the agent persisted, "I demand that you seize this book."

After a short argument the customs inspector called over his chief and said, "This fellow wants me to seize this book." Then the chief started to argue; he said that was ridiculous. But our agent had his way. He was right legally, and *made* them seize the book. So when the case came up, that was the copy in evidence.

Morris Ernst made a brilliant defense of *Ulysses* before Judge Woolsey, who fully understood the points being made. The trial, in which there was no jury, was over in two days, and though we had to wait quite a while for a ruling, the judge's attitude made us feel confident that we had won. Woolsey's famous decision, which took him some time to write, concluded that *Ulysses* "is a sincere and serious attempt to devise a new literary method for the observation and description of mankind." He ruled that it was not obscene and could be admitted to the United States.

The case was appealed once, before Judges Augustus and Learned Hand and Judge Martin Manton. The appeal was denied irrevocably, and that was the end of it. We published *Ulysses* in January, 1934, with Woolsey's landmark decision in it—and it is still included in our edition. The book has had an enormous sale; it is one of the leading Modern Library and Vintage Giants and sells thousands of copies every year. Morris Ernst has been getting royalties on *Ulysses* ever since, but he richly deserved them. We never begrudged him this. He's made a lot of money out of it but so did we, and of course Joyce made a fortune too. So everybody was very happy—except the bluenoses, the self-appointed censors.

The year after publication I presented our special copy of *Ulysses* to the Columbia University Library and wrote a letter explaining some of our strategy in the famous case:

May 21, 1935

Dr. Hellmut Lehmann-Haupt,
Columbia University,
The Library,
New York City.

Dear Dr. Lehmann-Haupt:

Various accounts of the "Ulysses" case have appeared in newspapers and magazines, but I think I can give you all the facts that you want most succinctly in this letter.

The reason that we chose to fight our case against the Government through the expedient of importing a copy and having it seized by the Customs was for the purpose of economy. Had the Government refused entry of the volume and had its claim been sustained by the courts, we would have been out only the cost of this single copy plus, of course, the advance that we had paid Mr. Joyce and legal fees. The other alternative was to set up the book in America and publish it and then wait for our tilt with the Government. This, of course, would have been a very expensive way of doing things.

Once we had decided to import a copy and have it seized, it became essential that the book actually be apprehended and not slipped through in one way or another. We therefore were forced to the somewhat ludicrous procedure of having our own agent at the steamer to make sure that our property was seized by the Government. The copy itself was a rather special one, since inside its blue paper cover (Columbia blue, by the way) were pasted critical essays on the book by leading authors and critics of both England and France. Only by having these reviews pasted inside the copy were we able to quote from them when the case actually came before the court.

In due course Judge Woolsey tried the "Ulysses" case, with the results that you know. It was only in the courtroom that we got a second look at our copy of "Ulysses." The impeccable copy that we had imported was already in the tattered, dog-eared condition in which you now find it. Obviously, everybody in the Customs department spent some time on this erudite volume. The District Attorney had also gone to the trouble of marking with a heavy cross every line of the book that he considered pornographic. This marking will undoubtedly be of great help to Columbia students who, I hope, will have a chance to examine this volume in the years to come.

Cordially yours,
Bennett A. Cerf

Ulysses was our first really important trade publication. We had already added O'Neill and Jeffers to our list, and we had done *Moby Dick,* which was an enormous success but was, after all, a standard classic. But here was a big commercial book—with front-page stories to help launch it—and it did a lot for Random House.

There's a very amusing story connected with this. We had never been able to do much business with the American News Company. Macy's was our big customer for Modern Library, but for new books at that time the American News Company, with branches all over the country, was *the* big customer. They distributed all the magazines, and they also distributed books, not only to the bookstores but to stationery stores and all the little miscellaneous outfits. The buyer for the American News Company was a very tough, very efficient fellow named Harold Williams. Donald and I knew Harold and liked him, and we played golf together occasionally. He was a great kidder, with a dry kind of wit. We had done only a little business with him—he had ordered about a thousand copies of *Moby Dick*—but here at last was a book that we thought was going to be a big national best seller. So I went to see Harold Williams down on Varick Street, where the American News Company had a whole building. I told him I thought we had a big book for him, one he could really sell in quantity.

He said, "Oh, I suppose it's that dirty book *Ulysses*. I don't think it's for us."

I said, "What do you mean, dirty? It's all been cleared by the court."

"Well, it's not really our kind of thing," he insisted. "But you're nice fellows, we'll help you a little bit. We'll take two hundred and fifty copies." This was for the whole country, of course! So I started screaming. I got him up from two fifty to five hundred; then, after some more screaming, he made it a thousand. Then, after considerably more battling, I pushed him up to twenty-five hundred, and finally, wringing wet with perspiration, I got him up through several stages to five thousand. He had started at two hundred fifty! Williams said, "Well, are you satisfied?"

I felt very proud of myself, and said, "Yes, at last you've given me the right order."

He opened a drawer and handed me a typewritten order, made out before I came, for five thousand copies! He said, "I thought I'd make you work for it."

It really was a masterly performance. Of course they sold them all, and thousands besides. *Ulysses* was a great best seller, partly because, I think, it was one of those books that are considered smart to own and which many people buy but don't read. Perhaps many did read the last part to see the dirty words; in 1934 that sort of thing was shocking to the general public. But *Ulysses* for a long time now has been an established classic, an important part of the curriculum in literature courses.

We almost lured Joyce to America once, but he was afraid of boats. At the last minute he welshed. By this time he had moved to Switzerland, and had received quite a lot of money from us. His *Portrait of the Artist as a Young Man* and *Dubliners* were also selling well for Viking Press. Harold Guinzburg, the founder of Viking, was one of my best friends, and I didn't want to harm that relationship. There are some publishers who respect the rights of others. Viking and Random House would never dream of doing anything to hurt each other. But some of the best-known publishers in America are veritable pirates. They'll have dinner with you one night and steal an author from you the next day, and if that's their game, we'll play it. But there are certain publishers we feel very close to, Viking and Knopf in particular. That's why we were able to get together years later with Alfred Knopf, because there was that bond of friendship and trust. I only wish we could have Viking with us, too. Phyllis and I love Harold's son Tom. We've watched him grow up. He's one of my favorite people, Tom.

The last time I saw Joyce was in Paris after *Ulysses* was already a big success and I had become a very favored friend. There was a girl I knew at the time whom I liked very much, a darling little girl from a very respectable, very rich Westchester family, who had arrived in Paris with her older sister and the sister's husband, a young Wall Street banker. I wanted to take my girl to Le Touquet for the weekend, but her brother-in-law said to me, quite rightly, "You're not going to take her unless you've got a chaperon. Not that I give a damn, but if her parents ever found out that I left her go off with you for a weekend, they'd kill me. So you get a chaperon—that's all I care about."

I didn't know how I could get a chaperon, and one night at dinner with the Joyces, I said, "I want to take a great girl to Le Touquet, but how the hell can I find a chaperon in Paris?" Joyce said, "I've got the perfect solution for you! My son and his wife would love a weekend in Le Touquet. You take them as chaperons and I promise you won't see them from the minute you get there until the minute you come back, but that will make it all proper."

Everybody was delighted, and the four of us went to Le Touquet together. We liked Giorgio Joyce and his wife, Helen, an American girl, so we actually spent much of the time together. When we were on the beach one day Joyce made a movie of me sitting with my girl and his wife, who was very pretty too. Eventually this girl married somebody else, but I kept track of her for quite a long time. She was a honey! Then in April, 1960, CBS did a television show with Janet Flanner, which had in it pictures of Fitzgerald, Joyce, Hemingway and others of that period, and somebody called me up from CBS and said, "You better watch that show on Sunday afternoon, because you're in it."

I said, "What are you talking about?"

He said, "You are in it—that I promise you."

We made a point of seeing the show, and sure enough, suddenly there was a short sequence of me sitting on a beach with two girls. I didn't have the faintest idea where the reel came from—I didn't even know who the

On the beach at Le Touquet

girls were. I was stunned at how young I looked; of course, I was some
thirty years younger. But *who* were the girls? The next day I borrowed the
tape from CBS and took it up the following weekend to Mount Kisco. I ran
that part of the tape over again on a small projector. A second time I didn't
know who in heck the girls were. The third time a light suddenly dawned.
It was young Joyce's wife and the girl I had gone off with to Le Touquet!
The producers had gotten hold of the film when they were combing Paris
for pictures of Hemingway, Joyce, Fitzgerald and Gertrude Stein, and in
Joyce's possession, along with pictures of his father, there was this shot.
Somebody said, "That's Bennett Cerf. Let's put him in!"

I had to find this old girl of mine, whom I'd finally lost touch with.
After about three days I tracked her down. She was now a grandmother
and had done very well for herself. I called her up. I hadn't talked to her in
thirty years. I said, "Sue—"

She said, "Bennett." She recognized my voice immediately. She said,
"I expected this."

I said, "You saw the show the other day."

She said, "Of course I did."

· 97 ·

I said, "Did you recognize it?"

She said, "You bastard, do you mean to tell me you didn't?"

I said, "Wasn't it something?"

She said, "Oh, goodness, I cried."

I said, "So did I. You've got to come down and have lunch with me."

And she said, "I should say not. I know how you look, I've seen you on television, but *you* don't know how *I* look, and that's the way it's going to stay." She said, "You remember me the way I looked in those days."

I wheedled and cajoled, but she said, "Absolutely no. You just remember me the way I looked then. I wish I looked that way now."

In the fall of the same year that we published *Ulysses,* we brought out Marcel Proust's *Remembrance of Things Past,* another important addition to the growing Random House list. Proust had first been published in this country by a fine old gentleman named Thomas Seltzer, the uncle of Albert and Charles Boni, to whom he sold his business in 1925 to avoid bankruptcy. Seltzer was a first-rate publisher, but he had no business sense at all and he was always short of capital. He would just go along doing a few fine little books a year, none of which would sell very well. When the Bonis ran into financial difficulties, we moved quickly and bought the rights from them.

Seltzer had always presented *Remembrance of Things Past* in seven separate volumes. (Sets used to be quite the thing. There were complete sets of Dickens, complete sets of Hardy. The reason they became obsolete was that most people no longer have room in their houses or apartments for them.) We immediately redesigned *Remembrance of Things Past* as a beautiful four-volume set in a wooden slipcase. It was one of the typographical masterpieces of 1934.

Like its predecessor, our edition used the famous translation by C. K. Scott Moncrieff, who died before he could complete the seventh part, *The Past Recaptured.* That was translated by Frederick Blossom, and for some reason Alexander Woollcott was greatly offended by it and wrote a snide review in *The New Yorker.* He thereby stirred up a controversy that went on for some time, with other critics defending Blossom, who joined them in attacking Woollcott—and he, of course, had some additional remarks to contribute. Needless to say, the whole argument had no ill effects on our sales, and Proust sold in our handsome set as he never had before.

In 1941 our fall catalogue announced a change in our presentation of *Remembrance of Things Past:*

> One of the most successful publishing projects in the history of Random House was the four-volume set of Proust's lifework, published in 1934. When the time came to reprint this set again, however, the publishers wondered whether the $12.50 price might not be discouraging to many thousands of readers who would otherwise be anxious to have a complete Proust in their libraries.

What we had done was to compress the complete work into two volumes which we could offer, boxed, at five dollars. The Book-of-the-Month Club used this set as a dividend and distributed over two hundred thousand copies. Meantime, we had gradually been adding, a novel at a time, the seven volumes to The Modern Library, until they all became available in that inexpensive series. Today *Swann's Way,* the first of the seven, still sells well in colleges, but demand for the others has dwindled. Someday, I am sure, there will be a big revival of interest in all of Proust.

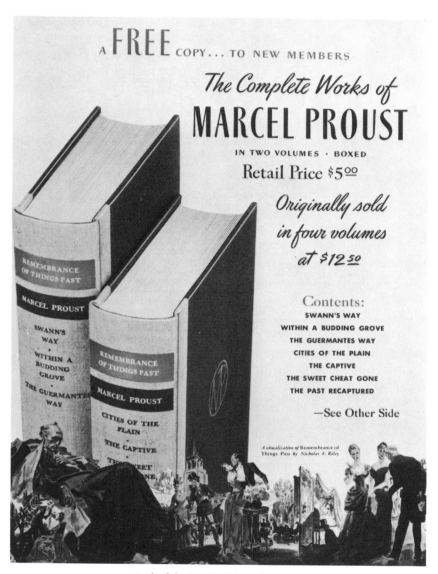

Book-of-the-Month Club mailing, 1941

The very successful *Autobiography of Alice B. Toklas*—written, of course, by Gertrude Stein—was published in 1933 by Harcourt, Brace. Shortly after it came out, my friend Carl Van Vechten suggested that we ought to publish some of her earlier work. I cabled her in Paris at once, with the result that we added *Three Lives* to The Modern Library that same year. Then early in 1934 we published the libretto of *Four Saints in Three Acts,* the opera she did with Virgil Thompson.

I first met Gertrude Stein and Alice Toklas in Paris, when Harold Guinzburg and I were on our way to Egypt and Russia.

DIARY, *April 20, 1934:*

> We had been due in Paris at about 5 P.M., & had arranged to dine at Gertrude Stein's, with la formidable Alice Toklas, but ship's deviation from its course made us hours late. Tied up at dock at Havre at 10 P.M., & didn't arrive at the Hotel Brillon, in Paris — dog-tired — until 1.45 A.M.

April 21

After getting our tickets for Cairo at the Airways office, I rode over to Gallimard's office. (They are the French publishers of Marcel Proust, and I wanted to explain what we proposed to do this Fall with Proust in America: a four-volume set complete for ten bucks.) Mr. Robert Avon, the American manager, however, was away for the day (chutzpa!) and I explained as best I could to a half-witted subordinate.

Walked up the Boulevard Raspail to 9 Rue Huysman, the abode of Helen and Giorgio Joyce, and had a most delightful lunch with Helen, Giorgio, Harold, Mr. and Mrs. James Joyce, Mr. and Mrs. Eugene Jolas, and Mr. Paul Leon. Joyce was in rare good humor, obviously delighted with the job we had done this winter on "Ulysses." I promised that we would send him 7500 dollars at once on account of royalties due him July 1, in order that he might have it before—or if—the dollar dropped further (it moved up to 15.05 today in French currency, making the franc worth almost 7¢—against 4½¢ when I was in Paris in 1930).

I left the Joyces at 3:30 and went round the corner to 27 Rue de Fleurus, where I spent an hour in the famous studio of Gertrude Stein, with Miss Stein and Miss Toklas, surrounded by countless paintings of Picasso and Matisse. Gerty was very pleasant and very voluble, and when she got around to trying to sell me the 4 or 5 hundred copies she had left of her early books (published by herself with the imprint "Plain Editions"), she reminded me very much of Edna Ferber. While this negotiation was in progress, Miss Toklas' imposing mustachio quivered with emotion, the while she interposed nervous comments intended to help drive the bargain home. I promised to consider the project when I got back to New York, and shifted the conversation back to safer ground: Scott Fitzgerald's new novel, "Tender Is the Night" and Miss Stein's latest artist discovery—a young Englishman named Francis Rose.

At 4:45 I left—regretfully—and taxied to the Gare de Lyons.

During my visit I suggested that Miss Stein and Miss Toklas come to America in the fall of 1934, when we would be publishing her next book, *Portraits and Prayers*. We wanted to make a big fuss over it—and over her! She decided to come—her first visit to the United States in thirty-one years. I promised we'd get her enough speaking and writing assignments to pay all her expenses.

Carl Van Vechten and I went to meet her at the dock, and when she and Miss Toklas disembarked, it was a front-page story—something we never expected. The papers thought this visit might make an unusual feature story and sent down their cleverest reporters to meet Gertrude Stein, whose writings were a great joke to many people. "A rose is a rose is a rose."

Gertrude proceeded to handle that bunch of fresh photographers and newsmen like the master she was. She was the publicity hound of the world—simply great; she could have been a tremendous hit in show business. They wrote funny stories about her, but they were mixed with love and admiration, because she was a great woman—a woman of authority. When she talked, she talked as plain as a banker. She knew what she was talking about, too, and all the incomprehensible mishmash appeared only in her writing. The press met a very direct, brilliant woman.

We took her to the Algonquin, and she immediately began telling me all the people she wanted to meet. She just took me over, and for the two or three weeks she was in New York, I was her slave. She ordered me around like a little errand boy.

I remember the morning after their arrival, Gertrude and Alice Toklas came to the Random House office. On the third floor of our building there was an employment agency for cooks and maids; it was a very elegant agency, patronized by all the society people. When Alice Toklas and Gertrude Stein walked into the elevator, the operator took one look at them and didn't even ask any questions; he dumped them off on the third floor. They finally got to our office, with Gertrude highly amused. It didn't bother her a bit. She said, "That damn-fool elevator boy thought we were a couple of cooks and put us off at the employment agency."

The mighty Alec Woollcott demanded to meet Gertrude, so I had a lunch for them in my apartment. As was his custom, Woollcott kept interrupting Gertrude until she stopped him cold and said, "Mr. Woollcott, I am talking." Woollcott actually shut up. She disputed him a couple of times, and he said, "People don't dispute Woollcott." She countered, "I'm not people; I'm Gertrude Stein." Woollcott was delighted, and they got along wonderfully. She disarmed everybody.

Next thing we knew, she was invited to the White House, where she stayed for a weekend. She became the rage, the big success of the season in New York, but still for a very limited audience. I wangled an NBC coast-to-coast interview for her and I acted as M.C. Miriam Hopkins came with us to the studio. (Miriam adored Gertrude, and Gertrude adored Miriam. She had Miriam running errands for her, day after day. It amused her—having a movie star calling for her shoes and having her clothes dry-cleaned. She ordered *everybody* around, and got away with it. Miriam thought she was the greatest thing that ever came down the pike.) I started the radio interview by remarking, "Gertrude Stein, here you are on a coast-to-coast hookup. This is going to be your chance to explain to the American public what you mean by these writings of yours." I added, "I'm very proud to be your publisher, Miss Stein, but as I've always told you, I don't understand very much of what you're saying."

She replied promptly, "Well, I've always told you, Bennett, you're a very nice boy but you're rather stupid."

On a coast-to-coast hookup! The studio audience let out a howl, and believe me, I didn't kid around with Gertrude for the rest of the interview. I was very respectful. She was superb, especially when she started explaining herself.

As we left the studio Miriam said, "You were wonderful, Gertrude. You sure shut Bennett up pretty fast. How much did you get for it?"

Gertrude said, "You mean they pay for this?"

I quickly explained, "There's no pay for this sort of thing—it's the best publicity in the world to get a coast-to-coast prime-time network interview."

Gertrude Stein

Miriam, who was a devil, disagreed. "Bennett ought to be ashamed of himself," she declared. "Gertrude, don't you *ever* go on radio again unless you get at least five hundred dollars for it."

So that became Gertrude's demand. We could have gotten her on a lot of shows for nothing and sold a lot more of her books, but Gertrude said, "Miriam said I should get five hundred dollars. I won't do it for less." That marked the end of her radio career.

Gertrude's lecture tour was a great success—front-page news in every city she visited—so we rushed production of a book containing the complete lectures so that we could publish it while she was still in America. Just before Gertrude and Alice were to depart in early May, I gave them a big farewell party which lasted until about four o'clock in the morning. As she was leaving, Gertrude told me how much she loved seeing her writing in print and asked me how I felt about it. I told her that anything she wanted to see in print, we would do.

So Random House became Gertrude Stein's official publisher. I continued to be frank with her about how bewildered I was by her writing, and when I wrote the jacket copy for her books I was equally frank with the public:

$2.50

The Geographical History
of America
or the Relation of Human Nature
to the Human Mind

By GERTRUDE STEIN
With an Introduction by
THORNTON WILDER

PUBLISHER'S NOTE

This space is usually reserved for a brief description of a book's contents. In this case, however, I must admit frankly that I do not know what Miss Stein is talking about. I do not even understand the title.

I admire Miss Stein tremendously, and I like to publish her books, although most of the time I do not know what she is driving at. That, Miss Stein tells me, is because I am dumb.

I note that one of my partners and I are characters in this latest work of Miss Stein's. Both of us wish that we knew what she was saying about us. Both of us hope, too, that her faithful followers will make more of this book than we are able to!

President
RANDOM HOUSE

She once began a letter to me with "My dear dumb ox Bennett," but it was nonetheless full of warmth and affection. She knew how I felt about her, and I expressed it clearly on the jacket of her novel *Ida*, where I described myself as "a publisher who rarely has the faintest idea of what Miss Stein is talking about, but who admires her from the bottom of his heart for her courage and for her abounding love of humanity and freedom."

The last time I saw Gertrude was in June, 1936. I was staying with Jo Davidson, the sculptor, and Gertrude invited both of us down to her château in Bilignin in the South of France for a weekend. Jo Davidson had turned down many of her previous invitations. He said, "I can't spend a whole weekend with those two crazy women. They're wonderful fun and I love them. But for a whole weekend—not on your life!"

Somehow I managed to talk him into coming with me. According to Gertrude's original instructions, we booked airplane tickets to Lyons, where Gertrude and Alice were to meet us. At the last minute she called up and said, "Go to Geneva; it's closer." Well, that meant one more hop after Lyons. We flew over the Alps in a little single-motor plane, and practically turned upside down en route. Jo got violently sick. Every time I turned to look at him, he was shaking his fist at me, he was so furious. We finally got down at Geneva, and Alice and Gertrude were waiting for us, laughing gaily. Gertrude said, "After I called you up, I found our home was much nearer to Lyons!"

We had to clear customs, of course, from Switzerland into France, which wouldn't have been necessary if we'd gone to Lyons. There was a great deal of excitement because Gertrude was bossing the customs people around. Then we started off, with Gertrude giving directions. She was a great back-seat driver. Alice Toklas did the driving. Gertrude got us lost completely—we went through one village three times. The third time the people waved at us, and Jo Davidson was going crazy. We finally arrived at Gertrude's villa. Everybody in town looked on Gertrude as the boss lady. People came to her with all their troubles—sicknesses, births, deaths, divorces, anything at all. Gertrude ruled the roost.

The way she got the villa is a typical Gertrude Stein story. She and Alice were motoring down through Southern France, and they had lunch in this little town. They were looking for a place to buy, and somebody showed them a château, which was near a big army post. It was perfect, but they were told that it was not on the market because some wealthy army captain owned it, and he had kept himself stationed there by refusing promotion. Gertrude decided she had to have that place, so she went back to Paris and began raising hell because this fellow had been neglected. He was immediately promoted to colonel, transferred—and Miss Stein got her villa.

Alice did the cooking—she was a great cook—and we had a wonderful weekend. I have in my study a little sketch that Jo Davidson drew of me while I was sitting in a deck chair out in the garden at Bilignin with Gertrude's poodle "Basket" at my feet.

Not long after that visit, the coming of the war put an end to my travels. With Alice, Gertrude withdrew from Paris to Bilignin after the fall of France. She sat out the war there, but she was working all the time; and soon after the liberation of Paris in August, 1944, we received a new manuscript from her.

Since Macmillan had just announced the publication of *Forever Amber* with a glamorous picture of Kathleen Winsor on the front cover of *Publishers Weekly*, we followed with a page of our own that announced Gertrude Stein's forthcoming book and featured a photograph of her and Alice B. Toklas that had been taken during their American visit. Gertrude was just as amused as everyone else was. I don't think I've ever met a better sport.

When the book came out in February, 1945, the title had been changed to *Wars I Have Seen*. It was Gertrude's account of what life in

Shucks, we've got glamour girls too!
COMING EARLY IN 1945 **Gertrude Stein's**
ALL WARS ARE INTERESTING

France was like under the German occupation, during which most of it was secretly written, and of what happened when the Americans arrived; it sold better than any of her previous books. The following summer we brought out *Brewsie and Willie,* her story of the conversations she had with the many American soldiers who came to see her after the liberation, when she had moved from her country place back to Paris. Five days after publication, on July 27, 1946, Gertrude died in Paris at the age of seventy-two.

Long before *Brewsie and Willie* was published, we had a big important volume in preparation: *Selected Writings of Gertrude Stein,* a wide representation of her work from 1909 to 1945, edited, with an introduction and notes, by Carl Van Vechten. Gertrude did not live to see it finished, but less than six weeks before her death she wrote a brief message for the front of the book. I was, to say the least, deeply touched by her concluding words:

> Then there was my first publisher who was commercial but who said he would print and he would publish even if he did not understand and if he did not make money, it sounds like a fairy tale but it is true, Bennett said, I will print a book of yours a year whatever it is and he has, and often I have worried but he always said there was nothing to worry about and there wasnt. And now I am pleased here are the selected writings and naturally I wanted more, but I do and can say that all that are here are those that I wanted the most, thanks and thanks again.

Every publisher worth his salt has to publish poetry, even some that he knows he's going to lose money on, and over the years we have done our share. The prestige this gave our company helped us on other fronts on which we also became active: finding younger playwrights and new American writers who had never been published before. We had started with Robinson Jeffers, and on April 25, 1934, *The New Republic* printed my letter announcing that Random House would become the American publisher of two young poets who had taken England by storm:

> SIR: I have noted Alfred Kreymborg's letter printed in your issue of April 4 asking why it is that no American publisher has yet imported sheets of Stephen Spender's poems. I am pleased to tell you that there resposes in the Random House safe at the present moment a contract whereby Random House will publish everything that Mr. Spender writes from now on. We are not importing sheets, but are setting up the poems anew, since we have high hopes that Mr. Spender's poetry will find a wide public in America. Incidentally, at the same time that we publish Spender, we shall publish a volume of another young English poet with exceptional promise—Mr. W. H. Auden.

A little later on, we signed C. Day Lewis and Louis MacNeice, so that in a very short time we had on our list the most promising of the young English poets. Auden stayed on with Random House, and it has always been a pleasure to publish him. There is more demand for Auden than for most poets, year after year, for his old books as well as his new ones.

W. H. Auden—early and late

O'Neill had given us our start in publishing plays, and we had immediately begun our program of signing up playwrights. This was my secret love, of course—a way to feel that I had one foot in the back door of the theater. Besides, plays weren't published much in those days—Samuel French was doing paperback editions, but they were mainly for actors—and the field was more or less open. We began to present plays as real books, attractively designed and hardbound, with illustrations of scenes from the actual productions, and we got them out while they were still running on Broadway.

We started off with George S. Kaufman, who had two plays in 1934. The first, which he wrote with Alexander Woollcott, was *The Dark Tower,* a successful melodrama, and we published it in January. Then, timed to its opening in September, we brought out the comedy *Merrily We Roll Along,* by Kaufman and Hart. (Moss Hart had had his first great success with Kaufman four years earlier, when *Once in a Lifetime* was produced. I had met Moss then, and it marked the beginning of a lifetime friendship.) Before long we were publishing such playwrights as S. N. Behrman, Sidney Kingsley, Clifford Odets, Lillian Hellman, Irwin Shaw and Arthur Kober. We continued to add others year after year, and we had our full quota of Broadway hits.

People thought and still think that I'm crazy to publish plays. They usually lose money, since most people find them hard to read and the audience is limited. Two cities—New York and Hollywood—account for about ninety percent of the plays that are sold, the other ten percent, I would say, being enough for the rest of the country. A certain number of people collect plays or anything to do with the theater, and some libraries buy them too, so even in the case of a total failure on Broadway, we can count on a sale of at least eight hundred. It's unusual for a play in book form to sell more than two thousand, but there are always exceptions. O'Neill was a great best seller, and the first play we did of his, *Ah, Wilderness,* sold over fifty thousand. In the 1930's we had to sell only about fifteen hundred copies to break even, whereas now we have to sell twice as many, even though the price has gone up so much. So we've had to cut down on publishing some of the failures, which we used to do just to please people we knew in the theater. Playwrights all like to have their plays published in permanent book form, and they'll fight for a play that runs only a week.

One thing to remember is that no one ever knows when a playwright is going to say, "I think I'm going to write a book next!" That happened with Moss Hart and *Act One*. It happened with Sam Behrman, with his biography of Joseph Duveen, the art dealer; *Duveen* was selected by the Book-of-the-Month Club. Behrman followed it up with a story of his own life, *The Worcester Account,* and a book about Max Beerbohm, *Portrait of Max,* both Book-of-the-Month. These books all came to Random House because we had published the authors' plays.

Since I had seen Horace Liveright go broke backing shows, Donald and I made an absolute rule that in spite of our great interest in the theater, we would never put a penny into a play. In some cases we passed up big profits, but on the whole, I think that anybody who invests in somebody else's business is a sucker. Angels are pathetic to me. In the old days the main reason they put money in a show was that they hoped to get at the chorus girls, which made some kind of sense at least: they got *something* for their money, but today backers are not even allowed to go to rehearsals. Producers take their money, and that's the end of it. We could have been in on all the Rodgers and Hart, and Rodgers and Hammerstein smash hits! Sidney Kingsley invited us to a run-through of *Dead End* when he needed money, but we had our rule and we stuck to it. By and large, it probably saved us a lot.

In 1936 I got the idea of doing a volume called *The Theatre Guild Anthology*, which was to include twenty of the big successes of the Theatre Guild. The two keystones of this volume had to be Eugene O'Neill's *Strange Interlude* and George Bernard Shaw's *St. Joan*, the Guild's greatest triumphs. We had no trouble getting permission to include any of the other plays we wanted, and Gene O'Neill presented no problem—I was his friend and his publisher—but the great stumbling block was George Bernard Shaw, who would not let any play of his be used in an anthology. What a shrewd old boy he was! I wrote him asking for permission and got back a very curt reply from his secretary, Miss Patch, saying simply that she was very sorry but Mr. Shaw could not accept our offer.

Since I was going over to England in the spring of 1936, I persuaded Lawrence Langner, the head of the Theatre Guild, to give me a letter of introduction to Shaw. I called up the day I got to London, and to my amazement, Shaw answered the phone himself. "I know you want my play," he said. "I won't give it to you—but if you'd like to meet me, come and have tea." He named a day for me to come to his apartment in Whitehall, which was right on the Thames between the Savoy and West-minster Abbey. It was a famous apartment house.

At that same time we had just brought out a work that had pre-viously been sold only to doctors: the four-volume *Studies in the Psychology of Sex* by Havelock Ellis. The rights belonged to Davis and Company, and I had gone down to Philadelphia and talked them into letting us do an edition for the general public. It had never been a trade book, and it was difficult for laymen to buy the medical edition. It was generally considered a "dirty" book, although it is done in such scientific terms that anyone who expects to get erotic excitement out of Havelock Ellis will be disappointed. But Ellis' *The Dance of Life* had become a big seller, and I knew that if we could buy *Studies in the Psychology of Sex,* we would do well with it. It exceeded our fondest expectations.

Now I wanted to meet Havelock Ellis, and by a great combination of circumstances, I had dates with Ellis and Shaw on the same day! I had to take a train to see Ellis. He was up toward Oxford—about a forty-minute train trip—so in the morning I went out to the country and had lunch with Ellis, came back in the afternoon and went right to George Bernard Shaw's apartment. What a day for a young publisher! Ellis was a very nice, charming man, rather shy, with a possessive housekeeper. He left no great impression on me except that of a quiet, dignified gentleman. Actually, he was a slight disappointment to me; he was getting old—didn't live much longer—and he didn't want to talk with a young publisher about sex.

So I said to myself, "Well, now comes Mr. Shaw. What's going to happen? How is he going to greet me? How long is he going to keep me waiting? Will he even remember our date?"

I went up in the elevator—one of those antiques with a rope you had to pull—and rang the bell, and the door opened and there stood George Bernard Shaw! He was in knickers; he had rosy cheeks, a long white beard and jolly, sparkling eyes. I was overwhelmed by him immediately. With Shaw you felt you were in the presence of a superior personality. Miss Patch arranged some tea for us and disappeared. She became quite a good friend of mine later on. She was a nice old lady, a real fussbudget. But Shaw sat down with me, and he was in a talkative mood. He told me all about a trip around the world he'd just made. In California he had met William

George Bernard Shaw

Randolph Hearst and Marion Davies. He couldn't understand why America didn't worship Mr. Hearst, because, as he put it, Hearst had all the qualities that America supposedly adored. He said, "Why is he feared and hated and made fun of, when he's got power, money, rather good looks, a beautiful girl—and a wife who lets him get away with it?" Everything about him, he said, was what America wanted. Marion Davies had absolutely captured Shaw's heart. She had been lovely to him and kissed him goodbye.

Then we began arguing about American journalism and what Americans were like. I said, "For a great man, you have some pretty silly ideas about Americans. You sound like any European tourist, not George Bernard Shaw. You obviously came over all prepared to laugh at us."

I seemed to amuse Mr. Shaw. He paid the supreme compliment of asking me to stay and have dinner with him. I couldn't—I was going to the theater—but we did make a date for dinner two nights later, just he and I.

Then I said, "Well, now, before I leave—"

He said, "I knew we were going to get around to this."

I said, "Of course we are. That's why I came. I need that play for our Theatre Guild anthology. Mr. Langner and Terry Helburn want it for us, too—you know, it will be a sort of celebration of their great plays, twenty Theatre Guild successes."

He said, "What you say makes sense, but I simply don't want any of my plays in anthologies."

I said, "Well, it certainly amazes me that a man like George Bernard Shaw has a set rule. Because he's never done it before, he won't do it once. That's not very progressive."

He said, "I'm too important to go in an anthology."

I said, "We've got O'Neill in it, and he didn't feel that way."

He said, "But you *publish* O'Neill." He knew—he knew!

I said, "Without you, Mr. Shaw, there'll be no book."

He said, "Oh, nonsense."

I said, "I'm quite serious. If we don't get your play, what's the good of doing a Theatre Guild anthology? *St. Joan* was their greatest coup."

He said, "Are you paying O'Neill more than the others?"

I said, "Yes, he and you are the most important playwrights."

Suddenly he proposed, "I'll give it to you if you pay me twice as much as you give O'Neill."

I said, "Isn't that pretty babyish?"

He agreed. "All right, it's babyish. Do you want it or don't you? Twice as much."

I said, "You know I'll give you anything you ask. We have to have it. You mean you'll let us use it?"

He said, "You give me twice as much as you give O'Neill, and you can have it."

We shook hands on the deal. I was delighted. But as we went to the door he said, "By the way, what happens if a book club chooses it?"

I said, "That's ridiculous. The Book-of-the-Month Club won't use a book like this."

He said, "Well, if a book club uses it, you've got to pay me twice as much as you said you would."

I said, "This is purely academic, but all right."

The price, I remember, was two thousand dollars for the use of his play; some of the others were from a hundred to two hundred. Sure enough, when we published *The Theatre Guild Anthology* in 1936, the Book-of-the-Month Club did choose it, and Shaw got four thousand dollars. He was a great businessman. There's a famous story about his having a fight with somebody or other who was explaining to Shaw why he couldn't afford much for the rights to a Shaw play, but that he was going to make a great motion picture out of it. And Shaw said, "There's no use in our talking about it because, obviously, you're a great artist and I'm just a businessman."

Two nights later we had our dinner together. I can't remember where we ate—some restaurant in the middle of town. But after dinner we took a walk, and one of the funniest things happened. Shaw walked very fast, which I like—great big strides—and we were heading down Piccadilly. He was talking a mile a minute—he loved to talk. Occasionally I listen, and this was one of the times. Suddenly out of the shadows a man appeared, grabbed Shaw's hand and said, "Mr. Shaw, my name is Rothschild and I think you're the greatest man alive today." Shaw, without pausing for one second, in full stride, said, "Goodbye, Mr. Rothschild," and pushed him aside and we walked on. We had gone about twenty steps when I let out a wild whoop, and Shaw joined in, explaining, "That's the way to get rid of them."

It was also in the mid-thirties that we made the acquaintance of three young writers whose names were not yet known to the public and who would later become successful and famous. The first books of all three came out under the Random House imprint, but ultimately, for various reasons, they would leave us and go to other publishers. How they first came to our attention is illustrative of some of the curious ways whereby publishers find new authors.

The first one came to us through our association with *Story,* a magazine devoted exclusively to publishing short stories. It had been started in Vienna in 1931 by Whit Burnett and Martha Foley, his wife, and by 1933, it had achieved an international reputation. The Burnetts moved to Majorca, continued to publish the magazine there for a while, but had to stop for a very unusual reason. Their printer had no w's in his shop, none being needed in Spanish, and when he bought some to do their job, the new letters printed up too sharply in contrast to the rest of his old battered type. When we heard of their dilemma, Donald and I, together with Harry Scherman of the Book-of-the-Month Club, bought the magazine from the Burnetts. We financed their move to New York in 1933, provided enough money for them to continue to edit and publish *Story,* and let them have space in our 57th Street office. We decided to sell the magazine in 1935, but meanwhile we had found a few authors through it.

One day Whit came in and said he'd turned up a boy with great talent. We wrote to William Saroyan and signed him up even before we met him. In fact, we never saw him until after his book, *The Daring Young Man on the Flying Trapeze,* came out in the fall of 1934. Then we brought him to New York.

Bill had never been east in his life. He came from the great vineyards of Fresno, California. He was a natural, an absolute natural—the cockiest young Armenian that ever lived—and he charmed everybody. He had never been to a show on Broadway, and the first thing we did was take him to the theater because he said he wanted to be a playwright. It was a very amusing evening. The play was *Ceiling Zero* and Osgood Perkins was in it, a superb actor, father of Tony Perkins. Those were the early days of commercial flying, and the locale of *Ceiling Zero* was an airport. After the first act—it was quite a hit and the lobby was crowded—we walked out for a breather, and I said to Bill, "Well, what do you think of a Broadway show?" expecting him to be bowled over. Bill said, "So that's a Broadway

William Saroyan

show. For God's sake, I could write a better one than that in twenty-four hours." That was his reaction to the first play he ever saw on Broadway—this hick from the vineyards of Fresno. But he did it! In 1939 he had not one, but two successful plays produced—*My Heart's in the Highlands* and *The Time of Your Life*, for which he declined the 1940 Pulitzer Prize.

He was an amazing man. Because he lent himself to bizarre stories, I could make up a lot of anecdotes about Bill to get his name in the papers. He was a cinch to publicize. For instance, the story that when we sent him his author's copies, he took them on a ferryboat from Oakland to San Francisco and went up to perfect strangers and said, "Look. This is my book. I wrote it," and sold them all. Also, that when he came to see me at the Palace Hotel in San Francisco, the phone operator called up, chuckling, and said, "Mr. Cerf, the greatest author in the world is here to see you," and I said, "Send Mr. Saroyan up." Bill came to believe these things really happened and they're in his autobiography. It's funny how people will accept anything that shows them in an amusing or friendly light.

Saroyan didn't stay with Random House for very long. After *The Daring Young Man on the Flying Trapeze*, he fished out of trunks all the stories he had ever written in his life and presented them as his second book. It would have come to about a thousand pages; we very carefully winnowed out about three-fourths of the stories and in 1936 did the ones we rated worthy in a book called *Inhale and Exhale*. Bill accepted the verdict.

About six months later, however, he came and said, "I've got a whole wonderful new bunch of stories"—and they were the same ones we had thrown out of *Inhale and Exhale.* I said, "Bill, I know you have a very low opinion of publishers, but if you think I've forgotten those stories, you're crazy. I didn't like them six months ago and I still don't." And he said, "There are at least ten publishers who would do them." He was by now famous. I said, "Maybe you're right. But we still don't want them." So he took them to Harcourt, Brace and they published the book. It was a complete failure, and I was very pleased with myself, but then in 1942 came *The Human Comedy,* which was a Book-of-the-Month Club choice and a great hit.

Saroyan was a good storyteller and had a great supply of material, but I think much of his recent work is very unfortunate. He doesn't take enough time with it. But he's got great skill and, as I said, incredible cockiness.

One night I introduced him to two sisters—very pretty and alert girls they were. Their name was Frohnknecht—German. The older one, Margaret, later married Arthur Kober. The other, Anne, married Eric Leinsdorf, the conductor. Bill was staying at the Great Northern Hotel, where I had gotten him a room. After we all got home, Margaret called me up, highly amused. She said, "Your friend William Saroyan just called me up and demanded that I come down and spend the night with him, and I said, 'Mr. Saroyan, I'm not that kind of girl. I'm a respectable girl.' Then he said, 'What difference does that make. Don't tell me you're going to turn down an invitation to spend a night with William Saroyan!' " Margaret concluded, "I couldn't get angry at him. He was so ridiculous. When I told him I wouldn't dream of coming down, he said, 'You wouldn't? Then what is your sister doing?' " Typical Saroyan.

I owe my first meeting with Budd Schulberg to a casual visit to the Dartmouth Club in the late fall of 1935. I picked up the undergraduate newspaper with the expectation of finding some such headline as "Coach Lauds Spirit of Big Indian Team at Conclusion of Most Successful Season." Not at all! The editor of this particular paper devoted *his* lead story to a strike then in progress at the marble quarries in nearby Vermont. What's more, he gave the strikers all the best of it. His story was terse, hard-hitting and thoroughly professional. To the trustees of a conservative institution like Dartmouth, this must have smacked of heresy. To a young publisher like myself (remember this was 1935!), it gave promise of an author who might one day go far.

I wrote the editor of *The Daily Dartmouth* a note of commendation. Would he come to see me in New York? He would—and did.

When Budd first presented himself at the Random House offices, I had no idea that the son of one of the most important film magnates in Hollywood would turn out to be a shy, self-effacing and incredibly vague youngster. Nor did I expect this reckless flouter of sacred undergraduate traditions to have a consuming ambition to write good books. I said, "When you do write one, I want it."

Some years later he did write it, and in 1941 we published his first novel, *What Makes Sammy Run?* It is probably the best book about Hollywood ever written. Six years went by before we brought out his novel about the prize-fight racket, *The Harder They Fall.* Then in 1950 came *The Disenchanted,* the story of the last days of Scott Fitzgerald, a Book-of-the-Month Club selection and a big seller. In 1954 he wrote one of the most successful movies that has ever been made—*On the Waterfront,* starring Marlon Brando—and then Budd rewrote the screenplay as a novel, which we published with the title *Waterfront.*

A succession of notable accomplishments has imbued Budd Schulberg with abundant self-confidence, and today, on his face, there's not a trace of diffidence or shyness. The vagueness remains. It's part of his charm. Appointments mean nothing to Budd. The blare of a be-bop band or the sound of a padded glove against a punching bag will distract him from a scheduled conference with a fifty-thousand-dollar movie contract at stake.

Budd Schulberg

When Budd puts pen to paper the vagueness disappears like magic. His prose is explosive and direct. His characters are three-dimensional and dynamic.

It is Budd's harmless conceit to tell interviewers, "My main claim to fame may be that I am the only writer I can think of who reversed the usual process: started in Hollywood and worked east, and to hell with Greeley."

After Saxe Commins, Budd's editor, retired from Random House, Budd, who always wrote slowly, seemed to lose his heart for writing books. He moved around a lot and got involved in causes. Finally, when he did show us the first hundred pages of a new book he was working on, I didn't like it. Then, I'm sorry to say, Budd and I drifted apart.

We first heard of Irwin Shaw in 1936, when his one-act play called *Bury the Dead* opened downtown. It is an antiwar play about six soldiers who have been killed in battle but refuse to be buried, and through their rebellion, convert live soldiers to their pacifist beliefs. Like so many young liberal writers of the thirties, such as John Steinbeck, James T. Farrell and Clifford Odets, Shaw was using a literary form to protest what he regarded as a social injustice.

Irwin's play got a lot of attention and good reviews. Both Donald and

Irwin Shaw

I were very impressed with it and I wrote to Shaw saying that we'd like to publish it. It was unusual for a young writer to have a one-act play published, and Irwin was delighted. We made a date for him to come to see us, and we were surprised to find that he was a great big bruiser of a fellow who was built like a longshoreman—I suppose because of the subject of his play we thought he'd be more ethereal-looking. Instead, he was dirty and sweaty and had a most infectious personality; his laugh was hearty and lusty and made you laugh with him. We liked him on sight. We knew that in spite of its critical acclaim, *Bury the Dead* was not making a fortune for its author, and so, after a moment's consultation, Donald and I decided to offer him a job at Random House. I approached the subject gingerly because I didn't want to embarrass Shaw by asking what he was living on, so I asked what he did. He said he wrote for radio, and my very next question elicited the fact that he was earning five or six hundred dollars a week. When we heard this, Donald and I burst out laughing. Here we were offering him a job and he was making more than the two of us put together. He was indeed already a very successful young man. It turned out that he looked so dirty because he had been playing touch football in Central Park.

We parted company with Irwin some thirty years later over money. Irwin's agent is a very slick fellow—Irving Lazar, probably the best-known agent in Hollywood. He's wonderful for his clients, but left to himself, could end up ruining all the movie companies—he gets so much more money for properties than they are usually worth.

We had a contract with Irwin for a new book of stories. After we had announced it in 1964, he suddenly decided that one of them could be expanded into a short novel. We were not very happy about the project; it was a good enough short story—not memorable, though certainly above average—but when padded out to make a novel, it didn't stand up. We went ahead with it anyway and got the manuscript ready to go to press and announced it in our catalogue for publication in the fall of 1964. Irwin, who had come back from Paris to go over editorial questions, complained that we didn't seem too enthusiastic about the book, and he was right; but we were doing our best with it and prepared to promote it up to the hilt.

Lazar walked into our office one day, obviously uncomfortable. He said that Dell had made Irwin a fantastic offer for three books—the so-called novel, a book of short stories, and a big novel to be written later. Lazar said, "Of course, if you'll match this offer, Irwin will be happy; but if you won't, he knows that you will be decent enough to release him from his contract."

I hit the roof. I told Irving, "You know perfectly well that this book has been under contract a long time." I was so angry, I said, "Get him out of here. I don't want to see him any more. He has an advance from us on this book—a considerable one." Lazar said, "Oh, he'll give you back the advance immediately." This was at least two years after our deal had been made—to Irwin's complete satisfaction at the time. I said, "That's very big of him. We have a contract. We could publish the damn thing and tell him to go to hell, but no, we'll send the manuscript back this afternoon. You send us the check for the advance, and let's forget about Irwin Shaw."

It was a sad ending to a nice story, because Irwin is one of the most enchanting men, and over the years we'd had a lot of good times and published many good books by him—*Sailor off the Bremen, Welcome to the City, Act of Faith, The Young Lions, The Troubled Air,* to mention a few.

Gradually, by adding authors old and new, we were building up a distinguished Random House list, so that when a great opportunity came our way in 1936, we were in a position to take advantage of it. It happened because Robert Haas had become a personal friend through our early adventure with *Moby Dick* and the Book-of-the-Month Club. He was a wealthy man and had retired from the Club, intending to devote the rest of his life to philanthropic organizations. But after a while he became bored doing only charity work, and in 1932 he formed a new publishing house with Harrison Smith.

Bob invited me to a party at his house in the country one night, and while I was there he told me about the trouble he was having with his new firm. They were getting good authors, but to make money with a very small publishing house was then—and is today—almost impossible. So I suggested that the firm of Smith and Haas join up with us. I said, "We've got The Modern Library, which is a pretty good business in itself, and we have a few famous authors and some promising new ones." This appealed to Bob, and finally it was arranged. Now, at one fell swoop, we had William Faulkner—imagine getting Faulkner for Random House!—Isak Dinesen, André Malraux, Robert Graves and Edgar Snow. Suddenly we became really important publishers. This meant there would be no more playing bridge and backgammon in the afternoon or going off to play tennis or taking long vacations. No more three-month trips. Now we had an expanding business to take care of.

Louise Bonino, one of the best juvenile editors in the country, came with the merger. Everybody adored her, and she was a wonderful asset. We also took Harrison Smith with the deal, though we didn't need him. "Hal" was without question one of the most amusing but irritating men in the world. He was charming and everybody liked him, but he was utterly undependable. He'd forget dates and he'd lose manuscripts. After about a year we managed to buy him out. Now Bob, Donald and I each owned one-third of Random House, and it stayed that way for a long time—until a few years before Bob died, when he decided that he wanted to retire again and we bought back his shares.

Our advertising was already being handled by Aaron Sussman, now a partner in Sussman and Sugar, which specializes in publishers' advertising. Aaron has been invaluable to us. We also had Horace Manges taking care of our legal problems. Horace has been one of my closest friends since college days, and I was best man at his wedding. When he became my lawyer he found himself more and more involved in book publishing, and before long he represented not only Random House, but among others, Harper, Scribner, Grosset and Dunlap and the Association of American Publishers. He's *the* publisher's lawyer and a wonderful man.

Then, to make our organization complete, we appointed Lew Miller, who had been at Doubleday, sales manager. He covered the country for us superbly, and everybody respected and liked him. There was never any nonsense about Lew. He put in a new discount schedule that some of the bookstores screamed and raged about, but he made it stick.

I was always very fond of Bob Haas; he was a most dignified and proper man but he had a great sense of humor. I loved to kid him, and he looked upon me as some sort of incorrigible pest. He liked me but he didn't approve of my frivolity. He'd always say that what I needed was more dignity. Bob himself was very severe-looking and held himself awfully upright. He was a captain in the Lost Battalion during World War I, won the Distinguished Service Cross, and came out of the war a great hero. He was a superior man.

I am given to making wild statements occasionally, which I find difficult to support if challenged. One day at lunch I told Bob about the clever press agent who promoted several things in America. He made "September Morn" famous. In that picture there is a naked girl standing in the water, covering herself with her hands. Some dealer, feeling that the American public would go for it, had imported fifty thousand prints of the picture from Europe. But they didn't sell. In desperation, he hired the press agent, hoping he could find some way of putting over "September Morn."

What the agent did was to get an art dealer on Broadway, right near the old Metropolitan Opera House, to put one of the biggest reproductions of "September Morn" in the window. Then he trained some kids to stand in front of it, snickering and making suggestive remarks. Then the agent called John Sumner, head of the New York Society for the Suppression of Vice, and told him there was a filthy picture in the window of a store on Broadway and that there were a lot of schoolchildren being perverted by it. Sumner came at once to see what was going on; and when the kids saw him coming, they went into their act. Sumner arrested the art dealer, so "September Morn" was reproduced in all the newspapers and thus became famous and sold magnificently.

Bob loved this story, so I told him another about what an agent did for a company that had thousands of cans of white salmon—and couldn't sell them. People were used to pink salmon and wouldn't buy anything else. The agent promptly came up with a wonderful idea. He ordered that a big notice be put on each can, saying: "Guaranteed not to turn pink in the can." It worked immediately, but then a canner of *pink* salmon went to court and said the notice implied that pink salmon was contaminated. He won the case, but all of the white salmon had been sold out anyway—so it didn't matter.

When I finished this story, Bob Haas said, "Very interesting, Bennett, but nonsense, there's no such thing as white salmon." Well, of course, I challenged him on this. I said, "There most certainly *is* white salmon." There was probably no subject that I knew less about. A tremendous argument ensued, and I finally said, "I bet you ten dollars there is white salmon." So Bob, always suspicious, said, "How are we going to prove it?" I said, "We'll write to Rufus Grady of the New York Aquarium." Bob looked askance at me and said, "All right, but I want to see the letter you write. I don't trust you."

So I wrote a letter to Mr. Grady, the head of the Aquarium: "There's been a slight bet here. One member of the firm says that there is no white salmon, I insist there is. You're the man who we feel can decide it. Is there or is there not a white salmon in this world?" Bob Haas read it sideways and upside down, to see I wasn't putting anything over on him. He mailed it, put it down the chute himself. Well, we waited for a few days. We had to. There was no Mr. Grady. I had made that name up on the spot, and to back it up, had stationery printed with the heading "The New York Aquarium," with his name on it.

When the answer came, which I had dictated very carefully and then mailed myself, I brought it in, still sealed, to Bob Haas. I said, "You open it. You don't trust me, for reasons that I don't comprehend." He opened the envelope. I'd begun the letter with my college nickname:

Dear Beans:

I cannot tell you what an enormous kick I got out of hearing from you after all these years. There are a hundred questions I would like to ask you about yourself and your activities, but first, what I want to know, is how in hell did you ever come upon the fact that there was a white salmon? As I recall it, you were elected most brilliant man in the class of '20 (I always felt that I was cheated), and now at long last I am beginning to suspect that maybe the boys were right about you after all.

Here are the facts about the white salmon. The only really pure white salmon are the land-locked variety, found in several lakes in northwest Oregon and Washington. If you want to be technical, the scientific name for these white salmon is Ouananiche albo. There is also another species of white salmon found in Alaskan waters called Onchorhynchus, but I am sure that even you could not have heard of this rare species, but I might add that some of the more ordinary run of salmon are such a very pale shade of pink that they pass as white salmon and, in fact, are permitted by law to be sold as "white salmon."

Now I want to know how much your bet was for. I think I ought to get a share of it anyhow! At least, come down and take me to lunch. I hear that things have gone well with you and that Dean Ackerman thinks you are the most brilliant product of his educational system. He always was a screwball!

I do hope you will call me.

As ever,
Rufe

P.S. How would you like me to write a book for Random House sometime on Ichthyology? I am not kidding.

Bob studied the epistle. It was the line about the book that got him. He forked over the ten bucks very reluctantly and said, "It was pure luck. I'm sure you just guessed at it."

Well, for several days I boasted about winning the bet and about my knowledge of fish. But I still had some sheets of "Aquarium" stationery, and I couldn't let well enough alone. I wrote myself several more letters, each time showing them to Bob. After the second one, Bob got suspicious, and after the third, he realized what I'd done. He instantly demanded his money back, but he did think it was funny. He even told the story on himself. But he was only biding his time, waiting for an opportunity to retaliate.

It came with *Beloved Friend*, by Catherine Drinker Bowen, the story of the famous romance between Tchaikovsky and Madame von Meck, who actually never met but knew each other only through correspondence. The story interested Bob Haas and he persuaded Catherine Bowen to write it. The book was promptly chosen by the Book-of-the-Month Club. It was a triumph for Bob.

Bob decided there ought to be illustrations at the head of each chapter and that they should be of high quality. We all agreed that this was a good idea. Three or four artists submitted sketches that Bob thought were suitable, but I rejected all of them. One day when I came back from lunch I found six little sketches on my desk, with a note from Bob: "What do you think of these?" I looked through them hastily, then went across the hall to Bob's office. He was not there, so I wrote "They stink," signed my name thereto and put the note on his desk. Bob's revenge was sweet. He couldn't wait to tell me the sketches were by Rembrandt. It was a great joke on me

Partners Klopfer, Haas, Cerf

and we both enjoyed telling it. We ended up by publishing the book without any illustrations.

Another story about *Beloved Friend* throws an interesting sidelight on Bob's character. Dick Simon heard that we were publishing *Beloved Friend* and called up Irita Van Doren, editor of the Sunday *Herald Tribune* book department, and said he would like to review the book. Irita felt it was rather unusual for one publisher to review another publisher's book, so she asked me, and I said that it was Bob's book and he'd have to decide. Bob said he'd be delighted, since Dick knew music well.

Irita saved the front page for the review, and the day it was due she called Dick Simon. He said, "Oh, I meant to tell you, I won't be able to do that review. I haven't got time." Irita said, "Dick, you were the one who asked to review this book, and now the day before we go to press, you tell me you're not going to do it. That's terrible." He said, "Things came up here at the office. I just can't do it."

So Irita called Bob and told him the bad news. This book meant an awful lot to Bob, and he was missing a front-page review. He phoned Dick Simon and called him every name under the sun and then slammed down the phone. He was fuming. Dick immediately got in touch with me and said, "Your partner, Bob Haas, just insulted me. I'm coming up there and punch him in the nose." I said, "What is this all about?" Dick told me, and

I said, "Bob's absolutely right. I've never heard anything so disgraceful in my life. You were the one who asked to review the book."

Dick was silent for a moment. Then he said, "Well, if that's the way you feel about it, I'm going home and write it." I said, "You do just that." He went home and spent the day writing a very good review and turned it in on time. But Bob Haas never forgave him.

Bob brought another important book to our list in 1938, a translation from the French. It was *The Tides of Mont-Saint-Michel* by Roger Vercel, a novel having as its background Mont-Saint-Michel and its great tides. It was a very good book, but we thought it was going to be one of those minor publications on which we would get good reviews and little else. Suddenly it was a selection of the Book-of-the-Month Club.

One day, years later, Bob came into my office with a letter written in French, signed by Roger Vercel. He showed it to me, and explained—Bob spoke and read French fluently—that the author, whom none of us had met, was making his first visit to this country. Since Vercel didn't speak a word of English, Bob said that he would take care of him but that I would at least have to meet him.

In due course Roger Vercel walked into our office—a typical French-man, with a beard and impeccably attired. He was very affable. I showed him around and introduced him to many people, including two of our top editors, Robert Linscott and Saxe Commins. When Vercel left, Bob Lin-scott said, "You know, it was very strange. No matter what I said to him, all Vercel said was '*Formidable!*'" Manny Harper, our treasurer, said, "Do you know who he looks like? He looks like Lew Miller." I said, "You're crazy."

Well, it was Lew Miller. Lew and Bob Haas had planned their joke for months. The letter had been a fake. Lew had spent two hours with a professional make-up artist having the beard put on, and I was completely taken in. Haas was exultant! Miller was so carried away with his success that he wore his make-up home to fool his two teen-age daughters. When they answered the doorbell, he greeted them with a low bow. They just looked at him and said, "Hello, Pop."

I guess I was the only one who was *really* fooled.

I forget when I first met William Faulkner, but it was before our merger with Smith and Haas. I do remember vividly the first time I read a book by him. I was selling our new list in Philadelphia to Harold Mason and David Jester, who had a lovely little personal shop there, the Centaur Book Shop, the kind you don't see much any more. Harold Mason told me, "Cape and Smith have published a new book by a man I think is one of the great authors of America. His name is William Faulkner." Five of Faulkner's novels had already been published, including *The Sound and the Fury* and *As I Lay Dying*. They had gotten good reviews but hadn't sold. This one was *Sanctuary*, and for 1931 it was a shocking book. So I took a copy and read it in my room at the Ritz-Carlton Hotel. I lost no time getting hold of his earlier books, which for some reason I'd not seen before.

I knew then I wanted to publish William Faulkner, and in 1932 we added *Sanctuary* to The Modern Library, with an introduction by the author. In 1934 we planned and actually announced a special limited edition of *The Sound and the Fury* in which the first section would be printed in different colors to indicate different time levels. A great deal of effort and negotiation went into the project, but it was finally abandoned when the printer let us down. Unfortunately, even the copy of the book that Faulkner marked with colored pencils has disappeared. So it was not until 1936, after we merged with Smith and Haas, that Random House published its first book by Faulkner, *Absalom, Absalom!*—but we published everything thereafter.

William Faulkner had a firm belief that the author writes the book and the publisher publishes it. He would bring in a manuscript, and I'd say, "Bill, do you have any ideas about the book jacket and the advertising?" Bill would say, "Bennett, that's your job. If I didn't think you did it well, I'd go somewhere else." The result was that William Faulkner got more attention in our office than most others, perhaps to prove to him that he was right in trusting us.

After we joined up with Smith and Haas, Bill wrote that he remembered me and was happy with the new arrangement. And I wrote back saying that getting him on our list was the best part of the deal. He didn't come to New York for quite a while thereafter. When he did, he often misbehaved.

One time he was going to be here for ten days, and we arranged all kinds of interviews for him—*The New York Times*, the *Herald Tribune, Time* magazine, and so forth. Everything was beautifully scheduled ahead of time. Faulkner arrived and he and I had dinner together. Hal Smith came along and also a gentleman named Dashiell Hammett, author of *The Maltese Falcon* and some of the best detective stories ever written.

Dash was quite a boy at putting away the liquor, and Hal was no slouch either. And as for Faulkner—well, I couldn't stand the pace. I went home, first saying to Bill, "Remember, there'll be a fellow from the *Times* at the office at ten o'clock in the morning." That was the last we saw of him until I got a call from the Algonquin Hotel several days later; Bill had gone into the bathroom, slipped down against the steam radiator and was badly burned. We rushed him to the hospital, where he spent a good part of his vacation. The day before he went home, I said, "Bill, aren't you ashamed of yourself? You come up here for your first vacation in five years and you spend the whole time in the hospital." Very quietly—he was always very quiet—Bill said, "Bennett, it was *my* vacation."

The maddening thing about Bill Faulkner was that he'd go off on one of those benders, which were sometimes deliberate, and when he came out of it, he'd come walking into the office clear-eyed, ready for action, as though he hadn't had a drink in six months. But during those bouts he didn't know what he was doing. He was helpless. His capacity wasn't very great; it didn't take too much to send him off. Occasionally, at a good dinner, with the fine wines and brandy he loved, he would miscalculate. Other times I think he pretended to be drunk to avoid doing something he didn't want to do.

Bill was one of the most impressive men I ever met. Though he was not tall, his bearing and his fine features made him distinguished-looking. Sometimes he wore what seemed to be rather weather-beaten clothes, but actually were outfits that he had had made to order in England. And he always took time to answer even the most trivial question. You'd say, "Nice day, Bill, isn't it?" and he'd stop and consider it as though you'd asked him something very important.

On November 10, 1950, when it was announced that William Faulkner had been awarded the Nobel Prize for Literature, he said he would not go to Stockholm to get the award. His daughter Jill, whom he adored, was by this time a young lady of seventeen, and when it was pointed out to him that the trip would be a wonderful experience for her, he finally consented. He called from Mississippi, gave us his measurements and asked us to rent a full-dress suit for him and have it ready by the time he arrived in New York.

Bill went to Stockholm and made a superb speech—but he came back a little annoyed because the suit I'd rented for him had only one stripe on

William Faulkner

the pants, and he discovered that European dress suits had two stripes. But he concluded, "You know, Bennett, I think I'll keep that suit."

I said, "What do you mean? I rented it. It's got to go back."

He said, "You just treat me to that suit. I'm going to keep it!"

I don't know whether he ever wore it again, but he took it back home with him.

Well, now he was famous and recognized as one of the great American novelists. His previous books began to be in demand, although a lot of them had gone out of print for a while. Today they are all in print and all sell. They're classics. *A Fable* put him suddenly into the best-seller class. He was on a rising tide, and more colleges were beginning to make him "Required Reading."

I got a call one day from the governor of Mississippi. At first I thought somebody was kidding me. (Norman Cousins of *The Saturday Review* was always identifying himself as the President, or something like that.) But it *was* the governor of Mississippi, and he said, "You've got to do me a favor, Mr. Cerf. This great sovereign state of Mississippi wants to give a dinner in honor of our Nobel Prize winner, William Faulkner, but he won't even talk to me."

I said, "What do you mean?"

He said, "I've called him about five times. He won't come to the phone. And all we want is to fix up a dinner in his honor. I want you to tell him this."

I said, "Well, he's in the middle of a novel. When he's working on a book, he doesn't like to be interrupted. But I'll see what I can do."

I immediately called Bill, who was in Oxford, and said, "Bill, I hear you won't talk to the governor of Mississippi."

He said, "That's right."

I said, "Well, all he wants is for the state to give a dinner in your honor."

And Bill said, "When I needed Mississippi, they had no respect for me. And now that I've got the Nobel Prize, you tell the governor of Mississippi he can go . . ."

When I called back the governor I couldn't quote Bill exactly, so I said, "It's as I suspected, Governor. He's in the middle of a novel. I'm terribly sorry, but he can't be disturbed."

How we laughed over this!

As a man he was so utterly without guile. He would come into the office—he made our office his headquarters when he came to New York—and peel off his coat. I had given him a pair of the red suspenders the Stork Club handed out to favored patrons, and Bill loved them. He would sit there in those red suspenders, smoking a pipe and reading mystery paperbacks. He liked mystery stories. When young writers would come in I'd say, "How would you like to meet William Faulkner?" This always gave them quite a thrill. I'd walk them in, and they'd see this man reading, with his feet up and the red suspenders and the pipe. And I'd say, "This is William Faulkner." And Bill would take the pipe out of his mouth and affably say "Howdy" and return to his book.

The first time Phyllis met Bill was once when he decided on the spur of the moment to come to New York. I said, "We'll come out to meet you at the airport—I want you to meet my Phyllis."

Phyllis was scared to death at meeting William Faulkner. She said, "What am I going to say to him?"

I said, "Phyllis, you won't have any trouble with Bill."

She waited in the automobile while the plane came in. We had arranged to take him with us to River House, where Quentin Reynolds and his wife were having a big cocktail party. Bill got off the plane in an old army trench coat and a dirty slouch hat pulled down over one ear. When I saw him I was delighted, as usual, and I took him over to Phyllis. I said, "Bill, you get up front with us." He hailed her as "Miss Phyllis," and that's what she remained forever after. Her first words to him were "Look at your sock!" The whole heel was out, and he was very abashed. Phyllis immediately lost all fear of the great William Faulkner. She said, "You're not going to a cocktail party looking like that." And so we went home and she made him change his socks. From then on they were great friends. Of course, he was the sensation of the party.

When he made his first visit with us in Mount Kisco, a very characteristic thing happened. At that time the main street crossed the railroad tracks, and the guarding gate was operated manually. When we got off the train Bill stood there watching a little old man open the gate by turning a wheel. I asked, "What's so fascinating about that, Bill?" He said, "I'm mighty glad to see *something* up North that's still done by hand." He knew he was being funny.

The very last time we were with him was at "21" in 1962. It was then that he talked to me about Albert Erskine, who became his editor after Saxe Commins died. Faulkner said, "You know, I think Albert is the best book editor I know." I said, "Golly, Bill, coming from William Faulkner, that's quite an encomium. Have you told Albert?" He paused for a minute, then said, "No, I haven't. Bennett, when I've got a horse that's running good, I don't stop him to give him some sugar."

It has always been Faulkner's plan that when he finished the third volume of the Snopes trilogy, it should be done as a set: *The Hamlet, The Town, The Mansion*—the three separate books about the Snopes family which he wrote over a period of many years. When the manuscript of *The Mansion* was delivered, Albert pointed out that there were certain discrepancies among the three volumes. Bill explained calmly, "That doesn't prove a thing, Albert. As I wrote those books, I got to know the people better. By the time I did the third volume, I knew a lot more about them than I did in the first volume"—as though they were actually real people. The Snopes family is probably his greatest creation—those Southern rascals who rose up from the fields by all kinds of connivance to become the richest people in the county, pushing aside the gentler aristocracy from previous generations.

Bill loved riding horses and hunting. In fact, I've a picture in my office, the last one he ever gave me, in his red hunting costume, inscribed: "To Random House—Love & Kisses—Tally-ho." He was very proud of that picture and proud of his riding.

Faulkner's last book, *The Reivers,* was a Book-of-the-Month Club selection and one of his most amusing. Phyllis, who adored him, said, "Bill, I love *The Reivers.* I think it's a terribly funny book." And Bill smiled that wonderful smile of his and said, "I think so too, Miss Phyllis. Every time I read that book, I laugh and I laugh."

What a lot of people don't realize, because of the tragic elements in most of his books, is that he was a comic genius, and *The Reivers* proves how funny he could be. He saw all of the tragedy of the Old South, but he also saw the humor. I consider him one of the great novelists in the history of American literature and I am certain that his reputation will survive for a long, long time.

On the sixth of July, 1962, early in the morning, *The New York Times* called me up to tell me that Faulkner had died. Within two hours I was on a plane on the way to Oxford. Over the years Bill had asked me many times to come down to visit him, but I had kept postponing it. Now it turned out that the first time I went was for his funeral. I was heartbroken about it.

I went with Donald and the novelist William Styron. *Life* magazine had called Styron immediately and asked him to cover the funeral. So Bill suggested we all go down together.

We landed in Memphis and spent the night there at a hotel, where Donald and I were interviewed by the newspapers as Faulkner's publishers. The next morning we hired an air-conditioned Chevrolet and drove ourselves from Memphis to Oxford, about seventy-five miles. When we got to Oxford we drove up to the courthouse. I felt I had been there before; Oxford is where they made the film of *Intruder in the Dust* and much of it was shot around that courthouse. I didn't realize how hot it was until we got out of our air-conditioned car. The heat was overpowering, like walking into a steam bath.

There were about twenty men sitting around on the steps of the stores. It was really a study in . . . not slow motion, but non-motion. We had had telephone calls from the publisher of the *Oxford Eagle*, and I had promised the editor that we'd call on her at her office so that she could show us some Faulkner items. We weren't due until noon at the Faulkner house, where the services were going to be held right after lunch. We had arrived at about ten in the morning, so we had a couple of hours to spare. We asked one of the men sitting on the steps, "Do you know where the *Oxford Eagle* is?" He just stared at us—didn't answer. Neither did a second. Finally, the third one we asked said, "I think it's over there." We walked around the corner, about twenty steps from where they were sitting. Of course they knew where it was, but they weren't going to have any traffic with city folk. You could see the hostility in their faces.

The editor turned out to be a bustling, energetic woman, quite different from what we had expected. She was obviously a go-getter. She showed us little pieces that Bill Faulkner had written, and took down all her files to show us things that she had printed, proving that she had recognized and understood the worth of William Faulkner even if the rest of the town did not. And she had printed, at her own expense, signs saying that "in memory of our great William Faulkner," every store would be closed from two to two-thirty that afternoon while the funeral procession went by. She had persuaded the shopkeepers to place these in their windows, and they did indeed close for that half-hour.

Then she told us, "We have time to spare. Let me show you the University of Mississippi grounds." So we rode out to the campus. There wasn't a soul around. It was a most peaceful sight—trees rustling in the breeze in this beautiful Southern scene. In less than three months this was where the whole James Meredith confrontation happened, and there was shooting right on this spot.

When we arrived at the Faulkner house a man got up and came to greet us, and he looked so much like William Faulkner that I almost fainted. It was John Faulkner, Bill's brother, who died about a year later. Sitting on the porch were about twenty of Bill's kin. Many of them didn't understand him or his writing, but at news of his death, they had all popped up. They had gotten there within twenty-four hours, and they had all brought—as is the Southern custom—turkeys and hams and pies and puddings. There was a great big table full of wonderful-looking Southern dishes.

Faulkner was lying in a great coffin in the parlor. Nobody paid any attention to him. The relatives were glaring at each other, but when we appeared, they had something new to glare at! I could see they regarded us as interlopers. Indeed, I had to do quite a bit of explaining before they would let Bill Styron in the house. John Faulkner knew who Donald and I were, but Styron was somebody new to him. And when I mentioned *Life,* he bridled. I said, "He's a Random House author and a great personal friend of mine, John. You've got to let him in. I brought him with me, and he's a great admirer of Bill's."

Don and I went upstairs to pay our respects to Jill and Estelle, who looked as though she had taken some kind of a sedative and was staring emptily into space. On Bill's bedside table was my anthology *Reading for Pleasure.* Of course this pleased me. And Styron found a copy of his *Lie Down in Darkness,* and he, too, was pleased.

When Donald and I went down to get something to eat, all the food was just sitting there, untouched. Suddenly one woman—I don't know who she was—said, "Aren't you that fellow we see on TV every Sunday night on *What's My Line?*" I said, "Yes, I am." Well, immediately they all came crowding around me and began asking me about the show. The hostility was gone. I was now one of the people who came to their house every week; I was an old friend. It was incredible to watch the change the minute they recognized me.

Finally the gray coffin was carried out to the hearse, and off it went, followed by six cars. We joined the procession in our car. Then a rather amazing thing happened. We went around the town square, in whose center the courthouse stands. The three or four policemen were standing there with their caps over their hearts. There must have been two thousand people in that square, standing in the streets or in the stores or on the balconies. They stood there absolutely silent as we drove by. There wasn't a sound; it was as though the town was in suspended motion. You could see that they realized they had lost an important citizen.

Then we went out to the brief, simple service at the cemetery. About fifty people were standing there in the hot July sun. As soon as it was over, Bill Styron and Donald and I got in our car and drove back to Memphis and flew home.

One day in the summer of 1937 my friend and lawyer, Horace Manges, brought me some extremely interesting news. A friend of his, Judge Samuel I. Rosenman, who had been counsel to Franklin D. Roosevelt during his terms as governor of New York, was going to edit Roosevelt's papers and speeches for publication. Great competition soon began for the rights to this historic collection. Everybody wanted it, and we were pleased and proud when we were chosen. One of the things in our favor was that Roosevelt had always been a book collector, and this was a time when the physical appearance of our books stood us in good stead. He liked the way Random House books were designed, and when I met him, he seemed to take a liking to me.

Sam Rosenman drove me up to Hyde Park on July 3, 1937. It was an exciting trip: I was going to meet one of my heroes, President Franklin D. Roosevelt! When we got there he was entertaining the mayor of Poughkeepsie. *Entertaining* is not exactly the right word; he was bawling the hell out of the mayor, and his voice carried. Mrs. Sara Delano Roosevelt, Franklin's mother, a very lovely lady, greeted us and kept saying "Tsk-tsk" when she heard Franklin berating the mayor, who obviously had done something the President didn't like. I don't know what it was, but the mayor left, very red-faced, a few minutes later.

Out came the President, wheeling himself. He manipulated that wheelchair like a racing driver. The house at Hyde Park had special ramps and he wheeled up and down like a bat out of hell. As he came out, my heart jumped at the sight of the President of the United States waving his hand; when he said "Hello, Bennett," I was ready to let him roll over me. We went in to lunch after a little while, and he had to be lifted into his chair at the table, which was a shock; but the minute he was seated, he was President Roosevelt. It was only his legs that were bad, and as he sat at the table I forgot immediately that he was a cripple. He was completely in charge and utterly and totally charming. When he wanted to be, he was irresistible.

He told us anecdotes about books and about his boyhood days. He had been, like me, a sucker for a complete Conrad, a complete Kipling. He'd order these sets but then couldn't pay for them. He'd hide them under the bed so his mother wouldn't see them, but she'd fish them out and make him send them back. Before he became President he was a customer at all the shops along 59th Street.

July 16, 1937.

Dear Mr. Cerf:-

I am looking forward to
seeing the books which you have sent to
Hyde Park. You were very nice to do it.

It was grand to have a
chance to talk with you.

My best wishes to you,

Very sincerely yours,

Franklin D Roosevelt

Bennett A. Cerf, Esq.,
Random House, Inc.,
20 East 57th Street,
New York, N. Y.

I left Sam Rosenman up there and drove home alone. I had gotten some autographs from Roosevelt and I was on top of the world—so happy that I got arrested for speeding on the way home. I said to the cop, "You can't arrest me. I've just left President Roosevelt," and he said, "Well, that's a new one." I showed him the autographs and settled for promising him a set of the Roosevelt papers when it was published. He got it, too!

The following December, Donald and I went down to Washington one night to see the President. This was heaven, to have time alone with F.D.R.! I had become very friendly with his secretary, Marguerite ("Missy") LeHand, and when we arrived, she said, "You can go right up."

So we went upstairs, and there in his study was the President. One purpose of our visit was to show him the binding and title-page designs for the forthcoming set and get his approval, but Donald and I had also brought with us a copy of our newly published satire *I'd Rather Be Right,* by George S. Kaufman and Moss Hart. We had had it inscribed to him by George M. Cohan, who played the part of F.D.R. in the show, and every member of the cast. The President immediately signed his own name in the book, remarking that he had begun to do this with all of his books to prevent some member of the White House family from making off with them. I said, "You can't be serious. Why, with your signature in them, I'm going to steal a few myself! Your books will disappear ten times as fast as they would otherwise." He said, "Golly, I never thought of that."

The night before publication I went down to the White House again with what seemed to me a very good idea: if the President put a set of books on his desk, they would be in all the photographs taken of him when he was posing with visiting dignitaries. He thought it was a great idea. Unfortunately, Sam Rosenman didn't. "If you think you're going to turn the White House into a publicity stunt for Random House, you're crazy," he said to the President. "What are you thinking of? You can't do that." He marched off with the books, the President and I looking after him very ruefully; but we knew he was right. Neither of us said a word.

I had to tell the President why I thought we needed that extra promotion: the advance sale had been quite disappointing. Always the optimist, Roosevelt said, "Well, how many have you sold in Washington?" We had sold about three hundred. The President took an envelope and began figuring on the back of it. I waited for a minute or two. As I have said, I'm not very patient, and I finally asked him, "What are you doing there, Mr. President?" He said, "Well, if you've sold three hundred-odd sets in Washington—there are nine hundred thousand people here and there are one hundred eighty million people in the United States, so if you've sold three hundred to nine hundred thousand . . ." He was figuring out how many we should then sell to a hundred and eighty million people. I said, "Mr. President, you must be kidding. All of the embassies are here in Washington and all the diplomats and all the people interested in politics and the politicians, so of course we'll sell plenty in Washington. As for the rest of the country—why, we haven't sold a book in Mississippi in three years." Roosevelt thought that was so funny, he told the press what I said. It came out in the papers, with the result that three bookstores in Mississippi closed their accounts in a rage, thereby costing us about nine dollars' worth of business a year.

The Public Papers and Addresses of Franklin D. Roosevelt came out in April of 1938, in a set of five big volumes at three dollars each—an incredibly low price compared to what they would be today. But after Roosevelt's attempt to pack the Supreme Court at the beginning of his second term, his popularity had slipped badly, and we soon discovered that almost anybody at that time who had fifteen dollars to spend on such things as books also hated Franklin Roosevelt. Furthermore, it was a rather dull collection, with very little exciting in it. And Rosenman had been very profligate; he had us set in type so much material that we had enough to fill ten volumes. Then after it was in proof, he decided what to take out, and the printer's charges for cutting and correcting were enormous. We thought this outrageous, but we had no say in the matter.

We printed fifteen thousand sets, which didn't seem an exorbitant number at the time; but it soon turned out that we were going to be stuck because a lot of booksellers hated Roosevelt, too, and wouldn't order any copies at all. We got letters saying things like: "I always thought Random House was a fine publisher, but we'll never buy another book with your imprint." I answered such people: "What you're angry about is that we published something by the President of the United States. How dare you say such a thing!"

A famous old bookstore in Boston made this offer: "We'll buy as many sets of the Roosevelt papers as you can deliver bound in his own skin." In one of the finest stores in Philadelphia the book buyer was an admirer of Roosevelt, and we arranged with him to have the set displayed on publication day in the center aisle of the main floor as well as in the book department. They were removed the next day on orders from a vice-president, who told our salesman, "Don't be angry with me. Roosevelt doesn't mean one thing or another as far as I am concerned. But our customers hate him."

There was no doubt that the sale of *The Public Papers* was going badly, and I found out from Doubleday that their two-volume edition of the public addresses and papers of Herbert Hoover had been a colossal flop—it sold only about two thousand sets. I knew Roosevelt was still optimistic, and I figured I had to temper him down a bit. I went up to Hyde Park and said, "You know, I'm a little worried about the project—I don't think the papers and addresses of anybody are going to have any huge appeal to the American public." He said, "What makes you say that?" I told him how Doubleday had done with the Hoover, and he let out a roar of laughter and slapped his knee and said, "Hoover sold two thousand—that means we'll sell a million!"

In the end we sold only about seven thousand sets, and were stuck with all the rest. A lot were returned by the stores, and I tried to persuade Sam Rosenman to let us send them out to libraries or schools at cost and get some rich supporters of Roosevelt to supply the funds. All we wanted was to get our manufacturing costs back, since we had already taken a terrible shellacking. Rosenman wouldn't do it. He thought we ought to give the books away, but we had lost enough money already, so we sold them finally for about four or five dollars a set to jobbers who specialized in selling publishers' mistakes at a discount.

The President was very offended. He didn't think we should have done it, but he had no other suggestions to offer. He was a rich man, but he took his full royalty and so did Sam Rosenman. The books were taking up a tremendous amount of space in the warehouse and we couldn't keep them there indefinitely.

I tried to explain it all to Roosevelt, but his pride was hurt. I said, "We can't keep them, Mr. President. We've taken a big beating as it is, and now we have a chance of getting over twenty thousand dollars back— selling about five thousand for four or five dollars a set." I told him that all those unnecessary author's corrections had already run us terribly in the hole. He was very angry at us, and I wasn't invited to the White House any more. I was even taken off his Christmas card list!

Later Macmillan and Harper each did another five-volume set of Roosevelt papers, but they had learned by our experience. Instead of printing fifteen thousand sets, they did only a few thousand, and they didn't do any publicity on them or waste money on elaborate ads and circulars the way we had. But I don't regret our loss on our venture one bit. I had a couple of weekends at Hyde Park with F.D.R. and one at the White House—and you can't buy that for money.

In 1939 Harry Maule had been for many years one of the senior editors of Doubleday, and probably would have finished out his career there had not the powers that be, in their great wisdom, decided that Harry Maule had outlived his usefulness, so they forced Harry to resign at the ripe old age of fifty-three.

Harry and I had lunch and talked. He said he would like to come with Random House, and told me he was very close friends with the authors he edited. Then he named a list that floored me, beginning with Sinclair Lewis, William McFee, Vincent Sheehan and Mignon Eberhart. Those were his plums, but he said, "I can't guarantee that any of them will leave Doubleday and come with me." I admired his honesty. I didn't think he was through by a long shot, and I was right.

Harry came with us and stayed with us—this man who was "through" in 1939—till about 1964. He was a superb editor. He brought us every author he had named—every single one of them. Harry was one of the gentlest, finest men that I've ever known. From the day he joined us to the day he left, so old he could barely walk, everybody in the place loved him, although once in a while you had to use forbearance with Harry. He was a little long-winded, and once he started, you couldn't stop him.

Every time William McFee came to the office—McFee was quite deaf, and like so many deaf people, shrieked at the top of his lungs and had a funny habit of grabbing you by the ear and screaming into it—he'd start shouting in Harry's ear, and Harry would try to quiet him down. I still remember how amused we all were at McFee and Harry. What a combination! He was a nice man—McFee—an old sea captain. Unfortunately, he drifted off and lost his popularity, but he did write three fine books—*Casuals of the Sea*, *Captain Macedoine's Daughter* and *Command*—that I think are as good as Conrad's sea tales.

Vincent Sheehan had already done *Personal History*, by far his best book, before he came to us, but we published a couple of great sellers of his. One, in 1943, *Between the Thunder and the Sun*, I guess outsold even *Personal History*.

Sheehan became a war correspondent during World War II and managed to make one wrong prediction after another. His book on Gandhi, *Lead, Kindly Light*, was a Book-of-the-Month Club choice in 1949. It was a good book, but Sheehan came back with a raft of crazy ideas he had picked up while researching it in India. For instance, when Douglas MacArthur returned as a hero and had a victory parade up Park Avenue, I was standing with Sheehan at a window on about the twenty-fourth floor of the Waldorf when MacArthur went by far below. Sheehan insisted to me that Douglas MacArthur had seen him up there and that they had had a communication by telepathy. That's when I realized I was talking to a man who was going off the beam. He got worse and worse. We did a couple of his novels. He's one of those men who write very good nonfiction but insist on writing fiction. Both novels were colossal failures, and of course he blamed us. Then Simon and Schuster offered him a lot of money to write a book about Oscar Hammerstein—not the author of *Oklahoma!*, but his grandfather, the Hammerstein who built the Harlem Opera House back in the late nineteenth century. We readily gave him permission.

The most important author who came with Harry Maule was Sinclair Lewis. I had first met Lewis, whom everyone called "Red," sometime in

Sinclair Lewis

the late thirties. He was not a personal favorite of mine—I thought he was a difficult man and a habitual drunkard, but I liked his books. His most famous—*Main Street, Babbitt, Arrowsmith, Elmer Gantry, Dodsworth*—had appeared back in the twenties and had brought him the Nobel Prize for Literature in 1930. Though his popular success had continued, his last book for Doubleday, *Bethel Merriday,* in 1940, was by his early standards a failure.

His next novel, *Gideon Planish,* was his first for Random House, and in 1943 our catalogue predicted that it would "stir up as much public comment as did any of Mr. Lewis' previous books." Unfortunately, our estimate was overly optimistic: *Gideon Planish* had only a moderate success because it was just not as good as some of the previous books referred to. One night when we were together, probably about the time of *Gideon Planish,* he propounded an interesting theory about writing. He felt that his had suffered in the thirties because during his marriage to Dorothy Thompson he had let her talk him into using professional typists to make the final drafts of his scripts. He now regretted following her advice, because he was convinced that if an author didn't do his own retyping—revising and improving as he went—he lost some control over his work. Maybe he had a good point; William Faulkner and John O'Hara, for example, did their own typing.

Red had separated from Dorothy Thompson in 1938 after a stormy ten years of marriage, but he remained bitter about her even after he had found a new girl—an eighteen-year-old would-be actress named Marcella Powers. Red was crazy about her and remained so for the rest of his life. I suppose the great difference in their ages embarrassed him; when he first started taking her out he introduced her as his "niece," but he soon got over that. She left Red several times and he'd always scheme and plot out ways to get her back, including having her mother come and live with him so Marcella would have to call his house. Finally she left him for good. During the Marcella days Red was on the wagon and stayed on the wagon.

We published Sinclair Lewis for the rest of his life, and though he could be extremely touchy and irritable, both Phyllis and I became very fond of him. He was a lonely man and the loneliness came mostly out of his own doing. For instance, he'd cut himself off from people by letting it be known that he didn't want to see them, and then getting hurt because they took him at his word. That's what happened to him in Williamstown, Massachusetts, where he bought a summer home. When he first arrived there, Red sent out word through the bookstore that he didn't want to be bothered by the local lights. He announced he was there to work, not to entertain them. This news was quickly spread through the faculty of Williams College and they left him strictly alone—obviously to his dismay,

Sinclair Lewis and Marcella Powers

for when we arrived for one of our many visits, Red complained bitterly of the snobbishness of the faculty, saying they hadn't the courtesy to pay him a call, or even the intelligence to take advantage of the fact that they had one of the world's greatest living authors in their midst.

In the mid-forties Red delivered two novels that matched—in sales if not in quality—his performance of the twenties. In 1945 *Cass Timberlane* was a Book-of-the-Month Club selection and a best seller; it was also made into a hit movie starring Spencer Tracy and Lana Turner. Two years later his novel about racial prejudice, *Kingsblood Royal,* was chosen by the Literary Guild and sold more than a hundred thousand copies in our edition. At that time it seemed that Red had pulled himself together and was regaining his former power.

The hope was not to last very long, however. In the fall of 1948 he brought in the manuscript of *The God-Seeker,* a historical novel set in Minnesota in the middle of the nineteenth century, which would prove to be even less successful than *Bethel Merriday.*

That fall, before he left for Italy, Red spent his last night before sailing at our house. Just as the three of us were finishing a quiet dinner at home, Bob Haas phoned to say that Bill Faulkner was with them for the evening and asked if we'd like to join them. I was so sure Red would be delighted that I said yes without even asking him. But Red said, "No, Bennett. This is *my* night. Haven't you been a publisher long enough to understand I don't want to share it with some other author?" So I had to call Bob back and decline.

We sat and talked for a while; then Red, who had to get up at the crack of dawn, said goodnight and went upstairs to our guest room on the fourth floor. Since it was very early, Phyllis and I were still sitting in the living room, two floors below, when suddenly Red shouted down the stairwell, "Bennett! Bennett!" We were afraid something awful had happened, so I rushed to the stairs and called, "Red. What is it?" And he said, "I just wanted to be sure you hadn't slipped out to see Faulkner."

Red stayed in Italy about six months, and while there he began to drink heavily again. When he returned he went up to Williamstown and rapidly finished a novel, *Lucy Jade,* and I can't describe how bad it was. I was visiting him in Williamstown in July and I had to read it there, part of the time with him sitting across the room staring at me as I read. It was very hard under those circumstances to tell him what I thought of the manuscript, but I did, and he was very angry with me. He had sold the magazine rights to Herbert Mayes at *Cosmopolitan,* and he said he was going to let Mayes read it and see what *he* thought. When Mayes told him it was even worse than I'd rated it, Red actually agreed to write it all over again. But he so resented our criticism that he took off on a binge so bad that medical help was needed to bring him out of it.

After he recovered, Red decided he had to get away, and on September 7, 1949, he took off for Europe again. Just before he sailed we had lunch together at the Weylin Hotel. That was the last time I saw him—on what turned out to be his last day in his native country. In Europe his health became progressively worse as his drinking increased, and in January, 1951, he died in Rome. But he had somehow managed to finish the rewriting of his last novel, and two months after his death we published it under its new title, *World So Wide.*

I must say that the revised version was just as bad as the first one. It was murdered by the critics. Here was a case of a man who kept on writing too long. His last two books were dreadful and should never have been published, but how can you stop a once very successful author from writing if he wants to continue? Some authors just get played out and know when to stop, but there are many who keep on after they have nothing more to say. Reviewers often blame publishers in these situations, saying that we have done an author a disservice by not turning down this or that book. But anybody who knows anything about the literary world should know that if we reject a manuscript by an author with a big reputation, somebody else will publish it, and we will destroy our relationship with the author even if it has been a close and long-standing one.

Just before Christmas in 1949, not long after Red Lewis had departed on his final trip, Phyllis and I went to a party at Herbert Mayes's house in Stamford. Herb was at that time the editor of *Good Housekeeping,* but he was also buying material for *Cosmopolitan,* in which he planned to publish the new Hemingway novel *Across the River and into the Trees,* and he showed me the part he had so far received. Rather early in the book comes the scene in Harry's Bar in Venice in which the narrator describes a man at a nearby table—unmistakably Red Lewis—in the most scurrilous terms, mainly about the condition of his face. Red had long suffered from a skin disorder which could not be cleared up and which had badly marred his face; he was extremely sensitive about it, and if he ever read this vicious scene, the effect on him must have been devastating. I don't know if he ever saw it—Mark Schorer, in his biography of Lewis, says it is doubtful—but I remember how furious it made me when I read it.

I also remember how excited I was when I first met Ernest Hemingway. A receptionist announced he was in our lobby, and at first I thought somebody was kidding me. But it *was* Ernest Hemingway, dropping in for a friendly visit. We had sold thousands of his *The Sun Also Rises* and *A Farewell to Arms* in The Modern Library, and as he was passing our office he'd decided to come in and say hello.

A few years after his death our interest in Hemingway really sharpened when A. E. Hotchner proposed to write something about him. We had published a rather unimportant novel by Hotchner, but now he told me about his great friendship with Hemingway and said he wanted to do a story of his month or so with him when they took a trip together from the Italian Riviera to Spain. It was to be more or less parallel to the successful though cruel book Hemingway had written, *A Moveable Feast,* of a similar journey with F. Scott Fitzgerald. We could tell by what Hotchner said that this was going to be rather a mean book, too. I questioned the propriety of doing it, whether it would be in good taste. But as Hotchner pointed out, Hemingway had written vicious things not only about Fitzgerald, but about Gertrude Stein, Sinclair Lewis and other friends of his. So why shouldn't it be done to Hemingway? In the last year of his life Hemingway had developed many very ugly and annoying traits and made a fool of himself with his "papa" routine, and Lillian Ross had inadvertently showed him up in her adulatory *New Yorker* piece. So we said, "Go ahead," and Hotchner's story expanded until it turned out to be a full-length book about Hemingway, ending with his dissolution and his finally killing himself after going quite insane.

We published *Papa Hemingway* in 1966, and it was a Book-of-the-Month Club choice and a big success. Mrs. Hemingway, the widow, the fourth Mrs. Hemingway, was outraged and said that the story of her husband's life was her exclusive literary property, which was the most absurd claim in the world. She sued, and of course the case was thrown out successively all the way up to the State Supreme Court.

One of my close friends was Harold Ross, the founder of *The New Yorker;* he was, I think, the greatest magazine editor we've ever had in this country. He was a strange mixture: people might imagine the editor of *The New Yorker* to be a polished gentleman, but Harold always looked as though he'd just gotten off a train from Sauk Center. He was a very naïve man and very prudish; he would never allow a bad word in *The New Yorker.* Anything salacious was killed by Ross, and that led to many fights with Alec Woollcott, who always tried to sneak in little off-color stories.

The book publishers very quickly got wise to the fact that *The New Yorker* was uncovering the smart young writers, and the minute Ross found one, sixteen publishers were after him. Of course, Ross would complain about this, and for that matter, about everything else.

I met Ginger Rogers through Harold; who adored her and was also a great friend of her mother, Lela Rogers. Though Ross was used to being waited on hand and foot, and nearly everybody was scared to death of him, Ginger treated him as somebody to be humored, laughed at and with. She would forget dates with him or come an hour and a half late, and he'd say, "That's all right." Ross took it absolutely meekly. Other people he would have screamed at if they were five minutes late. But Ginger was something else again! She's a great girl.

Once in a while Ross and I would go to the theater together; he'd bring Ginger and I'd take my girl of the month. I also spent many weekends at his house in Stamford, and one of those visits turned out to be a historic event. On Saturday morning, July 15, 1939, I picked Ross up and we drove over to George Bye's place. Bye was Eleanor Roosevelt's literary agent, who that day was throwing a big picnic lunch in her honor.

Ross had told me that Lela Rogers was coming for the weekend, bringing with her, as he put it, "Ginger's goddamn kid cousin." When we got back to Stamford that hot afternoon, everybody was down by the lake in their bathing suits—the kid cousin in a little red-and-white-checked one. She was absolutely the cutest-looking kid I had seen in a long, long time. Ross said, "This is Phyllis Fraser," and I walked right over and kissed her. She smacked me in the face. That's the way we met; I was a fresh guy. All the next day we lazed around at Ross's, playing badminton, croquet, Chinese checkers and backgammon. I was fascinated by Phyllis, of course, and spent most of the time talking to her.

She was just twenty-three at the time. I found out that she was born in Kansas City, Missouri, but when she was two her mother took her to Oklahoma, and when she was fourteen her Aunt Lela and Ginger took her to Hollywood to live with them. As small children Phyllis and Ginger adored each other and were like sisters, as they still are.

In Hollywood, Phyllis became a sort of baby starlet and was in several pictures. But she was a very smart girl, and even then she realized that she was getting parts because she was cute, not because she had any great acting talent. Also, she just didn't like being an actress. She began writing and selling a few pieces to movie magazines. Then she decided to go to New York, where she got a job in the radio department at McCann-Erickson.

Phyllis Fraser

When I met her she was working on two very popular daytime radio serials, one with Josephine Hull—a wonderful little woman who played in *Arsenic and Old Lace*—the other with Joseph Cotton and Martha Scott. Phyllis was editor of the productions and doing extremely well.

It didn't take long for our friendship to flower. I didn't immediately stop seeing other girls, but I started taking Phyllis out. On our first date, about a week after we met, I took her to dinner at the Hungarian Pavilion at the New York World's Fair. Later we started going to the French Pavilion, which was the great hit of the fair. That was the beginning of restaurateur Henri Soulé. It was also the beginning of Phyllis and Bennett. We often revisited Monsieur Soulé.

Then I began introducing her to my friends. I was a little sheepish about it because she looked like a child, about eighteen at the most, and I got quite a lot of kidding. She was small and quiet and darling. All my friends fell in love with her at sight, which had not been the case with several other girls I'd had. They immediately said, "This is for you. You've found the girl." There was never much question in my mind. It was inevitable.

When I took her to meet George Kaufman, I was terrified because George always scared me a little. He was a fine man but a savage wit, and he could make people nervous with his sarcastic comments. All the way down to Bucks County to George and Beatrice Kaufman's, I kept telling Phyllis, "Now, don't be too scared of George Kaufman." We got there and George was waiting at the portico. He had heard us coming up the driveway. Phyllis got out of the car, and George said, "So this is Phyllis." He held out his arms and Phyllis walked right into them. Beatrice loved her, too. That day Phyllis also met a man who has played a very important part in our lives—Moss Hart, who lived nearby and was working with George on the play *George Washington Slept Here*. Moss and Phyllis loved each other at once, and this meant a lot to me, because I adored Moss Hart; my eyes still get misty when I think of him.

Phyllis and I were seeing each other more and more, but I was fighting this thing because I was still recovering from an abbreviated and unsettling marriage, and a replay was not part of my dream at that particular time. In 1935 I had married Sylvia Sidney, but even before the honeymoon was over I realized I was not cut out to be the husband of a movie star. We had planned it that Sylvia would spend six months of every year in New York with me, and the other six in Hollywood, acting; but we saw very quickly how ridiculous and impossible that idea was. A star has to put her career first, so her husband comes second. The marriage lasted less than a year.

The bad part of being married to a girl like Sylvia and having it end is that you can't forget it quickly. I'd keep her out of my mind for a while, but then I'd turn a corner and see a flag in front of the Paramount theater—three stories high: SYLVIA SIDNEY. Or I'd open a paper and see a big picture of her looking absolutely beautiful in some new movie she was doing. Or I'd read an item about myself—for three years after the marriage it was always "Bennett Cerf, ex-husband of Sylvia Sidney," which used to drive me absolutely crazy. Gradually the tag disappeared and my memories of her disappeared too—the poignant ones, the ones that hurt.

I think you can tell when you're over this kind of affair: for a long while thoughts come unbidden into your head to haunt you—places you've been together, holidays you've shared—and then there comes a moment when you're cured but don't want to admit it to yourself, and you deliberately dredge up the memories, and you say, "I guess I'll suffer a little bit." It's like putting a record on the Victrola. Now it's no longer involuntary; it's something you do on purpose. I know myself so well that I soon caught myself doing this, and reflected: Why, you . . . stop this self-pity, you fool. You're doing it just to play games with yourself.

What completed my cure was meeting Phyllis. I loved her, I was mad for her, but I was scared—really scared. She's a great deal younger than I am, about seventeen years. It's a big difference. But finally I decided to put my fears aside, and we were married on September 17, 1940, by Mayor Fiorello La Guardia at the summer City Hall. It's been glorious, just about perfect.

At the time of our marriage I had a beautiful apartment that had been designed especially for me in the Navarro, on Central Park South. There were four rooms, and for a time it was big enough for us. My father was living upstairs in the same building in a little apartment I had gotten for him, and Phyllis would often make breakfast for Pop and me. In December, when it came time for Christmas—Pop and I had never had a tree or anything—Phyllis started the tree business, and I found I loved it. Pop, always discreet and delicate, put a little cradle under the tree for Phyllis, a hint that he would like to have a grandchild.

He didn't know, but one was already on the way, and we began to look around for another place to live, since we didn't have enough room for a baby. One day Neysa McMein said, "Why don't you buy a house?" For some reason that had never occurred to us, but luckily, almost at once, we were shown one we liked so much that we've had it ever since.

Our first son, Chris, was born in August, and two months later Pop died. A new life began for us.

Phyllis was bewildered at first by the number of people who seemed to be my intimate friends. The fact of the matter was that I would see many of them only once or twice a year, but they were still my good friends. She soon picked and chose the ones she liked best, and those are the ones that have been closest to us ever since.

It rapidly became evident that all our authors liked Phyllis because she's warm, she's intelligent, she's attractive. (Of course, she was busy at first with a little baby, and then, after a five-year lapse, Jonathan arrived.) Her judgment is in many ways impeccable. She doesn't pretend to know literature with a capital L. European moderns aren't Phyllis' act. But on American novels and nonfiction, her taste is excellent. I began to rely more and more on what she would say about manuscripts, and when I was in doubt about one I thought might interest her, I would very anxiously await her approval. It was Phyllis who signed up Marjorie Craig's *21-Day Shape-Up Program,* a best seller that presents a wonderful regimen of exercises. They are done faithfully every day by Phyllis and me and have been responsible for keeping us in very good shape.

Shortly after we were married she and my uncle, Herbert Wise, edited for Random House *Great Tales of Terror and the Supernatural,* probably the best anthology of its kind ever compiled, and a very big success.

It was Phyllis who was later responsible for my thinking seriously about the books we published for children. She felt we were not doing the kinds of books that could help our own children expand the knowledge they were gaining in school. As I began to read to, and with, Christopher and Jonathan, I realized how right she was, but still I didn't get personally very involved with children's books until Christopher got beyond the "read-to" stage. Now the juvenile department of Random House is one of the biggest in the country and probably the best, and no little credit is due to Phyllis, our sons Jon and Chris and, of course, our superb juvenile editor Louise Bonino, and the sales know-how of Lew Miller and later Bob Bernstein. When Louise came to us with the Smith and Haas merger, she was Bob Haas's secretary, and on the side, responsible for editing books for children, which were really "carriage trade books." The list wasn't large, though they had published three of the Babar series translated from the French by Robert Haas's lovely wife, Merle. At that time, except for classics, children's books were not a very profitable business, and few authors could afford to make writing for children their life's work.

The first juvenile book I personally signed for Random House was by the now famous Dr. Seuss—Theodor Geisel. He had written two juveniles for Vanguard Press, but the one he did for us in 1939 was *The Seven Lady Godivas,* intended for an adult audience, which I am sad to say it never found. In that same year we published his *The King's Stilts,* a juvenile which didn't sell very many copies, either. Then in 1940 came *Horton Hatches the Egg;* this was the first of many successful books that Ted would do for us.

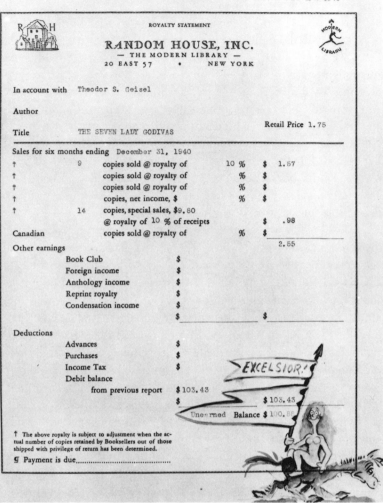

ROYALTY STATEMENT

RANDOM HOUSE, INC.
— THE MODERN LIBRARY —
20 EAST 57 • NEW YORK

In account with   Theodor S. Geisel

Author

Title   THE SEVEN LADY GODIVAS   Retail Price 1.75

Sales for six months ending   December 31, 1940

†	9	copies sold @ royalty of	10 %	$	1.57
†		copies sold @ royalty of	%	$	
†		copies sold @ royalty of	%	$	
†		copies, net income, $	%	$	
†	14	copies, special sales, $9.80			
		@ royalty of 10 % of receipts		$	.98
Canadian		copies sold @ royalty of	%	$	
Other earnings					2.55

Book Club	$
Foreign income	$
Anthology income	$
Reprint royalty	$
Condensation income	$
	$

Deductions

Advances	$
Purchases	$
Income Tax	$
Debit balance	
from previous report	$ 103.43
	$

EXCELSIOR!

$ 103.43

Unearned Balance $ 100.88

† The above royalty is subject to adjustment when the actual number of copies retained by Booksellers out of those
shipped with privilege of return has been determined.

¶ Payment is due..

Dr. Seuss annotates a royalty statement

The Cat in the Hat was the one which inspired Phyllis to ask Ted and his wife, Helen, to form a company with her to publish books for children just learning to read. The three of them set up a separate corporation of which they were the editors and publishers. Random House was the distributor— Donald and I, and Lew Miller, each bought a tiny interest along with Louise, our production man Ray Freiman and Manny Harper, our treasurer. Phyllis later gave a few of her shares to Bob Bernstein, but it was Helen and Ted and Phyllis who owned the bulk of the business. They called their firm Beginner Books. After a couple of years Beginner Books became so profitable that I wanted it for Random House. Phyllis didn't

"Outgo J. Schmierkase Award" to Theodor Seuss Geisel "for twenty-five years of dazzling accomplishment," October, 1962

really want to sell, but the others were interested in the capital gains; so we bought the firm, and it became a wholly owned subsidiary of Random House.

Phyllis finally bowed out of Beginner Books to start two series of her own: Step-Up Books, which are factual books for kids who can read at a level just beyond the Beginner Book range, and Take-Along Books, for the child still in the lap-sitting reading stage. Phyllis is a genius at that sort of thing, and her understanding of children is fantastic. She always involved our two sons, Chris and Jon, in whatever she did. During their summer vacations I put them to work as messenger boys. This way they learned all about Random House, including our employees' names and the functions they performed. I remember when Chris was about eight years old—a cabdriver querying him as to what he wanted to do when he grew up, and his answering, "I want to be a publisher, because all they do is laugh and talk all day." I'm glad to say he never changed his mind about what he

Bennett made honorary member of Harvard Lampoon, *May 4, 1961. In center: Marshall Field and Michael Frith*

wanted to be, but I think his on-job training taught him there was more to publishing than laughing and talking.

While Chris was still at Harvard, I gave him the task of surveying the lifetime sales of The Modern Library. Chris learned all about the series and we learned that some of the titles we loved had not sold as well as we thought. Phyllis prevailed upon Jon to help with a newspaper for New York schools that she and Jason Epstein wanted to try; it didn't work financially, but Jon learned a lot from it. The experience was valuable to him when he graduated from Harvard and started teaching school—and thus met a pretty art teacher named Rosanne Novick, whom he married, much to my delight. After Chris graduated from Harvard he and one of his best friends, Michael Frith, went to work at Random House in earnest. Mike worked for Phyllis, and Chris worked on another of our juvenile series—Pop-Up Books, with which he did quite well.

The series books are the ones which make money for a company, for if a child likes one, he'll go back to the store for more. We found that to be true with the Walter Farley books about horses, Ira and Mae Freeman's science series, and others such as the Shirley Temple storybooks, the Alfred Hitchcock mystery and ghost stories, the Wonder Books, Pop-Up Books, Dollar Flats, and my special favorites, Landmark Books.

Our son Chris suggested that we add numbers to each volume of our Landmark series so children would know there were more to be had. It was quite a suggestion. Actually, Chris was responsible for the whole Landmark series. I got the idea for them in the summer of 1948, when Chris was seven and Jonathan was two. We were up on Cape Cod, between Provincetown and Barnstable, in a house on the bayside. I was sitting on the beach one day with Chris—Jon was playing around somewhere—and I asked Chris if he realized that where we were sitting was where the Pilgrims landed. Chris, who had learned differently at school, said, "You're wrong, Dad.

Jonathan, Bennett, Phyllis, Christopher

They landed on Plymouth Rock." I said, "They did not land on Plymouth Rock. They landed right here at Provincetown, and they stayed here for about two weeks." I could see that Chris didn't believe me, so I said, "We're going down to the bookstore and get you a book on it."

The bookstore in Provincetown was run in the summer by Paul and Bunny Smith, who also had one in Chapel Hill at the University of North Carolina in the wintertime. Theirs was a first-rate shop because they were real book people. When we walked in I said to Paul, "I want to see all the children's books you've got about the Pilgrims." Paul said, "We haven't got any." I said, "What do you mean? In Provincetown you haven't got books about the Pilgrims?" He said, "I haven't got them for a very good reason. There aren't any." It was hard to believe, but it was true.

I began thinking about it, and suddenly it struck me that there should be a series of books, each one on some great episode in American history. By the time we left Provincetown, I had made a list of the first ten titles and had a name for the series: Landmark Books. I also decided not to get authors of children's books, but the most important authors in the country.

When I discussed this with Louise Bonino, she was a little dubious, and said, "In the first place, you won't be able to get such people to write books for children. Second, I don't know whether there'll be enough demand for a whole book about the Pilgrims or, say, a whole book about the first transcontinental railroad."

I went from one author to another, and every one of them jumped at the chance. They thought it was a great idea. The keystone of the whole thing was Dorothy Canfield Fisher, who, in addition to being a distinguished novelist, was a noted authority on children and a judge of the Book-of-the-Month Club. Bob Haas had a place up in Vermont right next to the Fisher home, and they were great personal friends. I wanted a book by Mrs. Fisher desperately. Bob said, "She's such a busy woman. I don't think you ought to disturb her." Despite Bob's apprehension, I made a lunch date with Dorothy. I told her about my idea, and then I said, "My dream is, Dorothy, that you would do one of these books for us." She said, "Do *one* of these books? You've shown me your list of the first ten, and I want to do *two* of them!" I almost fell off my chair.

She did one about the Declaration of Independence and the Constitution and one about Paul Revere and the Minute Men. Another of the first ten was *The Pony Express* by Samuel Hopkins Adams, one of the most successful, and Sam later did *The Santa Fe Trail* and *The Erie Canal*. Landmark Books took off like a rocket, and as the series grew, more and more well-known writers were happy to participate. Even those repetitious Westerns on television create a desire for knowledge of American history. For example, when the Daniel Boone craze was on, we had a Daniel Boone in Landmark Books by John Mason Brown. That book sold by the thousands and is still one of the most popular.

Then we got the idea for the All About Books—*All About the Weather, All About the Stars, All About the Sea*—and they hit the jackpot too. Television was booming, and kids had begun to ask questions about the sea and the stars and the weather and other things they'd seen on the screen and wanted to know more about. To the American history group we added World Landmarks; by the mid-sixties there were nearly two hundred titles available in the combined list, including books by such famous correspondents as William L. Shirer, Quentin Reynolds, John Gunther, Robert Considine, Richard Tregaskis and Vincent Sheehan—many of whom had written books for us about World War II.

$\mathbf{A}$t the time the war broke out in Europe, Donald and I had been partners for about fifteen years. At first very little changed in this country or in our business, and the Random House list looked much like those of the years before. In the spring of 1941 we published two hits—Budd Schulberg's *What Makes Sammy Run?* and Sally Benson's *Junior Miss*—as well as books by such authors as William McFee, Mignon Eberhart, W. H. Auden and Louis MacNeice. We also brought out *The Basic Works of Aristotle* and a generous selection of new Broadway plays. But the war was already beginning to show up in our catalogue, with entries like *The Battle for Asia* by Edgar Snow; *A Faith to Fight For* by John Strachey; and *A London Diary*, an eyewitness account of the blitz by Quentin Reynolds.

Then came the Sunday afternoon we won't ever forget. By this time Harry Scherman, head of the Book-of-the-Month Club, and his wife, Bernardine, had become close personal friends of ours (we had published Harry's extremely successful book *The Promises Men Live By* in 1938). That Sunday, Phyllis and I were sitting in the Schermans' house in New Jersey, playing bridge, fighting over a hand, when somebody called up and told us

Harry and Bernardine
(Kielty) Scherman

Pearl Harbor had been bombed. We all felt very foolish to have been squabbling over something so trivial, completely unaware that such a terrible and world-shaking event had taken place.

We were now in the war, and though Donald was thirty-eight, he immediately applied for a commission in the Air Force, and in the spring of 1942 Major Klopfer went off to England for the duration. He just barely

made it: his fellow officers called him "Pop." (One of them was Jimmy Stewart, the movie star.) I was already too old for military service—forty-three in 1941—so I had to stay home and mind the store, which turned out to be quite a job.

It was soon clear to everybody that our entry into the war would bring about great changes, changes not only in American life in general, but in personal lives as well; but what exactly these would be was impossible to predict, and people were worried. Things were going very badly for this country and our Allies at first, because, as is usually the case, the dictators were ready and the liberty-loving people were caught unprepared, as we were. Until we could catch up, we were in bad trouble. Publishers were concerned and uncertain. We had weathered the Depression all right, but would people who were preoccupied with the war, and deeply disturbed by the way it was going, still read? Before long, we knew the answer.

Soon a flood of books on the war began to be written, and we managed to get some of the best of them. Our first really big one was *Suez to Singapore*, the story of the sinking of two of Britain's biggest and newest battleships—the *Prince of Wales* and the *Repulse*—at Singapore a few days after Pearl Harbor. It was a black day in Allied history, another sweeping victory for the Japanese, who were now free to walk into Singapore, which in two months they did.

The author, Cecil Brown, a correspondent in the Far East for NBC-Radio, happened to be on the *Repulse* when it was sunk, and his broadcasts had been attracting a lot of attention. I hadn't heard him, but Howard Lindsay and his wife, Dorothy Stickney, who were in the middle of their long run as the stars of *Life with Father*, were up late every night and listened to Brown's dispatches. When they told me how good he was, I immediately sent him a cable saying "We want your book." I thought there was one chance in twenty it would reach him, but it did; and he commissioned his wife, Martha, to come to see me and draw up a contract.

Suez to Singapore was an immediate best seller. Cecil came back to New York and was with us on publication day in October, 1942. It was like celebrating the opening of a play. The Browns and the Cerfs had dinner together at the Stork Club and waited, the way show people do, for *The New York Times* to appear with a review. After dinner we had to go over to Third Avenue and 59th Street to find an open newsstand. The *Times* had a rave review, and the four of us literally danced down the street.

A few months later came *Guadalcanal Diary*, an example of energetic publishing. The author, Richard Tregaskis, was a correspondent for International News Service and his pieces were syndicated by King Features. Acting as agent, Ward Greene, head of King Features, had copies made of

Dick's manuscript and sent them to nine publishers at the same time, asking for bids—something that had never been done before.

I had just said the day before that the first book that came out about Guadalcanal was going to be a knockout because Guadalcanal marked the turning of the tide. Then in came this manuscript on November 11, 1942. I took it home, read it immediately, called Ward Greene at nine o'clock the next morning and said, "I've got to have this book." We signed it up before any of the other eight publishers had even started reading it. *Guadalcanal Diary* was just a day-to-day diary and the author was absolutely unknown, but within a week of our accepting it, it was chosen by the Book-of-the-Month Club; then Twentieth Century-Fox bought the film rights before our rush publication date, January 18, 1943. It was the first Random House book to sell over a hundred thousand copies.

While we were rushing *Guadalcanal Diary* into print, we already had in our office safe the manuscript of an even more sensational war book, but one which, for security reasons, we definitely couldn't rush. It was *Thirty Seconds over Tokyo,* the story of the famous group who, under the leadership of General James Doolittle, had bombed Tokyo on April 18, 1942. The author, in collaboration with Robert Considine, was Ted W. Lawson, one of the pilots who had participated in the raid. Ted's plane was one of those that came down in China. He, like many others, was led to safety by friendly Chinese. Ted's leg was badly injured in the crack-up and an infection developed before he could get proper treatment, and it had to be amputated.

We had the manuscript long before anybody knew, though many already suspected, that the planes that had carried out the surprise attack had come from a carrier. President Roosevelt had made his often-quoted remark that they had come from Shangri-la—the imaginary country in James Hilton's novel *Lost Horizon.* We were told that we couldn't publish the book until we got clearance from the Air Force, and naturally they were going to keep the lid on until all our airmen were brought to safety or otherwise accounted for.

Here we had a hair-raising book, but we were thwarted. I had to keep this secret and it was burning my tongue. I'm not very good at keeping secrets, but I kept this one because all the details were top security. Finally, on April 20, 1943—a year after the raid and months after we had received the manuscript—the Air Force released its official communiqué and we were free to produce *Thirty Seconds over Tokyo* for June publication. Again we had a Book-of-the-Month Club selection, and this time our first printing was a hundred thousand copies.

By the fall of 1942 I had become very friendly with Bob Considine, and he told me he wanted to write a book with a photographer named Sammy Shulman, who had been all over the world. He followed everybody. In fact, he was so omnipresent that one time in North Africa, when President Roosevelt was there for one of his big conferences with Churchill, F.D.R. looked around and said, "Where's Sammy?"—he was that accustomed to seeing him. And that's how Bob came to call the book *Where's Sammy?*

We had a date to meet Shulman one afternoon to draw up a contract, and that was a day Bob and I never forgot, because I said I had promised Dick Rodgers that I would go to an audition of a new show he'd done with Oscar Hammerstein. The Theatre Guild was producing it and they were looking for backers. I told Bob, "They've got some rich people coming to see it, and it might be fun. We'll see Sammy Shulman later." So we went to a performance of a musical called *Away We Go* (by the time it played up in Boston, it had been renamed *Oklahoma!*). There we sat while they sang "Oh, What a Beautiful Morning" and "The Surrey with the Fringe on Top" and "People Will Say We're in Love." The Guild was desperately trying to raise money. Bob and I could have put a few thousand dollars into the show and made a fortune. We didn't. It never occurred to us to invest. First of all, Donald and I had that strict rule never to invest in plays, and as for Bob, he was a newspaperman and didn't have that kind of money.

But we've often thought back. That was the day that fortune beckoned us. All we had to do was put up five thousand dollars. I think that if we each had put up that much, we would by this time have gotten back, probably, at least three hundred thousand. Everybody who went into that show became rich on it.

We met Sammy Shulman afterward and signed the contract for the story of his wartime experiences. When we published it in November, 1943, nobody bought it, and the reason I remember it at all was *Oklahoma!*

There's a nice story about Bob Considine. He had started in Washington, where he was a tennis champion, as a reporter on the *Times-Herald*, working for its formidable publisher, Eleanor Medill Patterson, who was known as "Cissy." She was very fond of Bob, and when he got a chance to go to New York to work for Hearst at a much bigger salary, she blessed him and said, "Go ahead. I can't afford to pay that much, but you're on your way." They remained great friends.

One time Cissy had a big fight with her brother, Joseph Patterson, who founded the *New York Daily News*. (Colonel Robert McCormick of the *Chicago Tribune* was her cousin. It was quite a family.) She called up Considine and said, "I want to answer an idiotic editorial of Joe's. I can tell you what I want to say but I can't write it, Bob. You have to write it for me." Bob naturally agreed. He loved her. She had started him on his way. She added, "I've got to have it right away. Get somebody on a train to bring it down here. I need it tomorrow." So Bob dropped everything and wrote the piece, which she loved. She ran it on the front page under her own name, of course.

The next afternoon she called up and said, "It was great, Bob. You did just what I wanted. How much do I owe you?" Considine said, "Cissy, I wouldn't take any money from you. This was for love." She said, "Don't be ridiculous. You're a newspaperman, and I don't get things for nothing. I ordered this from you and I'm going to pay you." Bob protested a bit more, and finally Cissy, very angry, said, "Listen, Bob, you had an article in this month's *Cosmopolitan*. What did they pay you for it?" Bob said, "I still tell you that I don't want anything, but since you ask, they paid me a thousand dollars for it."

She said "Okay" and hung up the phone. Two days later Bob got a check for seven hundred fifty dollars from Cissy Patterson with a little note pinned to it. The note read: "Dear Bob, I telephoned *Cosmopolitan*."

Our most prolific author of books about the war was Quentin Reynolds, who had started his career the way Westbrook Pegler did: in the sports department, covering the Brooklyn Dodgers and writing color stories. He joined the staff of *Collier's* magazine, and, at the outbreak of the war, was sent to London as a foreign correspondent. There it was discovered that he had a mellifluous and beautiful voice. So they transferred him temporarily into a star broadcaster, and with Edward R. Murrow he covered the big Nazi bombing raids over London. Murrow gave the news; Quent did the human-interest stories. He was very warm and colorful and a born optimist. He became a hero in England because his broadcasts brought hope to the people. It was very nice to hear his reassuring accounts of how the English were holding out—which, indeed, they were.

Quent was a very brave fellow. In August, 1942, he participated in the first invasion rehearsal at Dieppe. As expected, the raid was repulsed; the real reason for it had been to test the German defenses and plan for D-Day. We published Quent's account of this campaign, *Dress Rehearsal*, in February, 1943. Then, a year later, came his *The Curtain Rises*, a report from all the major battlefronts of Europe and Africa.

Among other war books we published was *Tunis Expedition* by Darryl Zanuck, head of Twentieth Century-Fox, who was a colonel in the U.S. Signal Corps, in charge of a unit that filmed the American campaign in North Africa. We had a very big sale on the book because the studio bought twenty thousand copies. One wonderful thing I remember. Zanuck was always a great one for sending eight-page telegrams; he'd send one the way some lovesick girl would write a mushy letter. When he came back to

Quentin Reynolds and Bennett

New York from Tunis, and before he went on to Hollywood, he had nothing to do, so he'd hang around my office and talk to me. He had a loud voice and smoked great big cigars. You could hear him all over Random House. He was fun, but you couldn't do any work while he was around. When he finally left New York, I gave him the galleys of Quent's *The Curtain Rises* to read on the plane back to California. The next morning I got one of his long, long telegrams, which started off with something like: "Dear Bennett: On page so-and-so, Quentin Reynolds mentions the so-

and-so hotel in so-and-so. It may interest you and Quentin to know that I was the first American officer to set foot in this hotel on the morning of so-and-so." And he went on with long details about what he had done and had for breakfast—all in the telegram.

Quent Reynolds was in New York, and I knew he never got up before noon. He was usually around the town all night, having a few here and a few there, and would stagger to bed in the wee hours. But I woke him up at nine o'clock, and he came to the phone mumbling. I said I had something so important to tell him, I had to call right away. Then I read Zanuck's telegram, and Quent gave forth a stream of profanity I'll never forget.

After the war we published several more books by Quent Reynolds, all very successful. Then came a famous episode. The *Reader's Digest* dug up a spine-tingling story about how a Canadian named DuPré had served in the English-Canadian Secret Service and performed great deeds of derring-do in Paris for the underground. He had been captured by the Nazis, but never talked although they tortured him for weeks. Finally he escaped and went back to Canada, where he was hailed as a great hero and raised fortunes for various Canadian funds by speaking in churches and government buildings and schools. He received every honor that Canada could bestow—medals and receptions by the governor general, and all that sort of thing.

The *Digest* got wind of the story and sent Quent to write it up. Quent was a most all-embracing man who loved everybody. No matter whom he met, he would come and tell you what a wonderful fellow he was. Well, he fell in love with DuPré, who was a very taking young man, and he said to me, "You know, I'm doing this piece for the *Digest*, but I think I can expand it into a book."

It sounded great, and we got permission from DeWitt Wallace, the head of the *Digest*, to proceed. We called the book *The Man Who Wouldn't Talk*. It got good reviews and was a substantial success.

Then one night when we were having dinner up at Mount Kisco, I had a long-distance call. The editor of the *Calgary Herald* was on the phone. I said to Phyllis, "What the dickens does the editor of the *Calgary Herald* want in my young life?" I soon found out! He said, "I'm afraid I have some bad news for you, Mr. Cerf. Your Mr. DuPré has just collapsed and confessed that his entire story is a hoax. There isn't a word of truth in it. His adventures are all things that he read in various news stories and spy magazines. He spent the entire war in England and in Canada and never got to France at all. The business of his being captured and tortured and the underground stuff was just his imagination. He couldn't stand the strain any longer; his conscience was bothering him. He is a nice little man and he didn't realize that his deception was going to be blown up to these dimensions. He was just romancing a little bit and suddenly he found himself a national hero! We're printing the whole story tomorrow morning, and I thought I'd give you a little advance notice."

Well, I had to break the news to Quent and to DeWitt Wallace. It was the *Digest* that had put Quent on to DuPré's trail, and I knew Wally would be distressed. I called him up and told him of the imminent exposé. He groaned, "Oh my God, what are we going to do now?" I said, "Well, I've had a little time to think about it, and there's only one thing to do. Imagine this little Canadian country boy fooling the entire Canadian government, not to mention *Reader's Digest,* Quentin Reynolds and Random House! The only way we can get out of this is to laugh it off. I'm going to call a press conference tomorrow. I'm going to tell them exactly what happened, and I'm going to say, 'Imagine this little man fooling all of us. Isn't it hilarious? We're going to announce that this book isn't nonfiction, but fiction, and we're going to change the name of it immediately from *The Man Who Wouldn't Talk* to *The Man Who Talked Too Much.*' " Wally was still worried, but he said, "Let's see what happens."

It worked like a charm. The press was delighted with the whole story and played it up, as I had hoped, as a harmless deception. Nobody was really hurt. The interesting thing is that the book sold about five times as well after the exposure as it did before. Suddenly everybody was talking about DuPré and chuckling over him. It's another example of how you can laugh things off. If we had gone into a frenzy, we'd have made fools of ourselves. This way, everybody laughed *with* us. Quent laughed right along too, but he continued to say, "He's a great guy, despite everything!"

The trouble with Quent was that like so many star newspapermen, he had a fondness for the bottle. He could really stow the booze away. He simply couldn't stop drinking. He'd swear he would, but he kept falling off the wagon.

Quent emerged a hero in a famous case in which he sued Westbrook Pegler for libel. Pegler had written a series of columns calling Quent a Communist (Quent was always on the liberal side, whereas Pegler was not), and also accusing Quent of being a coward. Here was Pegler smearing Quentin Reynolds, who had lived through the London blitz, gone with the expedition to Dieppe, and was shelled by Nazi batteries while on a boat one hundred yards from shore!

I went down to one of the courtroom sessions. People fought to get in because everybody hated Pegler and loved Quent Reynolds. It was really the case of the villain and the hero. Pegler was always finding Communists under the bed. The time I went was one of the great days, because Louis Nizer—Quent's lawyer and just becoming famous—confronted Pegler on the witness stand and demanded, "Do you think this is a Communist statement, Mr. Pegler?" He read a long paragraph. Pegler said, "It certainly is. That's typical Communist propaganda." Nizer said, "Mr. Pegler, I got that out of one of your own columns! You wrote it."

Well, the case was over right there. The courtroom audience burst into laughter and applause, and the judge simply couldn't restore order. Pegler turned the color of a beet. Quent won the case, though for a while his reputation was hanging in the balance. But eventually all of Pegler's charges were proven to be false and Quent was awarded damages.

Publishing during the war was not just a matter of bringing out war books. It was also business as usual—in fact, more business than usual. We soon found out that gasoline rationing and the military pre-emption of space on trains and planes made travel extremely difficult, so that many people even found it impossible to get to the movies very often (and of course there was no television). So people stayed home and read books, and the market expanded tremendously. The Book-of-the-Month Club, for example, more than doubled its membership during the war, and *Reader's Digest* doubled its circulation.

Our regular authors continued to produce, and we kept adding new ones. In the fall of 1942, much to my delight, Samuel Hopkins Adams appeared for the first time on the Random House list. I had known and admired Sam since my days at Liveright and had always wanted to publish him, but I never managed this until I presented him with a wonderful idea for a historical novel about the American West. The idea came to me when I met Byron Harvey, president and son of the founder of Fred Harvey, Incorporated. I knew, of course, about this flourishing enterprise, which now operates a chain of hotels and restaurants throughout the West, as well as many fine bookshops with which we do business. When I heard the fascinating story of its background, I immediately thought of Sam as the ideal man to write a book about it, and he agreed.

The company had its beginning in the last quarter of the nineteenth century, when the Santa Fe railway was under construction and pushing its way westward. Food for the passengers already traveling on the finished portion of the railroad was a real problem, since at that time there was no such thing as dining cars. To fill the void, Fred Harvey opened restaurants at various stations on the Santa Fe where trains could stop for breakfast, lunch and dinner. The passengers would get out for meals, then climb back on the train, and soon everybody got to know everybody else. Of course, it was rather leisurely, and it took longer to go a hundred miles in those days than it takes to fly across the country now.

Harvey needed girls to serve his customers, and since the only kind available along the Santa Fe were the tarts who had followed the railroad builders, he imported his waitresses from the East and Middle West. He was a very religious man, and before he hired girls they had to pass all kinds of tests to establish that they were churchgoing and respectable. They were soon widely known as the Harvey Girls. They were decent and attractive, and many of them married the most eligible men, becoming the social belles of the new frontier towns and founding many of the prominent families of the West.

Sam's novel, *The Harvey Girls,* was not only a big success as a book; it was made into the Academy Award-winning movie which featured Judy Garland singing that wonderful song "On the Atchison, Topeka and the Santa Fe."

Sam was not an "important" author, he was a popular one, and his books had authentic historical interest. We continued to publish him as long as he lived, and novels like *Canal Town* and *Sunrise to Sunset* were well

Samuel Hopkins Adams

received. In 1955, when Sam was eighty-four years old, his *Grandfather Stories* was a Book-of-the-Month Club selection.

Toward the end of his life he had dreadful arthritis, and it was painful to watch him get in and out of an automobile, which sometimes would take him five minutes. But he was a gutsy old man, and when he came to the office, if people tried to help him, he'd get furious and brush them off. We all loved him. He was a superb man—who courageously forced himself to finish his last novel, *Tenderloin,* which was just going on press when he died in November, 1958. We published it two months later, and afterward a successful musical based on it was done by another Random House author, Jerome Weidman.

At the height of the war we had an anthology, *Famous English and American Poetry,* done for Modern Library by poets Conrad Aiken and William Rose Benét, and I was distressed to discover that they wanted to include several poems of Ezra Pound, who was—I consider—a traitor to this country. He was broadcasting fascist propaganda from Italy—venomous stuff. It was later established that he was insane, and though I don't know whether he really was or not, he sounded just like Lord Haw-Haw, the traitorous Englishman who, from somewhere in the middle of Germany, was broadcasting to the Allies, trying to pervert American and British soldiers. That's precisely what Ezra Pound was doing in Italy.

I said, "I'll be damned if I'm going to publish Ezra Pound. Any book that has my name in it isn't going to have him in it." After a knockdown fight, we brought the book out without Pound. Aiken raised hell, and I discovered to my intense surprise and horror that almost every important critic sided with him and not with me. They said that it was a poetry anthology and I was acting as a censor and leaving Pound out because I didn't appreciate his political ideas.

I decided that when people I respected, like Lewis Gannett, the daily book critic of the New York *Herald-Tribune,* told me I was wrong, well then, I must have been wrong. I still in my heart don't think I was, but I had to admit that I was overwhelmed by people who felt the other way. I have never been ashamed to say I was wrong. I had to apologize, and the Pound poems appeared in the second printing.

The direction my own life would take was greatly affected by the war. From the time I left Wall Street to join Liveright, I had devoted all my working time to publishing. Now, almost twenty years later, the war diverted me into new activities that I had not foreseen, and as one thing often leads to another, I found myself embarked on a career of sidelines that converted practically all of my time into working time. With Donald away, my responsibilities at Random House were greatly increased, but I somehow found the energy to take care of them as well as to involve myself in new occupations.

It all began one day in early 1942, when Norman Cousins and Henry Seidel Canby of the *Saturday Review of Literature* came to see me. They were worried because they weren't getting enough advertising from publishers and were calling on various ones of us to ask how they could improve the magazine and what service they might offer that would lead to more advertising. I told them that one thing they could do was to put in more humor. Since Christopher Morley had stopped writing his column "Trade Winds," the magazine seemed too serious, even pompous and pedantic at times. I said, "There's plenty of fun in the book business, and this can be mined."

About two days later Cousins called up and said, "We've discovered how to provide the humor you suggested." I asked him what he had in mind, and he said, "The man we want to do 'Trade Winds' is you!" I was flattered beyond measure, but I said, "How can I do a column of publishing and book news? I'd have to say what I think, and I'd be stepping on the toes of other publishers—you know I'm not very diplomatic or tactful." Norman said, "That's just what we want. I'm sure the other publishers will understand." I said, "I don't think they will, but let me think about it."

I asked a few associates about it, and they all agreed that I couldn't possibly do it for the very reason I had given. As soon as they said that, I got my back up, though they had only echoed my own doubts, and I told Norman I would do three or four columns and see what happened. So I started on March 1, 1942.

Since it was a column of bits and pieces, I could write it at odd moments—a bit here and a piece there. If a usable anecdote came along, I'd write it up and put it in when I needed it. These columns—all of them—became material for future books. I invented a character I called Mr. Bump, and he appeared about once every three months. He was a publisher—myself, as a matter of fact—and some of my own funny experiences and gripes were presented under that name. The column caught on, and some publishers did indeed raise hell, but they were the ones who didn't like me anyway.

I had barely begun doing "Trade Winds" when I embarked on another project. In the spring of 1942, after we'd lost the Philippines and Bataan, we were pretty despondent in this country. Hitler and Japan seemed to be winning all over the world, and it occurred to me that what we needed was some humor, some laughter, just as we do this very day. So I conceived the idea of putting together a collection of war humor. Pocket Books was just getting under way then. At its head was my old friend Dick Simon; I proposed this idea to him and he was all for it. I compiled the *Pocketbook of War Humor*, which came out just about the time people needed it most. It consisted of war jokes and excerpts from humorous best sellers like *Dere Mable* and *See Here, Private Hargrove*. It was enormously popular and sold about two million copies.

Suddenly I became the Joe Miller of the day as a result of this one book, and I decided I would do another. I knew hundreds of amusing stories about all kinds of people that I could put together in a pocketbook of anecdotes that I would write myself instead of just collecting from already published sources.

I began to work on it, and it expanded. Since I was never able to write at the office, I did the work at home or on vacation. Several sections were written in Florida, where Phyllis and I went with Lew Miller and Saxe Commins for a brief winter vacation. I never learned to type, so all my writing had to be done in longhand. I soon found out that those big oversize legal pads were the most comfortable things to write on, and over the years I must have consumed thousands of them. Fortunately, Pauline Kreiswirth and, later, Mary Barber, were able to decipher my handwriting and would patiently type up what I had written, and I would then revise and correct it for the printer.

While I was working on what was to be my first book, I was already in my second year of "Trade Winds," and the column I wrote for July 17, 1943—a remembrance of my dear friend George Gershwin, who had died six years before—brought unforeseen results. I received many letters in appreciation of that piece, including a very gratifying note from Ira Gershwin, but the one that was to lead somewhere came from Dick Simon. He had managed to get an advance copy of the magazine, so even before it was published he wrote me that he thought it the best thing I'd ever written, and when the time came that I was ready to publish a book of my own, he'd like to put in a bid for Simon and Schuster. Since I was already working on just such a book, I showed some of it to Dick, who immediately said he thought it should come out in hardcover first, saving the paperback for later.

Dick and I had lunch together one day, and during that meeting—we've often wondered since who thought of it first—we decided to call the book *Try and Stop Me*. We used the Gershwin piece in the book, and since I have always been rather proud of it, and since it was an important episode in my life, most of it is included here:

IN MEMORY OF GEORGE GERSHWIN
(September, 1898–July, 1937)

On an oppressively hot Sunday evening six years ago, a group of people was gathered in a Bucks County remodeled farmhouse, engaged in various desultory pastimes. A spiritless bridge game was in progress in one corner of the room; a bout of cribbage in another. The host was tinkering aimlessly with the radio dials. Some of the guests were splashing about in the pool outside, although there was no moon and the night was pitch-black. The heat had everybody down. Suddenly the clear voice of a news commentator came over the air: "The man who said he had more tunes in his head than he could put down on paper in a hundred years is dead tonight in Hollywood. George Gershwin succumbed today at the age of thirty-eight."

Everybody at that party was a close personal friend of George. Two of them had collaborated with him on his brightest Broadway hits. We had seen him within the month—joshed him on his complaint of recurring headaches (he had been telling us details of his symptoms and disorders for years; nobody took them seriously) and on a front-page report that a little French picture cutie had entrusted him with a gold key to her front door. His unbelievable energy and vitality had astounded us for so long that we sat speechless at the thought that he was dead. Now six years later, his music is played so incessantly, stories about him spring so readily to mind, it is still somehow unbelievable that he is gone. Because he graduated from Tin Pan Alley, it has taken all these years to convince some critics that George Gershwin was a great composer—one of the greatest we have produced in America. Because his monumental but strangely unobjectionable conceit encouraged his friends to circulate hilarious anecdotes about him, some of them did not realize until he was dead how deeply they liked and admired him. The stories that I have gathered for this piece are set down in loving memory. George laughed at all of them himself. . . .

George Gershwin was born in Brooklyn on September 26,

1898. He was the second of four children. Ira, whose sparkling lyrics were so perfectly attuned to George's music, was the oldest. Another brother, Arthur, followed George. The youngest was their sister Frances, happily married today to Leopold Godowsky. The family moved as a unit, a mutual admiration society that was completely unaffected by temporary failure or dizzying success. Mrs. Gershwin was adored by everybody. "You must meet my mother," George would tell anybody who called. "She's the most wonderful mother in the world." On further reflection, he would frequently add, "And so modest about *me!*" The father, Morris, was one of those restless souls who embarked upon a new business career every year or so; the family was always ready to pull up stakes cheerfully at a moment's notice. George once figured that he lived in twenty-seven different houses before he finished school. . . .

When George was twelve, his mother bought a piano. The idea was for Ira to take lessons, but it didn't take long to discover that George was the one with music in his soul. At the High School of Commerce he was pianist for the morning assembly exercises. At fifteen he was a song plugger for the music publishing house of Jerome Remick. One of his chores took him to Atlantic City, where he pounded out Remick melodies at the local five-and-ten. Down the Boardwalk, Harry Ruby was doing a similar job for a rival outfit. At night the boys would dine together at Child's and dream of writing songs of their own.

His first song was published in 1916. It was called "When You Want 'Em You Can't Get 'Em," and it earned him an advance of five dollars. His next few numbers began to carry lyrics by Arthur Francis. That was brother Ira making his debut as a lyricist, using the first names of his other brother and kid sister as a pseudonym. His first real clicks came in 1919, when he did his first complete score for *La La Lucille* (remember "Nobody But You": "Billie Burke—Alice Joyce—none of them were my choice"?) and wrote a couple of numbers for the opening bill of Broadway's biggest movie palace of its time, the Capitol. One of the numbers was "Swanee," and I've heard it twice on the radio this very week.

Beginning in 1920 George wrote the music for *George White's Scandals* for five consecutive years. A few of the hits of these scores were "Drifting Along with the Tide," "I'll Build a Stairway to Paradise," and "Somebody Loves Me." Most of the lyrics were contributed by Buddy De Sylva, now head man at the Paramount Studios. In those days White was the great Ziegfeld's only serious rival. Gershwin didn't meet up with

Ziegfeld himself until 1929, when he wrote the score of *Show Girl*. Working with Ziegfeld was perfect training for a siege on Guadalcanal, but that's another story. After the contract with Gershwin was signed, Ziegfeld went to Carnegie Hall to hear "An American in Paris." At the symphony's completion, Otto Kahn rose and made a brief speech in which he declared that George was well-nigh a genius. "In fact," said Kahn, "someday he will be a genius, but geniuses must suffer, and George hasn't suffered yet." Ziegfeld turned to Larry Hart, who was sitting next to him, and said, with a sly wink, "He'll suffer!" . . .

George became internationally famous in 1924, when Paul Whiteman introduced his "Rhapsody in Blue" at a concert in Aeolian Hall. By now the family was located in a private house on West 103 Street, where George worked imperturbably amidst a hubbub that suggested Grand Central station on the eve of a Fourth of July weekend. The Rhapsody was written there in exactly three weeks; George had to meet a deadline! That year saw, too, the first of seven musical comedies produced by Aarons and Freedley, with music by George and lyrics by Ira. Five of them made Broadway history. They were, in order, *Lady Be Good, Tip Toes, Oh, Kay, Funny Faces,* and *Girl Crazy*. They made stars of Fred and Adele Astaire, Gertrude Lawrence, Ethel Merman and Ginger Rogers. "Fascinating Rhythm," "Do, Do, Do," "Sweet and Low Down," "Embraceable You," "I Got Rhythm," and a dozen other wonderful songs followed one another in dizzy succession. In addition, *Of Thee I Sing*, written with George Kaufman and Morrie Ryskind, won the Pulitzer Prize in 1932. George moved to a Riverside Drive penthouse, which became headquarters for a series of wondrous Sunday evening delicatessen suppers that featured Barney Greengrass's sturgeon and attracted the greatest wits and socialites of the town. That's when the Gershwin saga really started. George, who loved to play the piano for hours on end, and naïvely—also justifiably—took it for granted that nobody wanted to hear anything but his own music, would finally suspend operations to seek refreshments. His place would be taken by a surly young man who played George's music just as well as the composer. His name was Oscar Levant. . . .

George loved to go to parties, and thought nothing of playing the entire score of a forthcoming musical for his friends. This practice irked his canny collaborator, George Kaufman. "If you play that score one more time before we open," Kaufman once told him, "people are going to think it's a revival." Kaufman also deplored Gershwin's genial habit of inviting everybody he met to sit in on rehearsals. Kaufman left one run-through with a deep scowl. "It's going to be a prize flop," he predicted. "What makes you say that? I thought it went beautifully," protested Gershwin. "Not at all," grumbled Kaufman. "The balcony was only half filled!"

I accompanied George on some wonderful vacation trips. They were a succession of hilarious adventures and beautiful girls. He banged out the Rhapsody once in the parlor of the Colonial Hotel in Nassau at seven in the morning to please a girl he had met on the boat, and was indignant when the manager made him stop. "I guess he didn't know I was Gershwin," he consoled himself. In Havana, a sixteen-piece rhumba band serenaded him en masse at four in the morning outside his room at the old Almendares Hotel. Several outraged patrons left the next morning. George was so flattered that he promised to write a rhumba of his own. He did, too. His "Cuban Overture" was played for the first time at the Lewisohn Stadium in August, 1932. In Havana, George reached his greatest height of indignation. A lovely Cuban miss failed to keep a luncheon date with him. Later that afternoon he spied her on the Yacht Club terrace, and exclaimed, "Hey, do you know that you stood me up today?" "Oh, I meant to phone and tell you I couldn't meet you," said the contrite maiden, "but do you know something? I simply couldn't think of your name!" George didn't recover for days . . . He reserved one unpublished little waltz tune for affairs of the heart. "You're the kind of girl who makes me feel like composing a song," he would tell the enraptured lady of the moment, and lead her off to his suite. We would follow on tiptoe to hear him compose the familiar tune for her. "It will be dedicated to you," he would conclude soulfully. One day I happened to remark that the score of one of his infrequent failures, *Pardon My English*, was below par. George demurred. All of us were sunbathing in the nude; George insisted that we all go inside while he proved his point by going through the score from opening to finale. I can still see him sitting at the piano, stark naked, playing the songs and singing them, too, at the top of his voice. George belonged at a piano. I have never seen a man happier, more bursting with the sheer joy of living, than George when he was playing his songs. He would improvise and introduce subtle variations, and chuckle with childlike delight when his audience exclaimed over them.

The work that George Gershwin loved best was *Porgy and Bess*. He composed it in eleven months and orchestrated it in nine. Its initial production by the Guild in 1935, a bit too stuffy and pretentious, was only moderately successful. When it was revived seven years later, it really came into its own, and its songs seem destined to become part of America's richest musical heritage; the tragedy is that George wasn't living to see that come to pass.

George moved to Hollywood in 1936. He wrote the music for the Fred Astaire–Ginger Rogers picture *Shall We Dance?*,

George Gershwin and Ginger Rogers

which included one of his best songs ("Oh, No, You Can't Take That Away From Me"), and *A Damsel in Distress*. He was working on the Goldwyn Follies when he was stricken by a brain tumor.

The last years of Gershwin's life were almost equally divided between composing and painting. George took his painting very seriously, and indeed had a genuine talent for it. At a memorable dinner one evening he said, "A man told me today that I need never write another note; I could make a fortune with my palette and brush!" "Isn't it amazing," said one awed lady, "that one man should possess a genius for two of the arts!" "Oh, I don't know," said George modestly. "Look at Leonardo da Vinci!" At another dinner, apropos of nothing, George suddenly said, "Has anybody here seen my new cigarette case?" It was solid gold, and inscribed thereon were facsimile signatures of a score of famous men. It had been presented to him after a performance of his Concerto in F. The case was passed clear around the table. As George was putting it back into his pocket, his brother Ira produced a crumpled pack of Camels. "Anybody want a cigarette?" he inquired pleasantly.

But Ira, like everybody else who knew him well, adored George Gershwin. After his death, Ira wrote practically nothing for years. That he had lost none of his talent he proved, however, with the lyrics for *Lady in the Dark*. Now he is going to work on the screen biography of George Gershwin. The title role has not yet been filled, but Oscar Levant will play himself in the film.

George Gershwin expressed his credo in these words: "My people are American, my time is today. Music must repeat the thought and aspirations of the times." Six years after his death, his exciting songs are played more frequently than they were during his lifetime. One critic recently remarked, "George Gershwin brought to serious consideration a new idiom in American music, and forever changed its future direction." Last Tuesday twenty thousand people gathered in New York to hear a program dedicated to his memory. As the first familiar strains of the "Rhapsody in Blue" hushed the expectant audience, it was hard to believe that the composer had been dead for over six years. It seemed like yesterday that he had sat beside me in Cuba, listening to the same composition on the radio, and saying, "It *is* great, isn't it? But wait till you hear the one I'm working on now!"

Try and Stop Me was a good book; I have done many since, but none of them had its richness; after all, it was crammed with over forty years of stories that I had collected! It was also a great success; it became number one

on the best-seller list and stayed there for months. An Armed Services edition was done, and millions of additional copies were sent to our soldiers all over the world. It was just the kind of book they needed and appreciated—it made them laugh. Then came millions more copies in the Pocket Book edition.

I believe that humor books have a certain rhythm. Just as some people are born knowing how to write songs, and other people are born knowing how to write books, I have a certain skill at assembling anecdotes that makes them pleasant to read. I don't understand what it is myself, but I do know how to do it. I've always said I've learned how to exploit a very small talent to the ultimate degree, and mine is very small compared to people that I really admire. Something I'm genuinely proud of, however, is that I've gotten both the Yale and Harvard humor awards—from the *Yale Record* and the *Harvard Lampoon*—and both were made by the undergraduate body, not by any professional staff.

I sold individual chapters of *Try and Stop Me* to various magazines, and King Features bought the serialization rights. By the time they used up

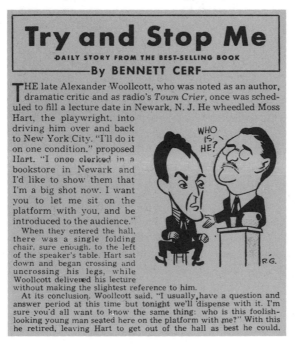

Try and Stop Me
DAILY STORY FROM THE BEST-SELLING BOOK
By BENNETT CERF

THE late Alexander Woollcott, who was noted as an author, dramatic critic and as radio's *Town Crier*, once was scheduled to fill a lecture date in Newark, N. J. He wheedled Moss Hart, the playwright, into driving him over and back to New York City. "I'll do it on one condition," proposed Hart. "I once clerked in a bookstore in Newark and I'd like to show them that I'm a big shot now. I want you to let me sit on the platform with you, and be introduced to the audience."

When they entered the hall, there was a single folding chair, sure enough, to the left of the speaker's table. Hart sat down and began crossing and uncrossing his legs, while Woollcott delivered his lecture without making the slightest reference to him.

At its conclusion, Woollcott said, "I usually have a question and answer period at this time but tonight we'll dispense with it. I'm sure you'd all want to know the same thing: who is this foolish-looking young man seated here on the platform with me?" With this he retired, leaving Hart to get out of the hall as best he could.

the book, they had several hundred newspapers signed up and wanted to go on with the column (which was called "Try and Stop Me"). This meant two or three new jokes every day. So I wrote them, but I decided that the best way to work it was to send them about ninety stories the first of every month and leave it to them to pick the order in which to run them.

For fifteen years I wrote the "Trade Winds" column, and it led to many other things. For example, one day I had a call from William Nichols, editor of *This Week*, the Sunday supplement of twenty-eight important newspapers all over the country, with a combined circulation of about eleven million. Nichols suggested that I do a weekly column for him. I hesitated for a while, and Phyllis was very much against it. She said I was doing too many things already, and this was even before *What's My Line?* came along. But any time anybody says I shouldn't do anything, I immediately want to do it, so on November 5, 1950, I started "The Cerf Board" in *This Week* on a temporary basis, and stayed with it for about ten years.

Since the *Saturday Review* was always just one step in front of the sheriff in those days, I think that even at the end, my payment from them was up to only a hundred and fifty dollars a column. I started with *This Week* for about eight times that! Finally, it was simply too much to do two columns a week; I couldn't keep up with it. So I told Norman that I would have to quit "Trade Winds." I wrote my final column for the March 20, 1957, issue, and they gave me a big farewell luncheon. In many ways I hated to give up "Trade Winds," just as I hate to give up anything, I guess. It was much more fun than my *This Week* stint, because everybody I knew read "Trade Winds." It brought me floods of letters from college professors, authors and real booklovers.

Though I had made some contribution with my humor books, I still desperately wanted to do something more directly connected with the war effort, so finally I joined up with the Treasury Department's bond drives. We discovered then, which I had asserted but didn't quite believe myself, that famous writers could sell bonds just as well as movie stars could. I said that to some people, well-known authors would be as big a drawing card as some beautiful little blonde, who might be much more fun to look at but not to listen to. We conceived the idea of sending out a group of authors who would appear together and talk for a while. They wouldn't try to sell bonds—they'd be no good at that—but people had to buy a bond to meet them. The price of a ticket to come to these meetings was the purchase of at least a twenty-five-dollar Victory Bond.

One tour I went on was hilarious because it included Kathleen Winsor. Miss Winsor, a very handsome girl, had begun writing a book while she was still a student at the University of California. It was *Forever Amber,* a whale of a best seller, which had just been published by, of all people, Macmillan. In our party were MacKinlay Kantor, Carl Van Doren and Miss Winsor. Mac Kantor and Carl Van Doren were both very convivial; we loved each other.

Miss Winsor was the big drawing card. Everybody came to see her because *Forever Amber* was the book of the day. They'd all go to her first, but when they found her so uncommunicative, they'd bounce right back to us. We'd do thirty or forty appearances a day at schools and factories, and in the evening there would be the great rally, with perhaps a couple of thousand people who had bought bonds. This raised a lot of money.

Kathleen Winsor was an amateur speaker at the time and she never learned her speech by heart. She'd come out on the stage and fish in her bag, which had everything in it but a live seal, and she'd finally come up with this piece of paper, which she'd carefully unfold. She'd then read in a colorless monotone. After about three days, of course, it became a source of some wild humor to Kantor, Van Doren and Cerf. We began to kid her; we couldn't help it. I'd begin introducing her in all kinds of crazy ways, and she withdrew more and more from the group.

As the years went by, however, she just seemed to remember that we had been old friends. About twenty years later, it became known that she had been working for years on a book about Montana. She was now married to Paul Porter, the famous lawyer in Washington. I was asked indirectly if I would be interested in publishing her book, and I said I'd be glad to see it. In came *Wanderers East, Wanderers West,* about the pioneer days in Montana. It was much too long—we couldn't get her to cut it—but it was a damned good story. We signed it, and it was distributed by the Literary Guild and by the Book-of-the-Month Club as an alternate selection.

The most interesting thing about *Wanderers East* was the reprint sale. The book never did what we thought it might; it sold only about thirty thousand, and Kay Winsor was very, very disappointed. But then one of the famous events in publishing history came about when we put her book up for paperback bids. We had advertised it very cleverly, I think, and made a big fuss about it before publication. It looked like a great best seller and everybody was after it. We set a final date for offers, and New American Library had bid two hundred thousand dollars. Then Bantam or Fawcett or somebody bid two hundred and ten thousand. We were going to close for that sum, which I thought was a terrific price.

Then into my office came the new president of N.A.L., a very nice young man named John Budlong. He introduced himself to me and said he wanted to talk about the Winsor book. I said, "There's not much to talk about. We said we were closing the bids, and your bid has been topped. It's

going to go to somebody else who bid ten thousand more than you did."
He said, "I'm not going to leave this room until you give me the Kathleen
Winsor book." I said, "I told you. It's all been settled." He said, "If I offer
you five hundred thousand for the reprint rights for the Kathleen Winsor,
will you give me the book right now?" I said, "Would you mind repeating
that?" He repeated it. I said, "Not only do you have a deal, but I'm going
to walk back with you to your office to see that you don't get run over
before you make out the contract."

That was the beginning of a wild period. Within three weeks I sold
three books to reprint for $1,700,000—the Winsor book for $500,000, John
O'Hara's *The Lockwood Concern* for another $500,000, and James Mich-
ener's *The Source* for a record $700,000!

As a result of the bond tours, somebody who had heard me at one of the big rallies suggested that I conduct a program on radio, which I named *Books Are Bullets*. Once a week I would interview somebody who had written a book about the war—either a correspondent or a general or somebody who had something else to do with it. We had such people as Quentin Reynolds and John Gunther, a couple of generals and Darryl Zanuck when he came back from his Tunis expedition. That was the first time I met Nan Taylor, who was working on the program. She introduced me to her husband, Frank, who later came to work for Random House.

Books Are Bullets

Again one thing led to another, and one day I got a telephone call from Colston Leigh, a lecture agent. He said he had heard me on a couple of the radio programs and asked if I'd ever thought of lecturing. I replied that I hadn't, and he said, "I think you'd be all right at it, and you can make quite a lot of money out of it." Of course I was intrigued. The mere thought of talking even for nothing delights me, and getting paid for it made it all the better! I said, "I'd certainly love to try it." So under Colston Leigh's management I did a couple of trial runs. I think the first one was up at some club in Pelham, New York. Since then I've done hundreds—all over the country. I found the time to do it because I've never prepared a lecture in my life; I've never even had any notes. I have an idea of what I'm going to say, and I just get up and talk.

I had learned something about lecturing from a very, very important gentleman. When I was at Columbia the students would invite people up to give talks; and being the Columbia School of Journalism, we got some pretty prominent people. Our all-time star attraction was one of my great heroes—Will Rogers. I was the chairman of the lecture committee that year, and I went downtown to collect Mr. Rogers, bringing him up in style on the subway. In those days we weren't fancy at all. He was quite content, and it never occurred to me to take him in a taxi.

Will Rogers attracted a crowd unequaled in Columbia annals. At that time his column was appearing in about every city in the United States. Two things impressed me deeply. One, he had no notes. Two, he didn't lecture to us—he talked to us. When we subwayed downtown together—I took him back to his hotel—I said, "You didn't use any notes!" Will Rogers said, "Of course I didn't. When a man gets up on a platform to talk, if he can't get by without notes or reading a speech, he's not a lecturer, he's an amateur. The way to intrigue people is to talk to them, not to lecture to them." Wonderful advice! I've never forgotten it.

Later on, luckily for me, I signed up with the Lee Keedick Agency. Lee Keedick was dead, but his son, Bob Keedick, owned the agency and there was a lady there, Elizabeth Schenck, who became a very important person in my life. She took care of all of my lecture activities and was absolutely wonderful. I became a top lecturer, getting very high fees, although I wasn't when I started, because you have to work your way up the way you do in the theater. I then brought Keedick lots of other people. One was Kitty Hart, who has now become a very successful lecturer. They already had John Mason Brown and Norman Cousins. I guess it was Norman who said, "Why don't you go to my agent—Lee Keedick." At that time John Mason Brown was the biggest lecturer in the United States; and Brown, Cousins and I made quite a trio.

The lecture business is a very peculiar one. The standard commission the agent gets is one-third of the fee, not ten percent, like theater or literary agents—they get *thirty-three and a third percent,* and you have to pay your own expenses. That's a mighty big take, but they do a great deal for you. They not only have to book you, but when you go out, they give you a dossier of every place you're going, what time your planes leave and all the necessary tickets and hotel reservations.

What is essential when you go on tour—I'll go out for a week, and I want to do as many lectures as I can during that time—is that the bookings and the reservations are planned so that you can make the jumps. For instance, once in a five-day period I did eight lectures in eight different cities. Now, that took a lot of arranging. These things have to be booked six or seven months in advance, because most of the forums in colleges, or wherever, plan their programs a season ahead and print up literature and sell season tickets based on the attractions they're going to present. Since I pay my own expenses, I feel perfectly free to take the best suite in the hotel and live like a lord.

Lecturing became an important part of my life—and an extra dividend developed from it. I went to towns where no book publisher had ever been before—no publisher of a big firm, that is. I would always go to the bookstores and meet the booksellers and chat with them and see where they had The Modern Library. I might say, "What do you mean putting Modern Library in the back of the store?" If they said they hadn't gotten around to moving it, I would help them. And when they weren't looking, I'd pull some of our new books out from where they were and put them in the front of the stand. For my own books, I'd sign anything they had in stock. In fact, there was a joke that if I ever got out of town leaving an unsigned Bennett Cerf book, it would be a rare and valuable volume!

Furthermore, when I talk and tell stories, a lot of them, of course, are about authors whom I know, Random House authors, and I consequently have to mention a lot of Random House books in the course of a lecture. So I'm selling at the same time; and I'm meeting heads of college English departments, hearing about any budding geniuses on campus—and you never can tell, you could be planting seeds. Of course, every time I go out our editors groan because a flood of trash starts coming in from people who have heard me say we like the young writers. They usually say, "Well, I'm a young writer and I have a work of genius," and in comes this unbelievable junk. But you never can tell: *Gone With the Wind* was found that way.

The only thing that had hampered our business during the war years was that paper was scarce and rationed by the War Production Board. We could have published many more books, but we couldn't produce them because our paper quota was based on what we had used in certain previous years. This led to a very interesting chain of events that had important consequences for Random House.

We had been preparing for publication a book called *The Basic Writings of St. Thomas Aquinas,* edited for us by Anton Pegis. The writings of Aquinas were available at that time only in a set of some twenty-odd volumes put out by a Catholic publishing house. By the time Pegis finished his work—two volumes containing over twenty-six hundred pages—we were right in the middle of the paper shortage, and had just enough for ten thousand sets. It was a very costly project, and with that size printing we would just about get our money back, but from then on, we'd have clear sailing.

What we did not know was that every Jesuit institution in the country was waiting for this two-volume set. Within a week of publication we got two orders for twenty-five hundred sets each from two we'd never even heard of. That was half the entire edition, and in about three weeks our entire printing was gone. We had thought they'd last five years. That's how brilliantly we figured!

We didn't have paper for any more at the time, and I thought we'd have to wait until the war was over, but one day my phone rang—it was a Monsignor from St. Patrick's Cathedral. He began in a deeply resonant voice, "Is this Bennett Cerf?" I said, "Yes." (Let's say that his name was Murphy.) He said, "This is Monsignor Murphy from St. Patrick's Cathedral. I just want to tell you that you're the stupidest publisher in the United States of America." I said, "Well, thank you for that sweeping compliment. What do I owe it to?" He said, "You're a fool. You bring out this beautiful two-volume St. Thomas Aquinas, and we're wondering how we can help you fellows, when what do we hear, three weeks after publication, you're out of print!" So I explained to him how we hadn't counted on orders coming in from Jesuits all over the country. He repeated, "You're a fool. I'll be right over to see you."

I went to our sales department and said, "This Monsignor can be coming from St. Patrick's for only one reason. He's going to offer us some paper!"

Well, in he came. There used to be a big movie star named Thomas Meighan, and this fellow was his double: a tall, dark-haired, blue-eyed, handsome, compelling person—hard to resist. He marched in and sat right down at my desk and lit a big cigar and began bawling me out, but I could see that it was all just an act. It was obvious that he understood the whole story. I waited patiently, and sure enough, the time came when he said, "It just so happens that we have some paper. If we give it to you, how do I know you'll use it for St. Thomas Aquinas?" So I did a little acting of my own and said indignantly, "I hope you're not accusing me of dishonesty. If you *did* happen to find some paper and gave it to us, we'd give you a printer's affidavit." He said, "I was only joking. Of course I know you'll use it for Aquinas. We have enough for about another five thousand sets." (They sold it to us for exactly what it cost them—and getting extra paper at any price was a miracle in those days.)

I said, "That's wonderful, Monsignor." He said, "Well, now are you happy?" And because something entirely unrelated was on my mind, I said, "No, I'm not." He said, "What else is bothering you?" I said, "As a matter of fact, we've just had notice that we've got to give up this office. IBM has bought the building. We all knew that we were living on a day-to-day basis—we couldn't get new leases—and we knew that somebody was going to buy the building, but we didn't know it was IBM and that everybody would have to clear out." In those days space was as unavailable in New York as paper. I said, "I've been looking at warehouses over in Gowanus . . . anyplace to go until the war's over. Next time you come up to tell me I'm the worst publisher in the United States, you'll probably find me operating from a rowboat in Central Park lake."

He said, "Well, let's see what we can do about it. How about the big building across from St. Patrick's Cathedral?" I said, "What building?" He said, "The palazzo, the brownstone building." I said, "That mansion with the courtyard?" He said, "Yes." I said, "Monsignor, besides being the stupidest publisher in America, I'm probably one of the poorest. We couldn't afford a building like that." He said, "Oh, nonsense. It's not one building—it's five." That was the first time I knew there were two wings, plus three separate buildings behind the wings. He said, "That north wing would be just about right for you. Joe Kennedy owns it now. We'll make him give it to you for what he paid for it." I said, "Wait a minute. I don't care what you could make Joe Kennedy do. We can't afford a building like that." He said, "You haven't even heard what it would cost you. Keep your shirt on!" He phoned his assistant at the cathedral and ordered, "Get me Joseph Kennedy." Kennedy was just a name to me. He had been ambassador to Great Britain, but the days of his great fame lay ahead.

The Monsignor and I sat talking for a while. I liked him more and more. He was a wonderful man. About fifteen minutes later the phone rang and he was told that Joe Kennedy was playing golf in Palm Beach. He said blithely, "Get him off the golf links." My eyes were popping. About fifteen minutes later Kennedy called up from Palm Beach. This Monsignor, whom I had just met for the first time, said, "One of our good young friends is in trouble and needs office space, and we want you to sell him that building across the street from the cathedral for what you paid for it." Well, I could hear Joe Kennedy fuming at the other end of the phone. He didn't think it was a good idea at all.

The building had been designed by Stanford White for Henry Villard, the father of Oswald Garrison Villard, and completed in 1885. At that time it was practically out in the country. Since it was intended for the whole family, it was built as five separate units. Shortly after it was finished Villard was wiped out in one of those Wall Street panics and had to sell the whole thing. Whitelaw Reid bought the south wing. Harris Fahnestock bought the north wing.

North wing of mansion: 457 Madison Avenue

Courtyard entrance

As the years went by, the Fahnestock family dwindled down to just Mr. Fahnestock and his son, who until the war started were living in that great big mansion with about twenty servants. Then the servants began disappearing, and it became ridiculous for two men to live in that big barn. In fact, they couldn't, so they sold out to Joe Kennedy, who then let the Free French use it as their office headquarters, and they had just moved out when this transaction took place. The building cost us somewhere around $420,000.

The first thing that happened was that the fire department, learning that we planned to use the building for offices, said we needed a fireproof stairway, which indeed we did. The building had been put up in the days when they made things to last, and breaking through those thick walls and putting in an extra stairway was a major undertaking. And steel was just as hard to get then as paper. I called up the Monsignor and we got our steel.

The Church helped us get the people to put in the stairway and they helped us get a mortgage—and in we moved to 457 Madison Avenue. So St. Thomas Aquinas became my patron saint, and I swore that the only way they'd ever get me to leave would be to carry me out.

We had many very pleasant dealings with Cardinal Spellman, whose residence was right across the street from us, behind the cathedral. He and I would have lunch together about twice a year. I'd usually take him out once, and next time I'd go over and have lunch with him. It wasn't a set rule, but that's about how it worked out. We were good neighbors, and I liked him even though he was so conservative. He was a decent man if you could get over his ideas, which I very often could not. But we knew when to stop talking. We understood each other and we had common interests, and both of us loved that building. That was one thing we shared. I would sometimes walk up Madison Avenue with him, and I always hoped we would meet somebody that I could impress properly, but somehow or other we never seemed to bump into anybody I knew.

When we had our lunches we talked about the stock market a great deal, and baseball too. One day he told me, "I once had to make a big choice: the Church or professional baseball." I expressed surprise, and he said, "I was a great catcher." Well, my dad had been a catcher too, so we had that in common. He said, "Where do you think I learned to kneel? I'll show you. I can still catch." He went out in the hall and called up and said, "Throw me my red cap." Someone threw down his little red cardinal's cap from way upstairs and he caught it and slapped it on his head. He was quite a human gentleman.

We often argued about books and movies and censorship—on which we were seldom in agreement. I remember one time when he seemed just a little bit put out with himself. It was just after a movie called *Baby Doll*, with Carroll Baker, had been released. It was a dirty picture, but nothing compared with what they do today. The Cardinal had issued a philippic against the picture, saying it was obscene and that nobody should go to see it. Until then it had done absolutely nothing at the box office, but within twenty-four hours it attracted lines two blocks long. He realized he had given the movie just the publicity it needed. He said he'd never make that mistake again.

A few years later we received a book by Honor Tracy, *The Straight and Narrow Path*—one of the funniest books I ever read. Honor Tracy, who is a Catholic, had been sent by the *Times* of London to write up life in a little Irish village, and had encountered some fascinating people. The priest had two new bathrooms in his house, and the rest of the town was starving to death because the priest was really using all the parish money for church purposes. The chapters were published first in the *Times,* and the Church in Ireland promptly sued them for libel. Well, the London papers had learned long ago that when this happened, you settled at once. You had about as much chance of winning as I would have of beating Rocky Marciano in the ring. So they settled immediately and apologized to the Church for the stories, saying that they were untrue; whereupon Honor Tracy sued the *Times,* saying that they had made her out a liar and that she could prove everything she had written. There has never been a case like it in literary history. She sued for quite a big sum, and the *Times* lost.

When the book came to us, we all read it, and laughed our heads off. At the last minute I got scared, and said, "Here we are across the avenue from St. Patrick's Cathedral. What is Cardinal Spellman, what are they all, going to say about this book? They're going to be outraged. I don't think we ought to do it." And Donald said, "All right. If that's the way you feel, we won't. But don't you ever tell me again that you're a liberal publisher." That, of course, was a stab right below the belt. So we published it in 1956, and we never heard one word from Cardinal Spellman. The book was a great success. It's still in Vintage Books, and I still think it's gloriously funny. Honor Tracy has written several books since, but none of them has been as successful as *The Straight and Narrow Path,* although one, *The First Day of Friday,* was a Book-of-the-Month Club selection in 1963.

We've done a lot of books with the imprimatur of the Catholic Church, and they've even given us several to publish. It's been a very pleasant relationship.

Gradually, the Church took over the other four sections of our building. They first got the Reid house and then one by one acquired the others. We owned the courtyard jointly with them—about twenty five percent to their seventy-five. Nobody knew exactly which part we owned. It was an undivided interest, a partnership, and neither of us could do anything without the other.

The two people who held out for keeping that mansion were Cardinal Spellman and myself, and when he died, I became a loner. The property became more valuable every day, and a lot of people both in the Church and at Random House long thought we should sell out and make an enormous profit. Our part of the building, which with all the improvements had cost about a half million dollars, had come to be worth about two and a half million, and we could make about two million dollars by selling it—more than we made in publishing in twenty years!

Finally, it was efficiency rather than profit that dictated our decision to move. Our business had grown to such an extent that we had five separate addresses in Manhattan, so in the interest of getting as many operations as possible under one roof, we moved into our new building at 201 East 50th Street in April of 1969. It broke my heart to leave the old house, and I never stopped believing that we should have kept it for our editorial offices.

"Carried out" by R.H. editor John Simon and Donald

As we have seen, the publishing business didn't suffer during the war, but it was profoundly changed by a new development, one that would affect us all. For many years in England and on the Continent, cheap paperbound reprints had been on the market and had flourished, and a number of futile attempts had been made to launch them in this country. Then, in 1939, Allen Lane, whose Penguin Books had been a great success in England, opened an American branch, with a talented young man, Ian Ballantine, as manager; and in that same year Robert de Graff, with financial support from Simon and Schuster, started a new American company, Pocket Books. It got off to a good enough start, but during the war years its sales expanded so rapidly that it attracted competitors. Paperbacks were here to stay, and a new era was on hand in book publishing.

Pocket Books was still the dominant company in 1944 when Marshall Field bought a controlling interest in it and in Simon and Schuster, and very soon after that event something else happened which demanded quick action on our part. Donald Grosset, the son of Alex Grosset, one of the founders of Grosset and Dunlap, came to me one day in a panic and told me that Field was about to buy their company. Through the machinations of Leon Shimkin, Simon and Schuster's financial genius, the deal had been all set up, and Grosset was afraid that he and a lot of faithful old employees were going to be fired. He was desperate and asked if we could buy the company instead of letting Marshall Field get it. He knew, of course, that no one publishing house could afford to buy Grosset; we hadn't gotten into high finance in those days. But Marshall Field was another story.

We immediately saw the threat to our business. Grosset practically had a corner on the hardbound reprint market, books that sold mainly in drugstores at seventy-nine cents and a dollar twenty-nine a copy. They were not really in competition with Modern Library; they reprinted more popular books than we did, and theirs were full-sized books. But with a Hemingway reprint, for instance, they could bring out their edition at a dollar twenty-nine, an inexpensive replica of the original book, while we would do it in a more compact Modern Library form for ninety-five cents. But paperbacks were beginning to cut into Modern Library by doing non-copyright titles like *Moby Dick* and *The Scarlet Letter,* books that we had more or less had a monopoly on. They were hurting us, and the thought of one firm, Simon and Schuster, controlled by Marshall Field, having the original publishing unit, the hardbound reprint and the paperback, too, was frightening. They could go to an author and say, "Not only can we publish your book. We can guarantee you the hardbound reprint and the paperback." That would be a package deal no other publisher could match.

I hastily called Harry Scherman, our good friend and president of the Book-of-the-Month Club. I found out that Donald Grosset had gone to him before he came to me, but Harry very wisely had said, "We don't want to be tied up with any publishing unit. We want to be able to operate independently, so that nobody can say we have a special interest." But he told me that if we were really interested, he'd reconsider, because he didn't like to see one firm owning all those properties.

Harry Scherman came up to our office, and we talked about whom we should ask to join us. Everything had to be done within forty-eight hours. The contract had been made out with Marshall Field and was ready to be signed. Shimkin had settled the terms with Field and with the son of the dead co-founder, George Dunlap, who was interested mainly in golf.

We wanted Scribner because they had Hemingway and Fitzgerald and several other important authors. We decided to ask Cass Canfield of Harper, and he said he'd be happy to come in. We wanted one of the Boston houses, Little, Brown or Houghton Mifflin, or both of them. We asked Alfred McIntyre of Little, Brown because he was a personal friend of mine, and I didn't happen to know anybody at Houghton Mifflin. When I got McIntyre on the phone, he came right down to New York.

Finally we called Charles Scribner, one of the most cautious men who ever lived. I said, "This has got to be done right away. We want you with us. I'd like to send over the papers and show you the figures." Mr. Scribner, this careful man, said, "How much would it cost me?" It was something like three hundred seventy thousand dollars for each one, except the Book-of-the-Month Club, which went in for two units and would own twice as much as any of the rest of us.

I said, "You have to think fast, Mr. Scribner." He said, "Well, are you and Alfred McIntyre and Cass Canfield and Harry Scherman all going into it?" I said, "We certainly are." He said, "If it's good enough for you fellows, it's good enough for me." I said, "You're with us?" He said, "Absolutely." I said, "Don't you want to look at the figures?" He said, "You've looked at them. If you're going to risk your money, I'm perfectly willing to risk mine." So Scribner came in without even looking at the papers. None of the rest of us had studied them very carefully, I must say, but the fun of snatching the prize away from Marshall Field was a very strong stimulus.

The total cost of Grosset and Dunlap was about two and a quarter million dollars. When the purchase was announced, the publishing world said, "They'll be at each other's throats inside of six months," but there has never been a more friendly combination in the history of publishing. We persuaded John O'Connor to run it, and this turned out to be a masterful stroke. John had had years of experience in the book business and at the time was vice-president of the Quarrie Corporation, which published the World Book Encyclopedia. A great diplomat, he managed the show beautifully.

The hardbound reprint division of Grosset dwindled to nothing in about two years, and the whole purpose for which the purchase was made had gone. Nevertheless, it turned out to be one of the most profitable investments any of us had ever made, especially after the Grosset juvenile department began to proliferate.

Then came another dramatic development. Ian Ballantine had parted company with Penguin Books, and in 1945 he approached Donald and me to try to get us to finance the paperback house he intended to start on his own. But Random House was growing very fast and we needed all the money we had; we knew that to start a rival to Pocket Books would take at least a million dollars, and we didn't have it. So I took Ian to Grosset, and we persuaded them to start a paperback house.

It took a lot of doing. Charlie Scribner was particularly opposed to it. He wanted no part of a paperback operation. I must say that Robert de Graff and Dick Simon did all they could to dissuade us, to tell us what the many hazards were. When Bob de Graff came as a "friend" to give us a talk about why we should not go into the business, we figured if he was that worried, it must be a damned good idea. That was what almost convinced Charles Scribner.

Then we all went to Philadelphia and sold the Curtis Publishing Company on going in with us. We had to have a distributor, and Curtis had a nationwide setup for distributing its magazines, which was ideal for handling paperbacks. Bantam Books was started, fifty percent owned by Grosset and Dunlap, which in turn was owned by us, and fifty percent by Curtis. We had our meetings in the Curtis office on old Independence Square in Philadelphia, in the board room of the *Saturday Evening Post*. It was sort of a dream for me; I had started out as a kid selling the *Post,* and here I was meeting with the board of directors!

It all worked out because the principals respected and trusted one another. There wasn't anyone in the combination who didn't have the full confidence of the others. If we had included one or two of the shadier characters in publishing, there would have been chaos. Or if we hadn't been fortunate enough to get a man like John O'Connor to run it, a man whom we all trusted implicitly. It was a huge success. There was never any doubt about Bantam Books. It began making money from the day it started.

Then came an unfortunate crisis involving Ian Ballantine. He was forced out of the business that he had brought to us. I thought this was shameful, but the others overruled me. Ballantine was a very difficult fellow to handle. He didn't know what diplomacy meant and he didn't realize that he was dealing with some very successful gentlemen who liked their prerogatives respected. Bantam had opened an English branch, to which, without getting the approval of the executive committee, Ian lent some sorely needed money. The sum involved was only twenty-six thousand dollars, but he had no right to do it, and for this minor offense they forced him to resign.

I was outraged and demanded another hearing. Ian had been foolish enough to confront these strong publishing men without a lawyer, and this time he brought one, but it was too late. They had made up their minds even before he could plead his case. Later we landed a real knockout: Oscar Dystel, who built Bantam up to be a huge paperback house. I guess it's number one today.

Everything went along beautifully for a long time, until all the other paperback houses began doing original publishing and Bantam wanted to follow suit. At this, Charles Scribner, Jr., who had long since superseded his father, rebelled. He didn't like the paperback business even though he was the owner of about one-twelfth of the profitable Bantam stock. Young Scribner is one of the finest and most honorable men I've ever met—though I think he was very foolish in this instance. He said he wanted to get out, and all he wanted back was the money his father had put into the business. We pointed out to him that his stock was now worth considerably more than what had been put in and we'd have to figure out a fair price for it, but he wouldn't hear of it. He got back his investment—a little less than four hundred thousand dollars—though his share of that business by 1967 would have been worth over three million.

Shortly afterward the Curtis Publishing Company had some financial trouble and offered to sell us their part of Bantam, so Grosset bought it, and owned Bantam Books fully—one hundred percent.

None of the publishers who bought Grosset liked the way Pocket Books was doing business, since they had almost a monopoly and could dictate exactly what they would pay for reprint licenses. The royalty paid by the paperback houses in those days had been set by Pocket Books: a cent a copy—or four percent—on a twenty-five-cent book for the first hundred and fifty thousand copies sold, and then a cent and a half—or six percent—on all additional sales.

When we started Bantam, I must admit we used the same royalty rate. At each meeting I would say that it was too low. When I would start every meeting with this, the others would say, "Oh, there goes Bennett again," half jokingly and half angrily, because none of them wanted to raise the rate.

Then, as the paperback business expanded and other competitors came into the field, they also adopted this same royalty rate. Nobody could help making money at first, but then came one year when so many paperbacks were printed, millions of copies had to be destroyed. I think some were used for land fill and some were dumped into Lake Erie. All the paperback houses had big setbacks. Gradually, as production costs increased, they were having to raise prices. The standard twenty-five-cent retail price was no longer feasible, and for too long they had been afraid to increase it. When they finally did, it made no difference in sales whatsoever, and quarter paperbacks disappeared entirely. They run up to two dollars and forty-five cents but the majority are from a half dollar to a dollar and a quarter.

It was the agents and the Authors League who finally put an end to the unfair royalty deals—aided and abetted by me. At last, the paperback houses raised their rate. Now some contracts are negotiated at royalty rates they can't really afford to pay. When the competition for a big title comes along and smart agents get into the picture, the deals are sometimes staggering. Instead of four and six percent, there have been agreements calling for as much as a twenty-five-percent royalty. The standard is ten or fifteen, and I'm just as much opposed to twenty-five as I was to four and six, because a paperback book can't afford twenty-five.

Of course, when a super best seller comes along, the profits can be enormous. In four months *Valley of the Dolls* sold eight million copies in paperback, whereas if a hardbound book averages eight thousand copies, we're happy. Eighty thousand is cause for cheering in the streets. Eight hundred thousand is virtually unheard of. Eight million staggers the imagination of a hardbound publisher.

As the prize became bigger and bigger, the Authors League, very rightly, got into the fight and protested that the traditional fifty-fifty division between author and publisher was not a fair split of paperback royalties. The League had always claimed the same thing about book-club rights too, but I don't think they had a leg to stand on, because the clubs distribute their choices to members at about the same time the books are published and are therefore in direct competition with original editions, so a fifty-fifty split of book-club royalties is justified, and publishers are holding the line.

I also think that publishers should have some share in motion-picture rights, as they used to. To me it's always been disgraceful that a publisher takes a book and works like the devil on it and helps edit it—and even retitles it in some cases—and makes a big hit of it, only to see, when the movies buy it for a big sum, that the agent, who has often spent a single day on the deal, walks off with a full ten percent while the publisher doesn't get a nickel. I think we ought to get a small share—not much, but something. If the agent deserves ten percent, the publisher deserves at least five percent, no matter how important the author is. Maybe the agent ought to give up a little of his ten percent, or split fifty-fifty with the publisher.

Also, I don't think agents have any right to get ten percent of an author's earnings above a certain limit. When the author earns a huge amount and the agent continues to earn ten percent, he's being overpaid. So when agents come to me, telling me that a publisher has been unfair on the fifty-fifty split, I turn the tables and point out that they are taking a full ten percent of everything, thus netting on a big deal as much as fifty or sixty or even a hundred thousand dollars. They change the subject mighty quickly! It always depends on who's being stabbed. I'm trying to be entirely objective and admit that everybody is guilty at one time or another of some stupidity or cupidity. It works out in the long run. That's why free competition is so important. You can tell it when you're riding on an airline that has no competition: you get a stale sandwich for lunch and the plane is two hours late. But where there are two lines competing, you get steak and arrive on the minute.

Competition brought about the changes in paperback royalties, and now some publishers are quietly breaking the fifteen-percent maximum-royalty rule on hardbound editions. We and most other publishers haven't done it, but I know one or two very respectable houses that will make a special deal to lure an author. We all know about it.

I don't believe that paperbacks will ever destroy hardbound publishing. First of all, most people who love good books want to keep them in their libraries. Paperback books are not made to last, and the type is usually too small for many people to read comfortably. The paperback has actually benefited publishing in more ways than one. Selling reprint and other subsidiary rights is now what keeps a lot of hardbound publishers from going bankrupt, because without a paperback sale, a book doesn't make expenses most of the time. Also, paperbacks encourage the reading habit; people start with them, and a small percentage will graduate to hardbound books. So new readers are created and books are provided for people who can't afford the hardbound ones—and that's the greatest advantage of all. For the student, it's wonderful. When I went to college, if we were required to read some rather expensive book, there would be two copies in the Columbia University libraries and a hundred and eighty-two students would try to get those copies at the same time. Today they can go out and buy what they need for about seventy-five cents. I think the hardbound publisher's got to be in on all this some way or another, and the one who

Jason Epstein

hasn't buttressed himself with an interest in a paperback house has been very short-sighted.

I credit Robert de Graff with starting paperbacks, but the man who really launched the *good*-book paperbacks was Jason Epstein, whose Anchor Books achieved fantastic results. Doubleday was practically conned into doing the series. Doubleday bigwigs didn't think much would come of it, but this brilliant boy, Jason Epstein, opened their eyes. Then, just as everybody had copied Pocket Books when they saw what a good thing it was, Anchor Books became the model for quality paperbacks: Knopf and Random House, for instance, with Vintage Books, which is today, I guess, bigger than Anchor.

Vintage Books was started by Alfred Knopf, Jr., who persuaded his father to try the experiment. They began with just Knopf books, and for a while, with such an incredibly wonderful list, they were able to prosper, but after a while they needed more titles, and they persuaded us to put in a few Random House books. That was when we began working together. But the actual merger came after we took over Knopf. Then we really expanded Vintage Books, which is today a very successful and distinguished series. We had lured Jason Epstein away from Doubleday, and he helped with the combined Vintage list.

After I first talked with Jason, I called up Doubleday's top man, Douglas Black, who is a very good friend of mine, and said I wanted to ask him about Jason Epstein. Doug got so perturbed about this that he said, "I'll come down. I want to talk to you about him." I said, "I'll come up." He said, "No. I want to talk to you down there." So he came over, only a few blocks away, and began telling me what a wonderful boy Jason was, but he said, "He'll drive you crazy. He almost drove me crazy." I said, "Why?" He said, "Every time I give him a raise it lasts for about two weeks, and then he's asking for another one." I asked him how much Jason was getting. I forget what it was, but it wasn't anything terrific. I said, "He must have started at about eighteen cents a week." Doug finally admitted that if he had given Jason a much higher salary to begin with, things wouldn't have been so difficult. But Jason is a very aggressive young fellow anyway, and he got on Doug's nerves.

With us he's worked out wonderfully. I call him "the cross I bear." (When someone told him I'd said this, he said, "Bennett is the bear I cross.") Jason is Jason. He's one of the brilliant young men on the New York literary scene. His wife, Barbara, is the co-editor of *The New York Review of Books,* and Jason is part of the literary establishment. He lords it around, but everybody loves him. He's very attractive, but is absolutely unmanageable. He does things the way he pleases; and anybody who tries to tell him how to do something another way is wasting his breath.

Of course, Vintage and Anchor Books cut into the Modern Library sales, and so do all paperbacks. But The Modern Library still offers real books, with very attractive bindings and jackets, and the type is kept immaculate. If the printing plates start wearing out, we order new ones. We watch that with loving care because The Modern Library was the keystone of Random House. But though in the beginning the series grew by leaps and bounds, when paperbacks came into favor, we were lucky to hold our own, and it was only by adding important new titles that we could keep The Modern Library going ahead. It's still a beautiful property, but no longer a "must" in all bookstores. They still stock it, but it's not the outstanding value it once was, since the paperback has overshadowed it for anybody who wants a book at the lowest possible price. Also, many publishers have started their own paperback series, so we've lost many outstanding titles. We make contracts that last for three or five years; and nowadays when a contract expires, we often can't get the original publisher to renew it. For instance, Scribner, when they started their own paperback library, took back Ernest Hemingway and F. Scott Fitzgerald. It broke my heart. For the same reason, when Harcourt started their Harbrace books, we lost Virginia Woolf and Lytton Strachey. But that's all in the game.

In recent years publishers have found that they can sell paperback rights for very big prices; and sometimes they have given us The Modern Library rights too, since we don't interfere with the paperback sale. We provide almost a third market; it doesn't compare in sales volume with the paperback, but many authors are proud to be in The Modern Library. It's a beautiful series, and an author feels that he's arrived if he gets on its list.

Magazines have been hurt by paperbacks, but not as much as by television. Many people used to buy a magazine just to pass an evening—a traveling salesman, alone in a city, for example, might buy two or three to take to his room when he was stuck in a town where he didn't know anybody. Today, in every hotel and motel room there is a television set, or if not, there's one in the lobby. The people who read only out of desperation can now just turn a knob and see all the trash on television. Why should they have to read it? When you study the groups around a television set in a small town, it's pretty discouraging. There they sit, glued to the set. They don't even know what they're watching. They sit there in a semi-stupor the whole evening. That has hurt the magazines—picture ones particularly. Also, trends are changing, and the magazine that doesn't change with the trends is like everything else. A while ago some professor at MIT said, "If it works, it's obsolete." Everything changes so fast, and you've got to keep on the ball.

The first magazines that went under were those that did light fiction—like *Bluebook* and *Ainslee's*. *Redbook* has kept up with the times—it has changed its character—but there were a lot that went on printing corny stories for a market that has disappeared. The *Saturday Evening Post* used to have three or four short stories an issue and one article, but gradually came to have maybe one story and the rest articles. When I started publishing, fiction outsold nonfiction four-to-one. Now that ratio is absolutely reversed, and nonfiction outsells fiction four-to-one. Occasionally a book comes along like *Valley of the Dolls* or *The Source* or *The Secret of Santa*

Vittoria or *The Confessions of Nat Turner,* and they'll sell more than novels used to, but the bulk of new fiction doesn't sell at all. It's heartbreaking to bring out a good first novel and watch it die virtually at birth. People just are not reading as much fiction, perhaps because life itself is too exciting. The fiction writer can't compete with the front page of the newspaper. More things happen now in a month than happened during our parents' lifetime; and life has become such a wildly exciting, chaotic affair, that just keeping up with actual news takes a lot of time. So it has to be a very unusual novel that will catch on—like *Hawaii* or *Dr. Zhivago.* For one reason or another, there will always be a few that become great best sellers, but most fiction finds it very hard going indeed.

By contrast, take the books that are coming out on various phases of world affairs. There have been probably a hundred books on Vietnam, and most of them have sold. There have also been hundreds of books on race relations, sold mainly to young people, and in paperback they outsell the hardbound by a huge margin because the college students who read them can't afford to pay seven ninety-five for a book. They *will* pay ninety-five cents or a dollar and a quarter.

A major financial problem for publishers is paying huge guarantees against future royalties to authors, sometimes months or even years before a book can be produced and start earning back its cost, sometimes even before the author has written one word. This can tie up large amounts of cash, which often has to be borrowed from banks, adding interest to the publisher's costs, which all too frequently are never recovered. Not too long ago, advances were far more modest—a few thousand dollars to tide the author over while he finished a book—but now they can reach six figures.

Several factors contributed to bringing this change about, not the least of which were the paperback explosion, which greatly increased the earning power of successful authors and the demands of their agents, and inflation, which drove up the cost of producing books and, consequently, their retail prices: a royalty of fifteen percent on a ten-dollar novel is four times what it used to be when novels were two-fifty.

Furthermore, it has become a custom for agents who represent not only authors but public figures—politicians, actors and actresses, athletes, and so forth—to offer their books, or sometimes only their intentions to write their stories, to many publishers simultaneously, and to sell to the highest bidder. We've seldom gone into such competitions, and for good reasons. Most of these memoirs receive advances for much more than they're worth. Furthermore, their value is diluted by the fact that the highlights are usually published first in *The New York Times* and in fifty other newspapers, as well as in magazines. Churchill worked out spectacularly for Houghton Mifflin, but he was one in a million, a fine writer.

Some agents are brilliant negotiators; I don't blame them for getting what they can. They put a big book up for auction, and there are always publishers who will start the bidding. Very often you will be tempted to buy it, not because you think it's a good book but because you hear Harper, Scribner, Doubleday and Viking are after it. It becomes a game, a contest.

The word gets around that there is hot bidding for a book, and you want to get in on it. You don't want to be left behind. In fact, I've often bawled an agent out for not sending me a book that I'd heard was going to be a big prize, only to be told, "I knew you wouldn't want this one. It's going for too much money, and it's not your kind of book." But I'm hurt that I'm left out, even if I wouldn't have bid anyway.

I know a couple of people Doubleday has given huge advances to and never heard from again—actors and such who proposed to write their autobiographies but never did. That isn't as prevalent as it used to be, but there was a time when everybody was trying to sign up every movie star for a book.

We've had those fits. One was with Judy Garland. When she was sick—she had hepatitis I think—she was up at Doctors Hospital. I've always loved Judy Garland. She's an irresistible little woman—but one of the most tragic in the world. I'm sure that one day she's going to do herself in. At any rate, she called and she was miserable. I went up to the hospital, and she said she was ready to write her autobiography. She had just the man to write it for her, she said, Freddie Finkelhoffe, who had written a play called *Brother Rat* and collaborated on the great musical *Finian's Rainbow*. His wife, Ella Logan, was the star of *Finian's Rainbow*. I gave Judy and Finkelhoffe an advance of thirty thousand dollars, fifteen to each.

Finkelhoffe wrote just enough pages to get the advance. Then he disappeared—just vanished into thin air. Judy felt very guilty about it. She's a good girl. When Herbert Mayes, then editor of *McCall's,* wanted to do a two-parter about Judy, she said yes, provided that *McCall's* pay us our entire advance. We got back our money, but there was no book.

Often, however, you'll give a big advance and never get anything back at all. That's part of the risk, and the publisher must allow for it. Random House alone has probably lost a million dollars in advances for books that were unpublishable when they came in, or that never came in at all—where the author just walked off with the money. Dorothy Parker, just before she died, had advances from several different publishers for books that she had no intention of ever writing. She, like many authors, considered publishers fair game.

When paperback people scream about the big advances they pay, I always point out to them that most often they are getting properties that are already proven successes, or that at least actually *exist*. A hardcover publisher, on the other hand, may never get the book he's contracted for, or, if he does get it, may find that it has no resemblance whatever to the synopsis he bought. I once playfully suggested to Ken McCormick, editor in chief at Doubleday, that a bunch of publishers should get together and sit around a table, each bringing with him three of his worst unfulfilled contracts; then, as in the game of hearts, everyone would discard to the publisher on his left his three bad contracts. Of course, all of us would be left with the same number we'd had before, but Ken and I agreed that at least we'd all have some *different* ones and not the same old boring ones that had depressed us for so long.

An interesting example of the responsible author was Dashiell Hammett, the father of the modern detective story. I think the Raymond Chandler and James Bond stories all derived from Dash Hammett. Hammett had an argument with Alfred Knopf, who had been publishing his books, notably *The Maltese Falcon* and *The Thin Man*. Knopf at that time, of course, was a very important rival and we went after the same kind of books. Hammett came to me one day and said that he had had a falling-out with Knopf and offered to come with us. Since Alfred and I were always friends, I called him and said, "I'm not going to poach on you, but Hammett says that he'll never talk to you again." Alfred said, "I want nothing more to do with him." When Alfred had a fight with somebody, it meant curtains! He threw out Irving Wallace and Harold Robbins, but he has never regretted it, I must say, even though they both made fortunes.

Alfred said, "Go ahead, but you'll have nothing but trouble with Hammett. He's a terrible man." Dash was *not* a terrible man. One of the reasons I remember him with particular fondness is that we gave him a five-thousand-dollar advance for a book, and after about two years he offered to give us back the money. That doesn't happen very often. I didn't want to take it. I said, "I think you'll do the book someday, Dash." But he said, "No. I'm afraid I'll never write it. I'm petering out." He knew he was getting sicker all the time.

Dashiell Hammett was a man who couldn't afford it, but he was so honorable that when he saw he wasn't going to be able to do a book, he insisted on repaying the advance. It was the fine gesture of a man with integrity.

You'll find honest authors and you'll find crooks. In this regard, there is no difference between authors and other people.

In my secondary role as writer, rather than publisher, of books, I performed a classical demonstration of two of the frequent areas of dispute between authors and publishers—advertising and sales. In 1948 Simon and Schuster brought out my fourth book, *Shake Well Before Using*, which sold about eighty thousand copies in hardbound alone, and after that I broke with them. They had done a glorious job for *Try and Stop Me*, but by the time *Shake Well Before Using* came along they had become enamored of Billy Rose and were promoting his book harder than mine. Like a typical author, I felt I was being neglected and I raised holy hell, as a result of which they took several full-page ads. In the end, my book outsold Billy Rose's about four to one, but I never forgave them.

I moved to Doubleday, which has done my books ever since, except every once in a while when I turned to Harper, which did *Reading for Pleasure*, one of my favorites, and *An Encyclopedia of Modern American Humor*—two books that I did not write: I *edited* them. *Reading for Pleasure* consists of stories that I liked best in my lifetime, not jokes. It's a good anthology and so is the *Encyclopedia*. Cass Canfield at Harper also did my *Out on a Limerick*, which fared well, and *Bennett Cerf's Treasury of Atrocious Puns*. Imagine a whole book of puns!

I think it is very impolitic for a publisher to bring out his own books, and most of my colleagues in the industry feel the same way. If you advertise yours, ten of your authors will probably say, "I see that you have money to advertise your own book. Why didn't *I* have an ad in the *Times* this morning? You're spending your time exploiting yours instead of mine."

There's also a great pleasure in dealing with some other publisher because you always get fed up at some point with your authors pestering you: "My cousin was in Des Moines yesterday and my book wasn't in the window of any store there," or "It wasn't in the airport at Shreveport," and all the other standard kicks that an author registers. "My royalty statement is wrong." "Why didn't you do this?" "Why didn't you do that?" When I get a bellyful of that now, I can always go over to Doubleday and make the same kind of nuisance out of myself, which of course I do.

At Doubleday when I would start arguing with John Sargent or Ken McCormick about advertising or whatever, we could hardly keep straight faces because we all knew the time-honored answers. I knew what they were going to say and they knew what I was going to answer. It was like a minuet. We'd go through the routine of my grumbling about something and their giving me the precise answer that I give my own authors. But it was always fun, and we usually ended up by going out for a couple of drinks together.

Opinions vary on the effectiveness of book advertising. I've always quoted Max Perkins, the great old Scribner editor, on the subject. He compared advertising a book to the problem of a car that's stuck: "If the car is really stuck in the mud, ten people can't budge it. But if it's moving even a little bit, one man can push it on down the road. By the same token, if a book is absolutely dead, all the advertising in the world isn't going to help. If it's got a glimmer of life, if it's selling a little bit maybe in only one or two spots, it's moving enough to be given a push."

That's a very good analogy, and I've used it many times with authors who don't believe one word that I'm saying, but it's true. You can take a full-page ad in the *Times* for a book that's dead and it won't sell fifty additional copies. We've proved it—to shut up an aggressive agent who hollers that we haven't done anything with a particular book and whom we consider important enough to pacify. We'll take a big ad, although we know it's throwing money away, just to keep the franchise. The ad will come out and we watch the daily sales. Invariably, a full week later, we haven't sold a hundred copies of the book all over the country, meaning that the ad is absolutely worthless.

The people who read advertisements are looking for new books that they haven't yet heard about, or that they have heard a little bit about and are reminded to buy. But if it's a book that means nothing to them, they just skip it. I even do it myself, and I'm in the business. When you're confronted with all those ads in a single issue of *The New York Times Book Review*, you look only at the ones that interest you.

Another favorite complaint of authors is that they can't always find their books in the bookstores. It's true that they can't, sometimes, and there are many reasons for it—some, beyond our control. Bookstores, which are generally run by people who love books, are not among the most profitable enterprises in the United States. The discount stores, because they don't carry a complete stock but do carry the best sellers, have hurt the small bookseller. In New York, for example, Korvette's, a discount store, is right across the street from Brentano's on Fifth Avenue and right down the street from Scribner's, and as a result, Scribner's and Brentano's don't sell as many copies of the top best sellers as they used to, because people go to Korvette's and get the same book for considerably less than the list price. Discount houses consider books "loss leaders" that lure customers into their stores, even though it's not always pleasant shopping there.

Of course, good booksellers have the stock that the discount houses haven't got. And that includes the unprofitable stock, books that might remain on the shelves for six months before somebody comes in and asks for one—if indeed anybody ever does—and if these stores don't get their share of best-seller sales, they lose even more by stocking books that sell slowly or don't sell at all and have to be returned. For this reason they are becoming more resistant to our salesmen's efforts to sell them books for which there will be a small, if any, demand—first novels, poetry, essays, plays. Some stores will not order any of these books, and those that do will take only one or two copies and then not reorder if the first shipment sells out.

But in spite of all these problems, authors are making more money than ever before because book clubs and paperback opportunities have greatly increased, as have the amounts earned from selling reprint rights to anthologies, textbooks and periodicals. The *Reader's Digest* is an especially generous source of extra income.

Back during the time I was doing "Trade Winds" and "Cerf Board," as well as the "Try and Stop Me" column, there was a powerful lot of Cerf material popping up in *Reader's Digest.* So DeWitt Wallace suggested that instead of paying me each time they used a squib of mine, they set a yearly rate that would give them the right to use anything I wrote. It was a very generous offer, which I was pleased to accept, but I told him, "You're not going to use that much material. To pay for each one of them wouldn't come to anything like what you're offering me now." He said, "Leave that to us," and for years it went on that way. As I stopped doing "Trade Winds" and then "Cerf Board" it became an outrageous fee, so, finally, it was reduced. They continued sending me too much and I thought it should stop altogether, but they kept on doing it. Wally always said, "You let us worry about that."

DeWitt Wallace is a remarkable man, and the *Reader's Digest,* probably the most successful publishing venture ever known, was entirely his own idea, one that had been forming in his mind before World War I. He was still in his twenties when this country entered the war; he volunteered, served in France and was seriously wounded the month before the Armistice. During his long months in a French hospital he perfected his notion that most magazine articles could be greatly reduced in length and still retain their essential content. Within a year after his discharge from the army he had produced a pilot edition of the *Reader's Digest,* dated January, 1920.

Then came disappointment, when publisher after publisher to whom he presented his sample issue refused to be sufficiently impressed to back it. But he stubbornly clung to his idea, and when the following year he became engaged to Lila Bell Acheson and found that she shared his conviction, they planned together the beginning of the *Reader's Digest.* In February, 1922, shortly after their marriage, they published, as co-editors and co-founders, Volume One, Number One, in a printing of five thousand copies, borrowing the money they needed to pay the printer. The rest is history: by 1941 the circulation had reached four million, and during World War II it doubled; by 1967 it was over sixteen million.

Besides being a very determined man, Wally is very direct. One day he called me up and said he'd like to see me. I thought, What now? but said, "I'll be right down." Wally said, "No. I'll come to see you. I want to talk to you about something personal." I couldn't imagine what was up.

Lila and DeWitt Wallace

Wally walked in and we had our usual exchange of a few jokes. He loves to tell stories as much as I do. Finally we got down to brass tacks. He said, "Have you any idea how much money the *Reader's Digest* has paid Random House over the last six years?" I thought, Here it comes. The Reader's Digest Condensed Book Club is a source of huge revenue, because if they choose a book, it's like hitting the jackpot. It is sometimes even bigger than a Book-of-the-Month Club selection. I quavered, "I don't know how much, Wally. I know it's an awful lot." He said, "It's over a million dollars." I said, "Really?"—dreading what this was leading to.

"Now," he said, "I want something from you. I am very much interested in a college out in St. Paul called Macalester. I want you to deliver a lecture there this fall." Well, all the weight of the world fell off at once, and I said, "Oh, Wally, I'll be delighted to." He said, "You're not going to do it for nothing, I don't think that way. But I have persuaded everyone I've asked to charge only half of his regular fee." I said, "I'll be glad to do it for nothing." He said, "No, no, no. What do you get for lecturing in colleges?" I said, "Well the standard college fee is a thousand dollars." He said, "All right, we'll pay you five hundred. I don't even want you to make a special trip to St. Paul. I happen to have found out that you're speaking at the University of Minnesota in November. If you'll come to Macalester that same morning, I've gotten permission from Professor Lombard at the University of Minnesota to have you do so."

So I went out to Macalester and spoke in the morning there and simply fell in love with the place. It's an excellent little college. The reason DeWitt Wallace loved it so much was that his father had been its head when it was so poor, they couldn't pay him any salary for two or three years. The Wallace kids had to go out selling newspapers—anything to enable the family to survive.

The president of Macalester, just newly appointed when I got there, was Harvey Rice—a very able man. When we went to his study after my talk, I said, "I don't want your check. I'd like to start a scholarship fund and I'd like to give the small income of it to the leading English student in the graduating class each spring." Harvey Rice said, "That's wonderful. I'm going to call up Wally right away." I knew this little gesture would please Wally, and I was pleased to do it too. Rice called Wally, who said, "That's good news. What did he give? Five hundred dollars? Make it two thousand dollars. I'll put in fifteen hundred." So the fund started with two thousand dollars. For the next several years I would take quite a good chunk of the money the *Digest* was giving me, and that I didn't think I deserved, and add it to the scholarship fund, and Wally always added to it, so that today the fund is, I guess, pretty close to thirty thousand dollars and the prize each year is over a thousand dollars.

The *Digest* people have always been wonderful to me. The first ones I met were Ralph Henderson and his late wife, Cliff—they were my idea of a perfect pair. Ralph came around to see us when they began buying material for the magazine, even before they started the Reader's Digest Condensed Books. He would go over our advance list with me, and we became very good friends. When the Condensed Books project was started, Ralph was more or less in charge of it. Though some publishers thought that such a book club might compete with their own sales, I was enthusiastic about it long before I realized how successful it was going to be. I thought of it as still one more way of getting people interested in books.

I felt the same way about my appearing on television when one day a man I'd never met, Mark Goodson of Goodson-Todman, called me and told me about the television show they were producing every Sunday night called *What's My Line?* One of the regulars couldn't be there the following Sunday, and they wondered if I'd like to take his place that night. I jumped at the opportunity, though some around our office felt that playing a game on television wasn't exactly appropriate for a dignified publisher.

I hadn't seen *What's My Line?*—though it had been on the air for about five months—but I'd read about it in the columns. A panel of four people tried to determine the occupations of contestants by asking them questions that could be answered with Yes or No. A special feature of the show was the appearance of the Mystery Guest—always some well-known person—whom the panelists tried to identify while blindfolded. On Sunday night, October 15, 1950, I played *What's My Line?* for the first time. I quickly observed that there were techniques of questioning that narrowed the field of possible occupations, and I handled myself rather well for somebody who had never been on the show before.

The sponsor at that time was Dr. Jules Montenier, whose product was Stopette, an underarm spray. When *What's My Line?* started, it was on only a few CBS stations. Everybody thought it would be one of those novelties that would last for a brief period and then vanish, but it caught on like wildfire. As it spread from city to city, of course, the sponsorship costs went up and up and up; but Dr. Montenier stuck with the program until it was running in practically every city in the United States, and the charges had become enormous. He couldn't possibly sell enough deodorant to pay for it, and that was his only product; so finally he had to give up the show. It broke his heart. His slogan was "Poof! There goes perspiration." The *Harvard Lampoon* had a picture in one of its issues of Dr. Montenier shooting through the top of a building, and the caption was "Poof! There goes Dr. Montenier."

After I had appeared on the show a few times as a guest panelist, on March 18, 1951, I joined it permanently. I thought it was fun and a good way to make our firm and our authors known to a wide audience. The other regulars at that time were the M.C. John Daly, moderator of many network programs and later head of ABC News; the actress Arlene Francis, Dorothy Kilgallen and Hal Block. John and I hit it off perfectly and started kidding each other at once. I'd always loved Arlene, who is one of the most charming girls in the world. All the cattiness that came out in Dorothy's gossip column didn't show when you met her, and I hit it off with her too. As for Hal Block, he had a style of humor none of us was too fond of.

Before long, Hal Block's place was taken by the comedian Steve Allen. Steve was a pleasure to work with, but after a little while he left for California to headline a show of his own. Then, to our absolute delight, one of the great men of show business—Fred Allen—came on the panel

What's My Line? *panel and M. C. John Daly*

and stayed with us until his death. What a superb man he was! Goodson-Todman never filled his place, but thereafter used guest panelists to sit in the fourth chair.

I could be entirely myself on that show, and I loved it. The personal fame that came with it I loved even more, and I made no bones about it. And even the doubtful people at the office had to admit that I had made "Random House" a household name. *What's My Line?* was a wonderful experience. We became like a close-knit family: the cast, the producers, the staff—we were all good friends. We spent nearly every Sunday night together for seventeen years.

There was only one Sunday during all that time that the show wasn't done in New York. We did it in Chicago for several very good reasons. The Democratic National Convention was being held there and John Daly was covering it for ABC. Dorothy was doing feature stories on the convention—she was a top reporter as well as a columnist—so she had to be there too. Our sponsors that year were Remington Rand and Helene Curtis. Curtis said that if we'd do the show from Chicago, they'd pay all the special costs of moving it for that one performance, figuring that the extra publicity justified it. Curtis gave a party after the show and it was big stuff all around. We had a ball.

The Mystery Guest that night was Perle Mesta. When the show was over, I asked John Daly, "Why in heaven's name did we have Perle Mesta? We had her only about four or five months ago." John said, "You don't know how happy we were to get her. You won't believe what happened. We were supposed to have—and what a coup it would have been—the ex-President of the United States, Harry Truman." John said that Truman, who was attending the convention, had agreed to appear on the show, but that then the producers had made a routine call to clear the invitation with our co-sponsor, Remington Rand. Their chairman was General Douglas MacArthur, whom Truman had relieved of his command on April 10, 1951, during the Korean War—an event I remember vividly, because Phyllis and I were having lunch that day in Washington with Anna Rosenberg, Assistant Secretary of Defense, and we learned what was about to happen just before it was made public. Apparently, when MacArthur learned who had been invited to be the Mystery Guest, the wires practically burned up. He said Truman was not going to be on any program he had anything to do with. Instead of telling MacArthur to go to hell, they went into a panic and told President Truman he couldn't be on *What's My Line?*

There they were, stuck in Chicago with no Mystery Guest and little time to find one. The city was crawling with prominent Democrats, but most of them were, or might turn out to be, running for something. The political equal-time requirement in broadcasting was in effect, and unless the network gave other candidates equal exposure, none of these Democratic aspirants could appear on *What's My Line?* So they dug up Perle Mesta, who was happy to oblige.

Bennett and Phyllis with Mystery Guest Jack Benny

Several years later, in June, 1960, I had an opportunity to meet Truman. The occasion, again in Chicago, was the American Booksellers Association Convention, during which Bernard Geis gave a dinner party to celebrate the publication of Truman's book, *Mr. Citizen*, published by Geis Associates and distributed by Random House. When I mentioned my regret that he had not appeared on *What's My Line?* he laughed and said, "Well, maybe that gave you some idea of what I had to deal with when we were fighting the Korean War."

I think that Harry Truman will go down in history as one of our fine Presidents, a man who came through when he had to, and I am grateful to Bernard Geis for giving me the chance to meet him—though I have mixed feelings about some of Berney's books that we distributed.

I had first met Geis when he joined Grosset and Dunlap in 1945. Later, when he started for himself, he devised this very clever idea of a sort of cross-pollination business by getting such partners as Gardner Cowles of *Look*, the publishers of *Esquire*, the Diners Club, Groucho Marx, Goodson-Todman and Art Linkletter. The idea was that they were all going to help each other. When *Look* or *Esquire* had any empty space, it would advertise some of the books of Bernard Geis Associates; Groucho Marx, Art Linkletter and Goodson-Todman would mention them from time to time on their television programs. Soon after he started, this became a sort of cause célèbre because of the quiz scandals on television and the plethora of these cross plugs. The government and the network heads themselves began screaming about it.

Thus the main point of Geis's business began to disappear, but by offering fancy royalties and making all kinds of special deals, he snagged quite a few money-making books. He's very good on publicity and also very clever at getting rights that most publishers don't get. Very often he'll pop up with twenty-five percent of the movie rights or more than half of the reprint rights. He was able to make these transactions because he was dealing with people who were not experienced writers.

When he suggested that we distribute his books, we agreed because he already had on his list, in addition to President Truman, Groucho Marx and Art Linkletter—quite a trio. He had Truman signed up for a book which was never written: a history of the United States intended for the juvenile market. Geis did publish *Mr. Citizen*, but not the one for children, which sounded like a million dollars in the bank. So we made a deal with

Geis that, I must say, we profited by enormously. It was a straight distribution deal; we had no editorial responsibility whatever for his publications.

For a while all went well: the Art Linkletter book and Groucho's book—Geis had many successes—Helen Gurley Brown's *Sex and the Single Girl*. Nobody really looked at *Valley of the Dolls* when it came in—I never read it—but when Jacqueline Susann came to the Random House sales conference to talk about it, she impressed us all. Twice a year our salesmen come from all over the country to be briefed on the next season's books, and the Geis presentations at the meetings were always rather amusing interludes, anyway. Our editors would outline our entries and Geis would then come up with all his trivia—puzzle books and crazy gimmicks. When he introduced Jackie Susann, who was quite a good-looking woman, she regaled the salesmen with her elaborate plans to push the book herself—and did she mean what she said! She got herself on practically every TV and radio show and into one gossip column after another. Her book became a huge best seller, and when it went into paperback, the rush was on. Then the movie broke records. *Variety* reviewed it as one of the most terrible pictures in ten years, but that didn't make a bit of difference, because it was pre-sold. *Variety* reported that in some town that had never run a movie more than three days in its history, it was in its fourth week!

We started shying away from Berney Geis when he began having scandalous books written to order about living people. They are called novels so that the person who is being crucified has really no comeback; the author can delineate a character in such a way that nobody can mistake who is meant, but also throw in fictional filth, all of which the reader will believe because of the true and recognizable parts. If the victim protests, the publisher can say, "What makes you think it's about you?" So by protesting, he appears to be admitting to all the filth in the book.

We became more and more worried as Geis's books got sleazier and sleazier, and since our salesmen had plenty to do selling our own books, we began to ask ourselves why we were bothering to distribute his. We warned Geis, and then he precipitated the final break when he brought in a manuscript he thought he had better let me look at. It was called *The King* and it was obviously modeled on the career of Frank Sinatra. Geis knew that Frank Sinatra is a very, very dear friend of Phyllis' and mine. I read *The King* with mounting disgust, because it was so obvious, with trash thrown in that was pure, or rather impure, fiction. I said, "I just won't distribute it." Geis had quite expected this. In fact, I think he had already talked to another publisher in case I wouldn't do it, and he got New American Library to distribute it. To my great pleasure, the book was a failure, and on my advice, Frank Sinatra did absolutely nothing about it. I

Frank Sinatra and Bennett

said, "All that he wants is for you to make a fuss—and the harder you holler, the better he'll like it." Now Geis, I understand, accuses Frank of keeping any movie company from buying it. But I don't think Frank had to lift a finger; no movie company would touch it.

Then came another book that was even worse: *The Exhibitionist*. I read it with complete revulsion, though I will say that *The Exhibitionist* is much better written than *The King*. The author, David Slavitt, can write, and there's no question that the book was publishable on its literary merits. But again it was a novel about recognizable people. We didn't want to go on with the arrangement any longer, so we told Bernard Geis to find himself another distributor.

In the early days of Random House, Donald and I had enough time to make all our own decisions, not only about what books to accept and how to present and promote them, but editorial decisions as well. But as our list grew, we gradually had to increase our staff and delegate authority, and one of our main problems—in common with other publishers—was finding editors whose taste and judgment we could trust.

A good editor, I think, like a good author, has to be born with some of the necessary talents, like a good memory and some imagination. But he also needs to have acquired a fairly broad range of interests, a working knowledge of the English language and a good supply of general information—the more the better—so that he can understand what an author is trying to do and be of help to him in doing it. An editor has to have read widely enough to be able to recognize and appreciate good writing when he sees it, but he must also have some sense of what kinds of books the public will buy, since no publishing house can survive if there is no demand for its books, no matter how well written.

One of an editor's most important functions is to try to keep in balance the interests of the authors he works with and the interests of the house he works for. These are often identical, but not always, and when they are not, the editor, caught in the middle, has to employ considerable diplomacy toward both sides, as well as patience -another indispensable quality.

An editor has to be able to get along with authors—which is not always easy. When the relationship is a good one, an editor can be extremely helpful by serving as a kind of sounding board for an author's ideas and intentions, and by making suggestions aimed at sharpening and clarifying what the author wants to say. Also, the editor can be of value in pointing out parts of a manuscript that should be cut out because they are repetitive, or dull, or unnecessary.

Authors differ greatly in the amount of help they need or want or will accept from editors. Since some of them refuse to accept even good suggestions, there has been many a book published that the author wouldn't allow to be edited, even though it badly needed it. What infuriates me is to read in a review: "Why wasn't the publisher doing his job?" Usually the editor has shed blood trying to get the author to make changes, but the author has refused. When a book is sold to the movies or to television, it's understood that they can do anything they want with it, but in publishing, the author has the last word. The only alternative to letting him have his way is to say, "I won't publish it at all."

If an editor offers too little help or doesn't show enough interest in an author and his work, or if he goes too far in trying to impose his own opinions, his relations with that author are in for trouble. Of course, any good author will tell an editor where to draw the line. Sometimes he'll demand another editor.

To my mind, the editors that go too far are usually frustrated writers themselves, and their temptation is always to try to rewrite books because they think they can do it better. We have to watch all of them on that. Saxe Commins, fine editor that he was, was a frustrated writer. When he himself wrote, it was purple prose, the kind of thing he would have laughed at if somebody brought it in to him. He infuriated John O'Hara with editoral suggestions to the point that O'Hara finally refused to work with him any longer. On the other hand, with James Michener, who came to Random House because of Saxe, the trouble was of a different kind. Jim brought in a manuscript that he regarded as an unfinished first draft and that he wanted to discuss with his editor before giving it the final polishing. When he learned that Saxe had copyedited the manuscript and sent it to the printer, he asked for a different editor. Though Saxe turned out not to be the right editor for O'Hara and Michener, he was adored and counted on by such literary greats as Eugene O'Neill and William Faulkner, and— beginning with their first books—he encouraged and edited Budd Schulberg and Irwin Shaw.

Actually, a publisher or an editor can be most helpful to a young author who *will* listen. For instance, an unknown named Mac Hyman once brought in a manuscript to us that had been turned down by three or four other publishers. It concerned the Korean War. I took it home and read it, and I had to put it down three or four times, just choking with laughter. The book was terribly funny but much too long. Of course we grabbed it anyway, and we persuaded the author to throw out the entire last half, and I thought of a good name for it: *No Time for Sergeants*. It was one of our greatest successes. What a fortune young Mac Hyman made on it! First of all, it was a Book-of-the-Month Club selection, then number one on the best-seller list for months on end; next it became a most successful play and then a long-running television series and a great movie.

Since we had done so well with *No Time for Sergeants*, we were on the lookout for another service comedy book, and in 1955 a group of short stories about navy public-relations officers was submitted to us. I read the manuscript on a plane going out to Cleveland. I called the office from the airport and said, "This is hilarious stuff. Get this book signed up right away. I want to talk to the author as soon as I get back." The author was

William Brinkley, on the staff of *Life* and a good writer. He immediately saw the validity of our argument that books of short stories usually don't sell as well as novels, so with our help he took the stories and strung them together with an admittedly flimsy plot—like putting pearls on a string. I named this book too—*Don't Go Near the Water*—and again we had a number-one book, another Book-of-the-Month Club selection.

If *No Time for Sergeants* and *Don't Go Near the Water* had been the authors' second books after successful first ones—and we had tried to tell them how to structure their books—they probably would have stamped furiously out of the office. But they were young, and eager to do what we suggested.

We have a rule at Random House that our senior editors can accept any book they want without question, unless an enormous advance against royalties is involved, in which case we have a discussion about it. There are two ways of doing this at Random House. One is regular meetings, committees, which I loath and detest and won't go to.

The other method is, when I want a meeting, I call together the people I need, and we talk—which is the way I think a publishing business should be run. For example, in 1969 Diarmuid Russell, who was Eudora Welty's agent, offered us an opportunity to bid against two other publishers for a contract for her next four books. A rather large advance was required, but since this was an auction, no one knew exactly how large. So Donald and two editors read the manuscript of *Losing Battles,* the first book submitted, and I sat down with them and thrashed out the problem. There was no question about our eagerness to get Eudora on our list, but we had to decide on an advance guarantee we thought was big enough to top our competitors but not too big to earn back. In short order, we came up with the right answer, and the following year we published *Losing Battles,* which received rave reviews and sold beautifully.

Another important editorial function, of course, is adding new authors to a publisher's list. This can be done in a variety of ways, but an editor who has a large number of friends in literary and academic circles who like and respect him obviously has a far better chance than one who, even though he might have the other necessary talents, doesn't get around much. Some highly successful editors devote most of their time to bringing in new manuscripts that are then worked on by others.

There's a big distinction between a working editor and the editor who goes out combing the sticks looking for properties and wining and dining authors and agents, though some are able to do both. The editor who dreams up "ideas" for new books is often more spectacular and might end up making much more money than the one who slaves over manuscripts and does the dirty work of publishing. He's like the poor fellow who's

From left: editors Jess Stein, Robert Linscott, Saxe Commins, Harry Maule, David McDowell

shoveling coal into the furnaces in the hold of the ship while the captain is sitting on the top deck making up to the prettiest girl on board. It's part of the mechanism of life today that few people have the time or the inclination to do painstaking work—like the man who used to make beautiful furniture by hand, the man who took pride in his craftsmanship.

Back during the thirties Donald and I and, later, Bob Haas had brought in the new authors, and though the company was getting bigger every year, most of the editorial work could still be handled by Saxe Commins and Belle Becker, who had come to Random House in 1930 as a receptionist. With some help from Saxe and her own natural talent, Belle taught herself to be an editor; she became an extremely skillful one and was helpful to many writers. When Quentin Reynolds and Sam Adams came to us, Belle became editor and good friend to them.

Since our growth continued during the war, it became clear that the editorial staff had to be expanded, and though we had already added Harry Maule, he had his hands full taking care of the many authors he brought in. In 1944 I finally succeeded in luring Robert Linscott down to New York. He had for a long time been a top editor at Houghton Mifflin, where I had met him in the days when I was selling books in Boston.

It was Bob Linscott who called my attention to Truman Capote. One blessed day he read or somebody told him about a story that had appeared in *Mademoiselle:* "Miriam," by an unknown writer called Truman Capote. That was the first thing of Capote's I ever saw, and what a fine story it is! It has such depth and such a haunting quality. We asked Truman Capote to come and see us.

Well, *that* was a day when Truman arrived at Random House! He had bangs, and nobody could believe it when this young prodigy waltzed in. He looked about eighteen. He was bright and happy and absolutely self-assured. We said we wanted to publish anything he wrote. He said he was writing a novel, and we drew up a contract for it immediately. It was *Other Voices, Other Rooms,* which we published in 1948, and it was an immediate success. Everybody knew that somebody important had arrived upon the scene—particularly Truman! Phyllis adopted Truman immediately. He was already exhibiting the charm which proved so irresistible that he soon became a society favorite.

When *Other Voices* came out we used the now-famous photograph of him, with his bangs and checkered waistcoat, reclining on a couch. It was

great publicity, but it's ludicrously simple to get publicity for Truman. For example, about a week before *Other Voices* was published, my friend Richard Simon called me up and said, "How the hell do you get a full-page picture of an author in *Life* magazine before his first book even comes out?" I said, "Do you think I'm going to tell you? Does Macy's tell Gimbels?" Dick said, "Come on. How did you wrangle that?" I said, "Dick, I have no intention of telling you." He hung up in a huff; and I hung up too, and cried, "For God's sake, get me a copy of *Life*." That was the

Truman Capote

first I knew about the whole affair! Truman had managed to promote that full-page picture for himself, and how he did it, I don't know to this day.

After *Other Voices* was published, Truman came wafting into the office one day and told me that *Vogue* wanted him to go to Hollywood for two weeks to write the impressions of a young writer who had never before been there. They offered him two thousand and expenses for two weeks, and Truman had demanded the cash immediately—twenty one-hundred-dollar bills, which was probably more money than he'd ever seen at one time. Truman brought them in, rolled up with a rubber band around them, to show me. So he went to Hollywood for his first time, and I couldn't wait to hear his story.

When he came back after his two weeks, he reported to me: "I spent the first week with Greta Garbo and the second week with Charlie Chaplin." It was absolutely true. He had gone to Hollywood with a letter of introduction to someone who had a party that first night. Greta Garbo met Truman there and took him right home with her. She said, "You're not going to a hotel. You're going to stay with me." After a week, at another party, Charlie Chaplin kidnapped him from Greta Garbo, and he spent the second week with Chaplin.

As Truman became more and more popular and knew more and more famous people, he was so busy going to parties and being the town's most desirable extra man that we had to keep after him to make him write. He is talented beyond belief, a born writer, but he must have the perfect word and will spend a whole day brooding over it. I've known him to do just that, and when he has a book finished, it's a polished gem. It needs hardly any editing. He proved that he was not only a good novelist but one of the great reporters when he wrote *The Muses Are Heard*—another great success—the often hilarious story of the production in Russia of George Gershwin's *Porgy and Bess*. Two years later his novel *Breakfast at Tiffany's* hit the really popular note.

Truman became famous not just for his books, but for two stories, *Christmas Memory* and *Thanksgiving Visitor,* which he and Eleanor and Frank Perry turned into award-winning television shows. Because of his personality, Truman is a gossip columnist's delight. He is always up to something that makes good copy. The party he gave in 1967 was the social event of the decade. *The New York Times* printed the entire guest list, and to be invited to that party was to be considered as having arrived. People who weren't invited were very disappointed. Guests came from Italy, France, Hollywood and all over for this affair, which was the greatest of its kind ever given, and Truman was ecstatic. It cost him a fortune, but he couldn't have cared less.

By a strange coincidence, I played a small part in the history of

Truman's great book *In Cold Blood*. I had lectured at Kansas State University in Manhattan, Kansas. I was there for two days, and besides lecturing, I had spent a day with the English classes, as I do sometimes. I became a great friend of the president, James McCain, the successor to Milton Eisenhower, who had made Kansas State a top university. I had made a lot of friends in those two days, and when I left, Jim McCain said, "We've enjoyed having you here, and if I can ever do anything for you, just let me know." I laughed and said, "What can you ever do for me in Manhattan, Kansas?" and gaily, off I went.

Shortly after that came the murder of the Clutter family—a man and his wife and two children murdered in cold blood—in Garden City, Kansas, and the case became known all over the country. Local police were frustrated because they had no clues. It seemed to be an inside job, since the murderers knew where to hide their automobile, how to get into the house and exactly where the wall safe was located. So they figured it must be somebody in Garden City. The whole town was suspect.

One day Truman walked into my office and said, "*The New Yorker* is sending me out to cover that murder case." I said, "You? In a Kansas hamlet?" That was the first reaction of everybody—the elegant Mr. Capote going to a small town in Kansas. He was quite indignant at my surprise, then said, "I don't know a soul in the whole state of Kansas. You've got to introduce me to some people out there."

That's what a publisher is for, I guess, and this was one time I could deliver the goods. I immediately remembered my friend Dr. McCain at Kansas State. I called him up and asked if he had known the Clutter family in Garden City. Jim said, "The Clutters were my close personal friends. I know everybody in Garden City, Kansas." I said, "One of our authors is coming out to write a series of stories for *The New Yorker,* and I hope it will also be a book. Can he stop off on the way and visit you?" He said, "Who is the author?" I said, "Truman Capote." Jim MacCain echoed me, "Truman Capote? Coming to Kansas?" I said, "Yes." He thought for a minute, then said, "I'll make a deal with him. If he'll spend one evening talking to the English department, I'll give him letters to half the people in Garden City." I said, "I accept for Truman right now. Great! He's bringing a young assistant with him, I've never met her, but I think she may be a distant relation of Truman." The girl was Harper Lee, author of *To Kill a Mockingbird*.

Truman and Harper Lee went out to Kansas, and two days later Jim called me up. He said, "I want to report on the visit of Mr. Capote and the girl with him. They're both great. Truman came waltzing in with a pink velvet coat on and announced, 'I bet I'm the first man who has ever come to Manhattan, Kansas, wearing a Dior jacket.' And I said, 'I'll go you one better, Mr. Capote. You're probably the first man *or* woman who ever came to Manhattan, Kansas, wearing a Dior jacket.' "

McCain continued, "I took him to meet the faculty, and when Truman and Miss Lee left at six-thirty this morning on the Santa Fe to go to Garden City, the entire faculty got up to see them off. Mrs. McCain and I got up too."

They went to Garden City, where Alvin Dewey of the Kansas Bureau of Investigation had been put in charge and was going crazy trying to solve the murders. He had turned up nothing, and people were getting angrier and angrier at him. Suddenly, to add to his troubles, Truman Capote arrived to cover the case. Two weeks later Truman was living in the Dewey house, and the Deweys and everybody else in Garden City adored him.

The minute the two killers were captured, who became their best friend in the world? Truman Capote. Before Perry, the one who was a poet, was hanged, he gave Truman his whole collection of books and all of his poetry. Each man was allowed one witness at the execution, and Perry insisted that Truman be his. Truman had to go back West for that double hanging, and Joe Fox, who became his editor at Random House after Linscott retired, and is one of Truman's closest friends, went with him. Just before going into the execution room, Perry asked that Truman come over and say goodbye to him, and he threw his arms around Truman and kissed him and said, "I'm so sorry." Truman collapsed, as anybody else would have.

In Cold Blood was an enormous best seller from the day it was published, a Book-of-the Month Club selection, and in the first month sold about fifty thousand copies a week. We'd never seen anything like it. Some time after it came out, Truman brought the whole Garden City contingent to New York City. Being Truman, he arranged a series of parties for them. The people from Garden City were in an absolute daze. They were meeting everybody from the President of the United States down. Kay Graham, head of *Newsweek* and the *Washington Post,* gave a big party for them in Washington, where they met every VIP under the sun.

When Truman comes to the house, I am always delighted to see him, although he sometimes annoys me by throwing his arms around me and calling me "Great White Father" and "Big Daddy" and such. I say, "For Pete's sake, cut that out." But I don't mind it somehow when Truman does it.

In 1945 a manuscript was submitted to Random House by a girl in Illinois. It was an extremely well-written first novel—but it was about incest, and she wasn't quite skillful enough to handle so tricky a subject. Back then—not so long ago either—incest was one of the forbidden subjects unless it was handled with great delicacy. I believe it was Bob Linscott who wrote her a detailed letter, telling her what was good in the book and what was wrong, and suggesting that she tackle something safer for a start and put this one away for later revision, because much of it was very good indeed.

She sent back a letter which had obviously taken a long time to write, saying that she never would have believed she would get from a well-known New York publishing house a detailed letter about a book it was rejecting. She said she would never forget it and that it had changed her whole opinion of the publishing industry. She said she would like to show her gratitude, then added, "As a matter of fact, I might be able to do you a favor right now. There's a girl in my block" (in Evanston this was, a suburb of Chicago) "who has written a book that I think is extraordinary. It's been turned down by one publisher, and the agent told her there was no sense sending it anyplace else, since nobody would publish it, so she's very discouraged. But I was fascinated by it. If you like, I'll send it to you."

So in came *The Snake Pit* by Mary Jane Ward. We published it the following year and I don't think ten changes were made in the manuscript—it was so nearly perfect. I always use that book as an example of why the publishing business is so exciting. It doesn't take genius to make a best seller out of books by John O'Hara or James Michener. But much of the fun of publishing is discovering somebody brand-new and bringing the book out and publicizing it properly and then seeing it possibly chosen by the Book-of-the-Month Club and the Reader's Digest Condensed Book Club, and then selling to the movies and watching overnight some unknown become famous. Then, of course, the author probably leaves for Hollywood and is never seen by you again. But while it's going on, it's mighty thrilling.

The Snake Pit is the story of an intelligent girl of medium circumstances whose mind suddenly snaps and she has to be committed—which is what had happened to the author. I called up Mary Jane Ward in Evanston and told her we wanted to do her book. I told her very gently, because I was worried about her, and I asked her to come to New York at our expense. She was an absolutely lovely young woman. I spent about an hour and a half trying to get her to change the title. I said, "Novels are bought to a great extent by women. Women hate snakes. If you call a book *The Snake Pit,* you're losing a big part of your audience just by using the wrong title. Women won't go near it." Well, thank the Lord, Mary Jane told me to go to hell. The title was absolutely perfect. To this very day asylums are called snake pits, which they were. They were horrible; great reforms were effected in New York and Chicago, among other places, but they're still terrible.

Things began to happen to the book right away. First of all, it was chosen by the Book-of-the-Month Club. Second, every movie company got interested in it. Many producers who inquired about the movie rights to *The Snake Pit* backed away at the last minute because a couple of big scenes involved shock treatment, and they thought the whole background of an insane asylum was too gruesome. But I finally sold the rights to Anatole Litvak, a close friend of ours and one of the most charming men in the world. "Tola" had become famous overnight when he directed a foreign picture called *Mayerling,* which was the story of the mysterious death of Archduke Rudolf and his mistress in Austria—a famous historical episode. It created a sensation, and Tola was immediately brought to Hollywood, where he became one of the leading directors and producers, with such outstanding successes as *Tovarich, The Amazing Dr. Clitterhouse, This Above All* and *Sorry, Wrong Number.*

I sold *The Snake Pit* to Tola one night while we were having dinner at the St. Regis Hotel. He bought it on his own, but finally had to get backing from Twentieth Century-Fox. He made the picture, which was a knockout and won a string of prizes. I remember the price: it was forty-five thousand dollars, which was a lot of money in those days, especially for Mary Jane Ward.

I've been very careful about telling authors they've bagged such big prizes ever since we published *Junior Miss* by Sally Benson—a difficult character in spades! The book was made up of stories she wrote for *The New Yorker,* about callow kids going out for dates for the first time—the seventeen- and eighteen-year-olds of yesteryear. The stories were delightful and so was the book, which we published in 1941, but nobody ever dreamed it would be taken by the Book-of-the-Month Club.

Sally was always broke, and when I called up to tell her about the book club, she let out a squeal and said, "How much does that mean for me?" I said, "I would say you'll probably make an extra twenty to twenty-five thousand dollars." Twenty minutes later the Buick agency called me up and said that a Miss Sally Benson was there and had given me as a reference—it hadn't taken her ten minutes to get her hat and coat on and go out and buy herself a car. I approved heartily.

The following year Sally had a new group of stories about her own girlhood in St. Louis, which she called *35 Kensington Street*. I persuaded her to change the title to *Meet Me in St. Louis*, from the name of an old fair song, "Meet Me in St. Louie, Louie," and to add another story to justify its use. She did, and the book was a runaway; in 1944 it was made into one of Judy Garland's most successful pictures. They still do it on the Late Show, and I watch it every time—it's such a heartwarming picture!

The events that led to our publishing *The American College Dictionary* started in the very carefully thought-out way I do many things in my life. I arrived at the office one day and cheerily announced, "Let's do a dictionary." To show how incredibly little I knew—we had two erudite editors, Saxe Commins and Bob Linscott, and I said that they could compile this new dictionary in their spare time. That was my brilliant, original plan!

When we started to discuss the project, I realized what a fool I was. When you do a dictionary, I discovered, you have to get experts in special fields to concentrate on various subjects, and the bigger and more ambitious the dictionary is, the more subjects there are. But I got more and more interested in the idea. Then we found out that Clarence Barnhart, who was considered one of the best lexicographers in the United States, had just finished the Thorndike-Barnhart dictionary and luckily was available. I sent for him and told him I thought it would be great to do a new college dictionary—a desk dictionary, not an unabridged. He said there was need, that there hadn't been a new one in years and that he would love to edit one for us. I asked him how much he thought it would cost, and he said it could be done for about a hundred thousand dollars—at which point I fell under the table. I had no such fancy notions!

We began to look into costs, and we found out that Barnhart's was a modest estimate. The project was bound to involve a lot of people and would take two years to do, but by this time I was determined that we were going to go ahead with it. We felt that we could get the money, since we weren't in debt to the banks for a penny. Bob Haas, the conservative member of the firm, was opposed; he said we weren't big enough and he didn't like the idea of borrowing funds, but we plunged ahead anyhow.

Then came a period of great dejection, because Barnhart turned out to be more or less of a visionary, and every time he came in, I said to myself, "Oh God, he wants another fifty thousand dollars." I was always right, too—unless he needed even more. Also, time was slipping by, but we found out that was more or less the normal procedure with a dictionary or a big reference book. At one time we were so discouraged by the way the costs were mounting, it almost became the greatest college dictionary from A to M that was ever put together. It finally turned out that Barnhart had been way off in his estimate of time and money, and the project cost pretty close to a million dollars and took over three years to finish.

Since publishing is a very seasonal business, we'd been in and out of the banks. We had often borrowed money to tide us over the fall season—our customers usually don't pay until the turn of the year—but we'd always been in the clear by February. But by the time the dictionary was published in 1947, we were in debt to the bank.

One wonderful thing about dictionaries, though, is that a good one always makes money. Once it's completed, it's the publisher's property, and if it starts selling in quantity, the costs are recovered rather quickly because there is no royalty to pay. *The American College Dictionary* won great critical acclaim and was a huge success. It was the first brand-new dictionary in a long time. Once again the old Cerf luck prevailed; and we soon got out of that pickle. It wasn't really a pickle: we were doing what is done by twenty businesses out of twenty-two in America. We were borrowing money from a bank, which we weren't in the habit of doing, but some people say that a good business should always use bank money to expand. Most of the big corporations borrow by the millions. Our debt was only about half a million before we were through, but it worried Bob Haas so much that he thought we ought to sell the whole project to Simon and Schuster.

One of the great things that came out of the venture was Jess Stein, who, as is so often the case in projects of this kind, was the assistant who really did the main body of the work while Barnhart took the credit. We greatly admired Jess Stein, and he became the head of our reference department and later of our whole college textbook department, which made him one of the most important people at Random House.

Curiously enough, some of the best customers for our *American College Dictionary* have been banks that offer giveaways to people opening new accounts or adding to old deposits. When we first thought of trying to get them to use dictionaries as premiums, we ran into some difficulty: because of rising costs, to sell *The American College Dictionary* for what they were willing to pay and for us to still make a profit was very tough. But we discovered that with a few economies here and there, we could—if we printed enough copies at a time and shipped them all together to the same address, thus saving in handling—make about fifty cents a copy at their price.

So we went out to sell the big banks on using our dictionary as one of their premiums. And if they gave a big enough order—five thousand, but preferably ten—I went with the packet for a day. That was a personal deal, and they had to pay me a good fee for it. I was happy to work for Random House, but I wasn't going to sit in a bank all day for nothing!

Usually I'd have to go the night before to a place like Minneapolis or Memphis or Houston or Denver. Almost always there'd be a party the night before. They'd meet me at the plane and give a dinner for the bank trustees and their wives and some important depositors. I was the guest of honor and it was great fun. Then they started off early the next morning, or even that same evening, with radio and television shows on every local station.

Often the morning television show started at seven-thirty, so I had to get up at the crack of dawn. I'd do the television interview and then there'd be a breakfast for the press so they could catch the evening papers. I would be there too late for the morning editions, but there were full-page ads in them, with a picture of the dictionary and a great big picture of me. Ham that I am, I loved it. In Houston they even used big billboards: BENNETT CERF IN PERSON. I'd stop and look at the signs with a lot of appreciation, and I liked the full-page ads—I like being a celebrity. At breakfast with the press, sometimes college kids were invited, and governors and senators who happened to be in town.

So we had the breakfast and then maybe another radio show was squeezed in, and then I spent the day at the bank, signing dictionaries. I think in Minneapolis—which was the most successful promotion we ever had because it was with the prestigious First National Bank—they used over thirty-thousand dictionaries, and made it the big feature of their fall campaign. The pitch was: Open an account of one hundred dollars or more and get a free dictionary for your child going back to school.

For lunch, I'd usually go with the bank officers, and late in the afternoon they would squeeze in a meeting for all the employees after the doors of the bank had closed. So by the time I finished, I'd worked for twenty-four hours—and we had sold thousands of dictionaries and gotten thousands of dollars' worth of free advertising.

The wonderful thing about dictionaries is that no one is ever going to have too many. With any other book, you sell one copy for a home, and that's that. But some houses will have as many as ten dictionaries—one in every room. Every kid has his own desk dictionary, especially when his parents have gotten it for nothing! People walk out of the bank sometimes with as many as four or five dictionaries in their arms, because every time they open an account with a hundred dollars they get one, so they start an account for every blessed kid they have. It's wonderful; you see the books going into the hands of the consumer! Between the TV and the radio and the newspapers, what an ad all this is for the ACD.

At first the bookstores raised hell with us, until they suddenly discovered that with all the tremendous free advertising, they were selling ten times as many copies of *The American College Dictionary* as they had before. After all, a lot of people didn't bother going to the bank. They saw the ads and sometimes came in to gape at me—and then went to buy a dictionary at their favorite bookstore.

After *The American College Dictionary* was launched, a gleam began to come into our eyes: an *unabridged* American dictionary. The main competition was the big Merriam-Webster, and their third edition, which they brought out in 1961, was received with hostility by many critics. In fact, a great many college people prefer the old second edition to the third. So we figured the field was wide open.

Of course, this was a tremendous undertaking. For the unabridged *Random House Dictionary of the English Language,* we had at one time almost four hundred people working on it, top authorities in every field. For each subject we had an important man as consulting editor, so our new dictionary is superb. Jess Stein was editor in chief. The cost, I would say, was between three and four million dollars, and it took about four years to do; but we were able to swing it, especially since we got help from two sources. The Book-of-the-Month Club bought the book-club rights the year before publication for a very handsome advance. Then we made an arrangement with Time-Life whereby they could make a prepublication mail-order offer of the dictionary below our own retail price, and they sold almost a quarter of a million copies before the official release date. Thus the two together paid us back a good portion of our original outlay before the dictionary even came out.

A few years after Bob Linscott joined our editorial department, it was again enlarged, though at that particular moment we had no great need or any such plan. It came about because two young men—Frank Taylor and Albert Erskine—both experienced editors and officers of the firm of Reynal and Hitchcock, became discontented and resigned. Taylor came to see me and offered their services; since they had performed well together, they wanted to continue to work as a team.

Hiring two senior editors at the same time was a rather big order, and we were hesitant. Since I knew Taylor and thought well of him, I felt he would be a valuable addition, but I didn't even know Erskine. So Taylor brought him to our house to meet me, and by the end of the evening I knew I wanted Erskine too, and both of them came to Random House in 1947. Immediately they started adding authors to our list, and among the first were two who had been under contract at Reynal and Hitchcock and whom we have published ever since—Pulitzer Prize poet Karl Shapiro and Ralph Ellison, whose novel *Invisible Man* would win the National Book Award in 1953 and become a classic, in constant and increasing demand.

About a year after he came, Taylor was offered a great job as producer at MGM and left for Hollywood; Erskine, who was made to order for Random House, stayed with us and became one of my very best friends. I love Albert Erskine. Albert is a Southerner, and he won't overwork. When he thinks he's slaving, other people don't think so, but he has his own pace. Nobody would dream of telling him what to do. I wanted him to be editor in chief, but he didn't want to be bothered with all the details involved; he already had his hands full working with a long list of authors, including some of our most famous.

One of these is Robert Penn Warren, whom Albert signed up almost as soon as he came to Random House. Warren's *All the King's Men* had already won the Pulitzer Prize for fiction. His first book for us, the novel *World Enough and Time,* was a Literary Guild selection, and so were *Band of Angels, Wilderness* and *Flood.* These were great sellers, and I think there's a great deal more to come from him, because his talents are numerous and varied. Warren is one of the country's leading poets, and we have published many volumes of his poetry, including *Promises: Poems 1954–1956,* which won both the Pulitzer Prize and the National Book Award 1957. He is the only writer to have been awarded the Pulitzer Prize for both fiction and poetry. He is also a brilliant critic and teacher, and his textbooks have been broadly influential. A liberal Southerner, he has written two important books on race relations; *Who Speaks for the Negro?* was an outstanding success.

When "Red" Warren came to Random House, he and Albert had been friends for a long time; they were practically like brothers. He soon became a close friend of mine, too. Talk about authors it's a pleasure to do business with, Red is the greatest, the nicest, the most agreeable, the most willing to listen. If you want to see Southern charm—he is irresistible. He knows how good he is as a writer, but he is reticent about it, doesn't throw it in your face. When he comes to our office, everybody is happy to see him. No wonder his students at Yale absolutely fell at his feet.

Robert Penn Warren

"Red" and Eleanor Warren

Phyllis and I were delighted when Red married the extremely talented writer Eleanor Clark. Albert and I persuaded her to be published by Pantheon, which had become part of Random House. How wise we were; her first book with them, *The Oysters of Locmariaquer,* won the National Book Award, and five years later her novel *Baldur's Gate* was a Book-of-the-Month Club selection. She works slowly and meticulously, and the results are beautiful.

Red's best man at his wedding was Albert Erskine, and some years later this was reciprocated. During most of the 1950's Albert was single, and he was one of Phyllis' favorite extra men at our parties. Then he met and fell in love with an Italian countess, Marisa Bisi, who is one of the loveliest women in the world. They decided to get married and move to Connecticut, much to the chagrin of some authors to whom he would no longer be available around the clock; and Phyllis, though she gained an attractive couple for our parties, had to find another extra man. The wedding was in our house, and Red and Eleanor Warren stood up for the bride and groom.

Relatively late in their lives, Marisa and Albert had their daughter, Silvia, a beautiful, enchanting little girl. Watching them with her when she was tiny brought tears to your eyes. Ecstasy—adoration. When she crossed a doorsill, they worried that she might hurt herself. If she coughed, they went into a frenzy. At first it seemed she might be smothered in love, but she turned out to be a great kid.

I understood their love for her—she's a darling. Proud and pleased as I am to be the father of two fine sons, I've always harbored a wish that we had a little girl too. So I've sort of adopted the girls of my friends. Bob and Merle Haas's Priscilla is a particular favorite, as are John and Barbara Hersey's Brook, Moss and Kitty Hart's Cathy, Rose and Bill Styron's Susanna, and Charlotte Ford's Elena Niarchos.

Another wonderful little girl even became a Random House author—the Warrens' daughter, Rosanna, who when she was only ten wrote a story that I thought could be a huge success. A lot of people in our office read the manuscript and were delighted with it, but some, including Albert, were afraid that publishing a book by a ten-year-old girl might spoil her. Red and Eleanor were worried, too, so we all talked it over. I said that maybe we shouldn't do it, but Rosanna was so happy at the thought of its being published that her parents gave in. We all had a lot of fun, though I was terribly disappointed when the book didn't really sell well. I still believe it should have. Incidentally, Rosanna wasn't spoiled a bit—not even by the publication luncheon I gave for her at the "21 Club."

About the time Red Warren came to Random House, we also signed up James Michener—one of our greatest coups. It was one of those glorious accidents, and when people tell me what a good publisher I am, I must admit that often I've just had dumb luck. Jim Michener was a textbook editor at Macmillan, just back from his service in the navy, when he wrote a book of connected short stories which his company published quietly in 1947. Of course, it couldn't be expected to do very much—a book of short stories by an unknown author. Meantime, Michener had submitted a second book, so George Brett, the head of Macmillan, called him in and gave him a heart-to-heart talk, the gist of which was that Jim really didn't have much future as an author and that therefore he should stick with his editorial job and not waste his time and effort on writing. Macmillan would agree to take the second book, but obviously without enthusiasm. Brett said he didn't think they ought to publish the work of employees.

So Michener, who had met our editor Saxe Commins and liked him, came to see me, and we got along immediately. We promptly agreed that we would publish his second book, which was to be his first novel, *The Fires of Spring*. About eleven days after we signed the contract, that book of short stories which nobody had paid much attention to won the Pulitzer Prize. It was *Tales of the South Pacific*. A little later, of course, Rodgers and Hammerstein wrote *South Pacific*, based on several stories from the book, and Jim Michener became an enormous literary success overnight. Every time I would meet Brett after that, he'd grumble, "You lucky bastard." Well, it was luck. But it was Brett who had let him go!

Michener's books have become one of the great literary properties of the world. Two of his novels made fabulous sums of money—*Hawaii* and *The Source*. Our advance from Fawcett for the paperback rights to *The Source* was, at the time, probably the biggest in history. *Hawaii* and *The Source* go right on selling; in fact, although Michener's books have been out in paperback for a long time, they all continue to do well in our hardbound editions.

Jim Michener, besides being a great craftsman, is a man who works very closely with editors, and he and Albert Erskine get along wonderfully. When Jim finishes a book, he and Albert go through every page together, and he's open to sensible suggestions. Then our indispensable assistant managing editor, Bertha Krantz, who has been with us a long, long time,

James A. Michener checking proofs at plant with Albert Erskine and Bertha Krantz. In background, Joe Levy of Book Press and designer Bernard Klein of Random House

goes through the whole thing again. It is always a great comfort to any author and his editor to know that Bert will be working with them on a manuscript.

Jim's a most meticulous workman. For *Hawaii* he had fifteen books of notes before he started writing. For *The Source* he lived in Haifa and other cities in Israel and Syria for more than a year, picking up history and folklore and learning how those people live. For *Iberia,* even though he had been in Spain over and over again from the time he was a college student, he went back and stayed for months of extensive research before he produced that marvelous travel book, which, like so many of his others, was a best seller and a Book-of-the-Month Club selection.

A wonderful thing about Michener is that every time he does a new book, it's about another part of the world. He seems to have a genius for selecting well ahead of time subjects in which a broad public interest will develop.

But with all his triumphs, Michener is the same today as he was before he won the Pulitzer Prize. He's modest, though quite confident of his own ability—and why shouldn't he be? His wife, Mari, is a charming and brilliant girl who was born of Japanese parents in this country. She travels all over the world with him and makes life comfortable for him wherever they are.

Jim Michener is the ideal author as far as a publisher is concerned—a man who lets us do the advertising, as Faulkner did, and trusts us. And we break our necks for him. He thinks that the publisher has his function and he has his, which is correct. You very seldom meet a really great author who doesn't say, "If I didn't think you were a good publisher, I wouldn't come to you." The "dream" author is *interested* in the advertising and the jacket and the design of the book and would prefer to approve of them, but he respects his publisher's judgment and realizes that we are just as anxious as he is to sell as many copies of a book as possible. Some authors seem to think that the publisher is deliberately trying to kill their books, which is obviously ridiculous.

Bennett and Jim Michener at Pearl Harbor

In 1949 David McDowell came to work for Random House as an editor. Sterling North, a leading book reviewer and author, was an old friend of mine, and he called me up one day and said he thought Dave would be great for us. So we saw him—a very polished Southern boy, very intellectual—and we liked him and gave him a job.

One day Dave, who was rather on the conservative side, came to my office and told me Whittaker Chambers was downstairs and wanted to talk about a book. My first reaction was "Get him out of here." This was not long after Alger Hiss had been convicted of perjury in the famous trial in which Chambers testified against him. Dave then used the same tactic with me that Donald does. He said, "Well, you're a fine liberal publisher—a liberal with all the people who are writing what you want them to write; but if someone comes along with something you don't agree with, you don't even want to talk to him." I was ashamed of myself. I said, "What *is* he going to talk about?" Dave said, "He has finished two chapters of his book and he thinks Random House would be a good publisher for him. He doesn't want to go to one of the right-wing houses. He'd rather have a liberal house do it. He deliberately picked Random House." I said, "Bring him up," and Dave went down to fetch him.

It was the first time I ever saw Chambers. He was pudgy and sloppy, and not a very prepossessing-looking man. When he started talking, and I discovered that he was a Columbia graduate and that we had lots of friends in common—Clifton Fadiman, among others—I found myself interested in him. But I was still a little hostile, since in my mind Hiss was still the hero and Chambers the villain. At any rate, I took home the first two chapters of *Witness,* and they were superbly written. Henry Luce once said that Chambers was the best writer he ever had working for him in the whole history of *Time* and *Life,* and Fadiman told me that he had the makings of a truly great poet.

I didn't know what to do. Since I consider myself a liberal, publishing Whittaker Chambers seemed shocking to me at first. I showed those two chapters to several friends of mine whose opinion I respected and who felt the same way about politics that I did—Robert Sherwood, Moss Hart, Laura Hobson, and even a fellow I knew who was way over on the left. I wanted to get their reactions. Every one of them said it was so well written that I had to publish it and let readers judge for themselves. So we signed up the book, and it was a huge best seller as well as a Book-of-the-Month Club selection.

When *Witness* came out, some of my liberal friends reacted just as I had at first, and wouldn't even read it. They said we ought to be ashamed of ourselves for publishing it, so I decided to give a dinner party at our house to which we would invite the ones who wished to question Whittaker Chambers. He agreed to face this veritable inquisition.

Before that night I had never met Chambers' wife, Esther, but from all the stories Whittaker had told me in the office, I knew that she must be a remarkable woman. He had met her first during a strike in Paterson, New Jersey, where she fought with him side by side, and they later got married. She was hesitant about coming to this big party, since she knew we had invited a lot of people. I seated Esther between Moss Hart and me at dinner; I had told Moss he had to help me. Both of us turned on the charm—and we made her feel at home. By the time dinner was over, she had lost her nervousness and said that she hadn't laughed so much in ten years. She had had some pretty bad times.

After dinner Chambers sat in a big easy chair and everybody sat around him in a semicircle on the floor. They threw their questions at him, and he answered every one without the slightest hesitation. This man—I'm convinced—was telling the truth. Several of the things he told us were proved later on. There was one man, he said, who was working for a big company—he wouldn't tell us his name—who was going to be picked up because he was part of the case. By God, he was arrested less than a year later. He worked for General Electric and had reproduced some of the papers which Hiss brought home. I believed what Chambers said that night. He summarized, "You know what the trouble with this case is? We're cast wrong. I look like a slob, so I should be the villain. Hiss, the handsome man who knows all the society people, is the born hero. It's bad casting. If it was the other way around, nobody would pay any attention to the story; but because of the way we look, all of you people think he must be telling the truth. That's what has made him so valuable to the other side."

The papers Hiss stole were absolutely worthless. The famous pumpkin papers were called that because Chambers hid them in a pumpkin long enough to go and get the district attorney in Westminster, Maryland. According to Chambers, they were used only to establish the method by which later on really valuable papers could be purloined.

Curiously enough, it's in Westminster, Maryland, where Chambers lived, that we eventually built the Random House warehouse. I'd forgotten all about it until I went down to look at the new building. I said to myself,

"I've been here before." I suddenly saw the main street and remembered that this was where I'd visited Whittaker Chambers.

Whit and Mrs. Chambers had invited us there for a night, and I remember our trepidation before we went—what were we going to talk about? Well, I found myself sprawling on the back porch with Whit, who was a lazy gent. Esther did all the work. She cooked the meals and cleaned the house and took care of the two boys. We found ourselves grumbling together about the Columbia football team—the last thing in the world I thought he and I would talk about. Columbia was losing every game, so we were both very annoyed and we agreed that the coach was an incompetent. Suddenly I burst out laughing. I said, "If anybody could get a tape of this conversation . . . I didn't know what we would be talking about . . . and here we are gossiping about the football team and various professors at Columbia!"

What a strange man Chambers was! I was preconditioned not to like him, but I repeat that I think he was telling the truth. I've never heard Hiss's story. I didn't meet him until years later, when I was introduced to him in a restaurant, and needless to say, he was not very cordial when he met me, nor do I blame him. Interestingly enough, Knopf did a book on the Hiss side of the case, written by Alistair Cooke, a friend of mine, who defends Hiss. I'd like to sit down with Alger Hiss sometime and listen to his version. I don't know whether that will ever happen; probably not. I think he will never forgive me for publishing *Witness*.

If it hadn't been for David McDowell, I would have refused to see Chambers, which would have been entirely wrong of me.

A few years after we brought out *Witness*, I had an experience that was in a way connected with publishing Whittaker Chambers. One of the boys who had been at Columbia when I was there, a couple of years ahead of me, was the campus leftist George Sokolsky. He used to come to classes looking like a ragamuffin. How he managed to afford Columbia, heaven only knows. I was sorry for him because he looked as though he never had enough to eat, and several times I took him home for lunch or dinner, just to give him a free meal. My father and my uncle were outraged every time I brought him over to the house. He wasn't always washed, but it was rewarding to feed him because he was so brilliant and extremely interesting to listen to.

When he got out of college Sokolsky went to China, and when he came back the flaming radical had turned into a flaming reactionary. He became one of the most important columnists in the United States; the Hearst papers made a great feature out of him, and when World War II came along, he was a power in our land.

We would see each other occasionally, especially at the Dutch Treat

Club in New York, where publishers and suchlike meet. George never forgot that I had been kind to him at Columbia, and he was embarrassingly grateful. He'd always bring it up, but he would kid me a little bit, too. When I walked in, he sometimes greeted me with "Here comes Bennett, the pinko publisher." I didn't like it and didn't think it was justified. So one day I called him on it. I said, "Have you ever looked at our list, George? If you had, you'd realize that we print a lot of books that some people might call fascist." George immediately said, "Oh, I'm only kidding." I said, "Nevertheless, I'm going to send you our catalogue," and I did.

Sokolsky called me up and said, "I apologize. That's a very impressive list. I had forgotten you did *Witness*. What did your 'pinko' friends have to say about that?" I said, "Plenty," and laughed. George suggested that we have lunch and talk about old times, so we made a date to meet at the Stork Club. I reserved a table in the Cub Room, way in the back. Sokolsky got there before I did, and when I came in he was waiting with a sardonic smile on his face. He said, "I see that you selected a spot at the back of the room. You're afraid that your friends are going to see you lunching with me." I said, "George, you're too smart. You're exactly right. If people see us dining together, they're going to say, 'What the hell is Cerf doing with that son of a bitch Sokolsky?'" The liberals hated Sokolsky and feared him. He was considered a dangerous character, and closely connected with the ill-famed red-hunter Senator Joseph McCarthy. He had also had a lot to do with the blacklisting of a lot of decent actors and writers. But he got one or two people out of trouble—people who were under a cloud. If I could ever convince George that somebody was not a Communist, he would move heaven and earth to help them, and he was powerful enough to do it.

We had our lunch together, reminiscing about Columbia. Then George said, "You know, you're one of those liberals that give me a pain in the neck. A liberal is supposed to be in the middle. At one end is the Communist, and at the other, the reactionary like myself. You're the guy in the middle. I've met a lot like you. If you lean over, you never lean to the right side but always to the left. Every liberal I know is a little bit to the left of center, never to the right of center." I said, "That's a lot of bunk," but I must admit there was a great deal in what he said.

We had a good time together because he was a very engaging man. He said, "You say you'll publish books on the right side. If I ever come to you with a book on the right, if it's good enough, will you publish it?" I said, "You're damned right I will," shaking a little bit, wondering what was going to come. Well, we parted with some affection. We had many roots in common, and I liked him.

Later that fall George called me and said, "Do you remember our conversation? Suppose I were to bring you a book, a story about the FBI, giving its good side, authorized and with an introduction by J. Edgar Hoover. Would you publish it?" I said, "George, are you kidding me? Every publisher in America would give his right arm for a book like that. We've all been trying to get an authorized book on the FBI." He said, "Well, if you want it, it's yours." I said, "You must be kidding, because this is not something you're showing me up on. This is something that I could probably be eternally grateful for." He said, "Tomorrow afternoon we're meeting for lunch at the Lotos Club, you and Louis Nichols of the FBI and myself." I groaned and said, "Tomorrow afternoon's the second game of the World Series. I've got tickets." George said, "Do you want the FBI book?" I said, "I certainly do." He said, "Give the tickets away." So, with a breaking heart, I gave them away.

I had never met Lou Nichols before. He was the number-three man in the FBI—right behind Hoover and Clyde Tolson. He later resigned and became vice-president of Schenley because, like so many FBI men, his pay was so low that he couldn't afford to stay. Lou Nichols was a wonderful guy and we got along immediately.

Of course I was delighted when he said we could have the book, *The FBI Story*. "Now we've got to find somebody to write it," Nichols said. "You're going to pick him, but we have to approve, since we're going to have to show him all kinds of secret records. We're going to temporarily give him an FBI badge so he can walk unimpeded through our whole headquarters, so it's got to be somebody we trust completely. I don't want to butt in, but I have a suggestion." I said, "Who's that?" He said, "Well, Don Whitehead, who's just won his second Pulitzer Prize for reporting." I said, "That would be wonderful, but he's the head of the Associated Press in Washington. We can't get him." Nichols said, "Try. What have you got to lose?"

I went back to my office and called Allen Gould, the vice-president of the Associated Press, whom I had known at Columbia, to see if I could spring Whitehead loose. I didn't think I had a chance. Allen said immediately, "I hear we've got to give you Don Whitehead." It was already arranged! I said, "We just want to borrow him." He said, "Yes, and we're not very happy about it, but we've got to give him to you for six months!" I said, "You know this wasn't my idea." He said, "You don't have to tell me, I know." So Whitehead was given a leave of absence to write *The FBI Story*.

I became a close friend of Lou Nichols, and I went down to spend a night with him and his family at their home in Alexandria. He met me at the Washington airport. As we were driving to Alexandria, I was telling him that even though the book wasn't out yet, there was an enormous advance sale, great interest, and that it would be a great success. I said, "You

Clyde Tolson, Jonathan, Bennett, J. Edgar Hoover, Phyllis, Christopher at FBI Headquarters

know something, Lou—what particularly pleases me is that your giving me this book means I must be in pretty good standing with the FBI. My record must be clear." Lou Nichols said, "Just, my boy, just." I never knew whether he was kidding me or not.

We published *The FBI Story* on November 28, 1956; in fact, when Whitehead turned in his manuscript, it was already too late to announce the book in our fall catalogue, but we rushed it out and it was a sensational success. Over fifty thousand copies were sold in the first two weeks, and we began to run into difficulties getting enough copies produced to meet the demand.

A few days before Christmas, I had a phone call from Helen (Mrs. Ogden) Reid, of the family that owned and operated the New York *Herald Tribune*. She said she had been unable to find a copy of *The FBI Story* anywhere in New York, and since she had promised to get it for a friend, she was hoping that I had one I would let her have. I had to tell her we had already stripped every shelf in our offices, that there was not a single copy left, but that we expected another printing in a few days. She said, "Bennett, I know where a copy is. If I tell you, will you promise to let *me* have it?" I said of course I would, and she said, "It's in one of those little display windows you have on your Madison Avenue side." "Helen," I said, "I'm sorry. We took that one out last week. What you see there now is just a jacket wrapped around some old book."

The FBI Story went right on selling after Christmas and into the next year. One morning in January the phone rang just as I arrived at my office, and it was Lou Nichols calling from Washington. "Bennett," he said, "what's wrong on the book?" I said, "What do you mean, what's wrong? It's selling as fast as we can print it." Then he said, "As of this morning, I must tell you there are no copies of *The FBI Story* in Brentano's or Scribner's and none in the Doubleday Shops, or for that matter, in any shop or department store in mid-Manhattan. None in Penn Station; none in the Wall Street area. So I ask you: what's wrong?" I tried to explain that this wasn't bad, that the book was selling faster than the stores could reorder or we could deliver them, and I guess I convinced him.

I was so amused by this switch on the usual report about the author's aunt who couldn't find a single copy of his book in any shop in Schenectady, I couldn't wait to tell somebody. So I went to the office next to mine, where Jim Michener, just back from the Austrian-Hungarian border, was putting the final touches on *The Bridge at Andau,* which we were rushing for March publication though he had finished it after our *spring* catalogue was already printed. When I told Jim about my phone conversation, he said, "Well, with all those agents checking bookshops, this would have been a great day for somebody to rob a bank in New York."

Generally, editors find a publishing firm with which they and their authors are comfortable, and stay with it for the rest of their working lives. Hiram Haydn was an exception. At the beginning of 1955 Hiram came to Random House as editor in chief. He had been at Crown Publishers before becoming the New York editor of Bobbs-Merrill, the Indianapolis firm, and I began hearing about his professional skill. I knew he was the editor of *The American Scholar,* the Phi Beta Kappa magazine, was teaching a writing course at the New School, and had under his wing a number of coming new writers, including William Styron. He had also written several books himself. When I heard that he was unhappy at Bobbs-Merrill, we got in touch with him and signed him up.

I admired Hiram—a wonderful fellow, although very exasperating in some ways. He had a great passion for first novels that other people thought were terrible. There was no way to convince him he was wrong, because he loved to help young writers—especially girls. The time he wasted with young women whose books were obviously destined to sell 918 copies! There was nothing we could do about it. He truly had us buffaloed!

Hiram had been with us for about four years when we negotiated a new employment contract with him—something unusual for us, but he insisted on having one. At about that time I went to Jamaica in February, 1959, with Moss and Kitty Hart for vacation. When I came back Donald told me that Hiram wanted us to tear up his contract. I said, "What are you talking about?" He said, "Pat Knopf has had a fight with his father, and Pat and Mike Bessie and Hiram want to start a new publishing house." When Hiram came in to discuss the matter, he said, quite logically, "You can understand this, Bennett. It's not that I'm leaving you to go to some other publisher, but that I want to go in for myself. You did it. *You* wanted to have your own firm." We had no alternative, so we tore up the contract—reluctantly, because during the four years he was at Random House he brought us a number of authors we were very happy to have and who remained with us after he left.

The first of these was Ayn Rand, whose *The Fountainhead* had been published by Bobbs-Merrill while Hiram was there. I had never met Ayn Rand, but I had heard of her philosophy, which I found absolutely horrifying. *The Fountainhead* is an absorbing story, nonetheless. She was very dubious about coming to Random House, she told Hiram, because her sycophants had told her that we were way over on the left and that she didn't belong with us. But this rather intrigued her—being published by a liberal house rather than one where she would ordinarily be expected to go. Furthermore, she had heard about me—one of the extra dividends you get from being known. She had lunch with Hiram, Donald and me at the Ambassador Hotel, now unfortunately torn down, and asked us a lot of questions. I found myself liking her, though I had not expected to.

She has piercing eyes that seem to look right through you and a wonderful way of pinning you to the wall. You can't make any loose statements to Ayn Rand; she hops on you and says, "Let us examine your premises." I am likely to shoot off my mouth occasionally and make statements that I don't quite mean or can't quite prove, and Ayn, again and again, would nail me. We liked each other; that's the answer. She asked me an infinite number of questions. Later on, after she came to Random House, she showed me a chart she had kept. She had visited about fifteen publishers, and when she got home she rated them on all the things they had said. I didn't realize, of course, that I was being examined this way, but I came out very high because I had been absolutely honest with her. I had said, "I find your political philosophy abhorrent." Nobody else had dared tell her this. I said, "If we publish you, Miss Rand, nobody is going to try to censor you. You write anything you please, in fiction at least, and we'll publish it, whether or not we approve."

She was just finishing *Atlas Shrugged,* and by the time we published it, we had an enormous advance sale. It was her first novel since *The Fountainhead,* and we printed a hundred thousand copies, knowing there would be tremendous interest in it. Then the reviews came out. The critics were hostile, as they always were to Ayn Rand, and the sale was badly crimped for a while. We thought it was going to be a failure, but the fact of the matter is: the book has gone on and on and on, through many printings, even in spite of its availability in paperback. Incidentally, the reprint made history. *Atlas Shrugged* was very long, and there was no possibility Ayn would cut it. So for the first time its publisher, New American Library, dared to price a mass-market paperback above fifty cents—they priced it at ninety-five.

At any rate, Ayn and I became good friends. What I loved to do was trot her out for people who sneered at us for publishing her. She would invariably charm them. For instance, Clifton Fadiman, who had snorted at the idea of our publishing Ayn Rand, sat talking with her until about three in the morning. George Axelrod, author of *The Seven Year Itch,* toward the end of a long, long evening at Ayn's, disappeared with her into another room and we couldn't get him to go home. Later he said, "She knows me better after five hours than my analyst does after five years."

Ayn is a remarkable woman, but in my opinion, she was not helped

Ayn Rand

by her sycophants. She's like a movie queen with her retinue, or a prize-fight champion who's followed by a bunch of hangers-on, or a big crooner and his worshippers. They all come to need this adulation. These people tell her she's a genius and agree with everything she says, and she grows more and more opinionated as she goes along. You can't argue with Ayn Rand. She's so clever at it, she makes a fool out of you. Any time I started arguing with her, she'd trick me into making some crazy statement and then demolish me.

But for some reason or another, Ayn liked me. She told me that one of the characters she put into *Atlas Shrugged* near the end was inspired by me. She was determined to save me, as she called it, because I was a very nice person with a very good brain that I was wasting on all the worthless causes I believed in. She was trying to convert me to her way of thinking; she didn't have a prayer, of course, but I did like to hear her expound her cockeyed philosophy.

A very peculiar thing happened early in our relationship—the first time Phyllis met her, Ayn came to our house and said to Phyllis for openers, "We have met before." Phyllis said, "Oh, Miss Rand, you must be mistaken." Ayn Rand said, "We have met before." Phyllis said, "It's impossible. I certainly would remember if I had met you." Ayn said, "No. You wouldn't. Do you remember when you were a baby starlet at RKO in the movies?" Phyllis said, "Yes." Ayn said, "I was working in the costume department there at twenty-five dollars a week, and I handed you several of your costumes." Incredible, but true.

Ayn's a very simple and modest woman. We were on our way to lunch in Radio City once, and as we passed one of those junk shops with all kinds of statues and knickknacks, she saw a little blue bracelet in the window, and like a twelve-year-old girl, Ayn said, "Isn't that a beautiful bracelet!" So I went in and bought it for her. It cost exactly one dollar, but she was as happy as a child.

She's so brilliant at expounding her theories! When she appeared on *The Tonight Show* with Johnny Carson, he had planned to have her on for only a few moments, but he ended by throwing out the rest of the program and even asking her to come back. He said that the mail he got from that show was enormous. People react violently to her iconoclastic statements. She's entirely against any religion. She thinks that strong, utterly selfish people should prevail, and that, in reality, two percent of the population is supporting the other ninety-eight percent. She says, "That's all wrong. The two percent should really be the gods instead of being reviled by the people they are supporting. Charity and all of this public welfare is the bunk." *Atlas Shrugged* is a story about capitalists who finally go on strike. They leave the industries to labor and say, "All right, you run them." The natural result, according to Ayn, is that everything goes promptly to hell. There's a lot in what she says.

Ayn believed that the critics were out to get her, and they really did tear her books apart. She wanted me to have reviewers fired or go to the *Times* and complain about them. I said, "I can't. If they gave your book to another critic, you'd get the same kind of review, Ayn. Whether you like it or not, most people don't agree with your ideas, and it's your ideas they're attacking."

Anyway, she began doing a series of articles for a magazine she and one of her disciples publish—*The Objectivist*. Ayn collected them to be done in book form, and I said we were happy to have a new book by her, but when somebody at Random House read the manuscript—which I certainly wasn't going to do—and found that one of the essays likened John F. Kennedy to Hitler, saying that their speeches and objectives were basically the same, I read the piece and absolutely hit the roof. I called her and said we were not going to publish any book that claimed Hitler and Jack Kennedy were alike. Ayn charged in and reminded me that I had said when she came to us that we would publish anything she wrote. I reminded her that I had said fiction. I said, "You can say anything you want in a novel, but this is something I didn't foresee. All we ask is that you leave this one essay out."

Ayn was enraged. But as I said, arguing with her was like running your head against a stone wall. I remember when *Atlas Shrugged* was being edited by Hiram Haydn. The hero, John Galt, makes a speech that lasts about thirty-eight pages. All that he says in it has been said over and over already in the book, but Hiram couldn't get her to cut a word. I very angrily said to him, "You're some editor. Send her in to me. I'll fix it in no time." So when Ayn came in and sat down, looking at me with those piercing eyes, I said, "Ayn, nobody's going to read that. You've said it all three or four times before, and it's thirty-odd pages long. You've got to cut it." She looked at me calmly and said, "Would you cut the Bible?" So I gave up.

At any rate, during our final meeting about the book of essays, she wouldn't stop haranguing. I kept telling her, "Ayn, I've got to go home." (It was about six o'clock and Phyllis and I were giving a dinner party that night.) As we left the building Ayn was still repeating that I had promised her I wouldn't ever change her copy. I finally got into a taxicab, and she was still standing there on the sidewalk, talking. Finally she gave her ultimatum, "You're going to print every word I've written—or I won't let you publish the book." I said, "That's that. Get yourself another publisher." I was adamant about it. Imagine putting our imprint on such a book! Well, some other publisher took it. I must say, I don't think anybody ever read those essays. I never heard one word of criticism, and I never even saw a review of the book. When Kennedy was assassinated that fall, I wrote Ayn to ask if she didn't agree now that she was wrong. She didn't agree at all. She said the assassination had nothing to do with what she had to say. It didn't change her opinion one iota.

I liked her and still do. I miss her. I thought she was one of the most interesting authors we've ever had. Many people who disapproved of a lot of the books we publish worshipped Ayn Rand; and wherever I go lecturing, somebody is sure to pop up and say, with adoration, "Tell me about Ayn Rand." When she gave a talk at Harvard, the hall was full of students who came to hoot but stayed to applaud. They weren't convinced by her but they were impressed by her sincerity. This is a brilliant woman.

Hiram Haydn was also responsible for bringing Jerome Weidman to Random House, and in January, 1958, we published *The Enemy Camp*, our first book by him. Jerry is a most amusing man, and he and his wife, Peggy, a wonderful girl, are two friends we love dearly. Jerry is a very prolific novelist, and he's written his full share of best sellers, but in between he's

Bennett, Jerome Weidman, Phyllis

dashed off several books that are not so good. His first novel, *I Can Get It for You Wholesale,* made history in 1937.

The Enemy Camp is an example of how an author can set his sights too high when dealing with Hollywood. He received an offer—which we at Random House thought was very generous—of a hundred thousand dollars for the movie rights; but he and his agent decided that was not enough, and in the end, they never sold it at all. Authors can sometimes overreach themselves. But *The Enemy Camp* was a Book-of-the-Month Club choice, and the following year Jerry's hit musical *Fiorello!* was produced and won the Pulitzer Prize for drama in 1960. *The Center of the Action* was written out of his own experience in the publishing business. Its main characters will be familiar to people who know the inside history of Simon and Schuster, where Jerry was once an editor. It's thinly disguised, and anyone who knows the idiosyncrasies of Dick Simon and Max Schuster will recognize them.

In June of 1960 we published *Set This House on Fire* by William Styron—a great addition to the Random House list and one of those we are proudest of today. Bill came to us with Hiram Haydn, who had published his first novel, *Lie Down in Darkness,* at Bobbs-Merrill. *Set This House on Fire* did not get the same critical reception as *Lie Down in Darkness.* It was a faulty but nonetheless brilliant book. Since authors frequently go along with editors who move to other publishing houses, it was a great source of satisfaction to us that Bill decided to stay with Random House when Hiram left. Phyllis and I had become quite fond of Bill and his wife, Rose, and we saw a lot of them.

The main reason Bill stayed with us, however, was that we had on our staff two editors, Robert Loomis and Bertha Krantz—both prize acquisitions we owed to Hiram, who recommended them to us and who was mistakenly confident that Bert would follow him to his new firm. Loomis and Styron had been friends since their student days at Duke University, and Bill thought—rightly, it has turned out—that Bob would be a good editor for him, and he had been highly pleased with Bert Krantz's work on *Set This House on Fire*. Bob is one of those painstaking editors in the old tradition and has been helpful to a great variety of writers of both fiction and nonfiction, including two Pulitzer Prize-winners: John Toland *(The Rising Sun)*, and Seymour Hersh *(My Lai 4)*. He also edits Shelby Foote, whose monumental history of the Civil War is nearing completion, and Jerzy Kosinski, whose *Steps* won the National Book Award for fiction for 1968.

Bill Styron devoted seven years to the research and writing that produced *The Confessions of Nat Turner*, which I regard as one of the finest novels of the past twenty-five years. It was a Book-of-the-Month Club

William Styron

selection, jumped right to the top of the best-seller list and stayed there for a long time, and it won the Pulitzer Prize for fiction in 1968. I am convinced that this book will be used in history and literature classes for many years to come.

Sometimes authors are responsible for bringing other authors to a publisher's list, and it was Bill Styron who told Bob Loomis about a friend who was writing some fine stories that Random House might be interested in publishing. When Bob pursued the matter, he found that Philip Roth was already under contract to another publisher. We were chagrined to miss that book, *Goodbye, Columbus,* which immediately made its author famous; but the matter didn't end there. Bob heard that Roth, who was staying at the American Academy in Rome, was not too happy with his publishing arrangements. Since Donald was planning to spend a few days in Rome, he made a date to see Roth and tell him how interested we were in publishing him. The result was that when Roth got back home he came to see us and talk things over, and we became his publishers. Our first book by Roth was the novel *Letting Go* in 1962, which was followed five years later by *When She Was Good.* Our belief that Roth would become one of the successful young authors was confirmed in 1969, when we published *Portnoy's Complaint,* which was an immediate sensation and one of the fastest-selling novels in the history of Random House. Unlike most young authors whose works we have published, Philip Roth is one I've never felt close to; he has always seemed withdrawn, unwilling to make close ties.

There are many people I like but only a few I truly love. Moss Hart was one of those in my life that I loved. In many ways he was the most remarkable person I ever knew. To me, Moss represented the theater. Everything he did delighted me. His plays delighted me and his humor delighted me. He was such fun to be with.

Just before Christmas in 1961 Moss died suddenly in California, and shortly thereafter his grief-stricken friends in the East arranged a memorial service for him. It was held on January 9, 1962, at the Music Box Theatre in New York, where his first successful play had opened thirty-two years before. Howard Lindsay presided, and after Brooks Atkinson, Dore Schary, Edna Ferber and Alan Lerner had presented their tributes, I spoke the following words, from my heart:

> All of the words that the name Moss Hart brings to mind are beautiful ones, and of special importance in a world like ours today: gaiety, warmth, understanding, laughter, gusto, loyalty, integrity, delight.
>
> Whatever Moss did, he did with all his heart and soul. He was as interested in your problem as he was in his own. Everything to Moss was a production problem. He could hear about the most mundane domestic disturbance and build it into a drama with national significance. He could invest the drabbest, dullest characters with a majesty and fire that turned them into fascinating ladies and gentlemen. What's more, the characters began living up to Moss's conceptions immediately and saw themselves for the rest of their days as Moss re-created them.
>
> All of his life Moss Hart suffered periodic attacks of almost unbearable depression. Analysis provided only a partial cure. Never once, however, did I know him to let his own troubles keep him from throwing himself completely into performing a task he had undertaken, or heeding a call for help from one of his innumerable close friends.
>
> Moss was the kind of guest a hostess dreams of. No sooner did he appear at a party than he automatically assumed the role of co-host. Immediately, furthermore, everybody in the room became a little brighter, a little more assured, just because Moss was there. What warmer tribute can you pay a man?
>
> Moss never left anything to chance. When we would congratulate him on some particularly successful achievement, he

would chuckle and remind us, cheerfully, "You know my father didn't leave me the money." When anybody ascribed his success to luck, Moss would counter with, "Nobody is sitting up there saying 'Now what can we do for Moss Hart today?' Luck is what you make it." He even undertook the supervision of this very memorial service we are attending today. "If you want to have a service for me," he told Kitty, "remember, I won't be there to make the arrangements—so you all will probably set it for an hour when the actors who were my friends can't be present." Sure enough, the first date we selected was tomorrow—matinée day. It was Moss's oldest friend, Joe Hyman, who set us straight.

Moss understood the true purpose of money possibly better than anybody in this theater. Not for him little notebooks that showed a constantly increasing credit balance at the banks and brokerage offices. Money to Moss was something you spent. And what joy the spending of it gave him! He didn't buy things by ones—he bought them by sixes, whether they were dressing gowns, porch swings, desk sets, household pets, or houses to put them in.

And how perfectly his wife Kitty fulfilled his life. She not only made him a family man with an irresistible wife and two irresistible children—a picture of himself that he cherished deeply—but she gave him just the right amount of opposition to his most outrageous extravagances before admitting graciously, "You were absolutely right, Mossy. The room wouldn't look the same without that six-hundred-dollar flower pot in the corner." That always made Moss's joy in his newest possession complete.

In my thirty-eight years in the publishing business, I never have seen an author derive such unalloyed delight from a best seller as Moss Hart did from *Act One*. To hear the relish with which he read his fan mail to me over the phone each morning was to understand what fun can be had in this life by a man who knows how to live it. It made no difference to Moss whether the letter came from an Adlai Stevenson or an unsung housewife in Wichita Falls. He saw a little old man trudging along Madison Avenue one day with a copy of *Act One* under his arm, stopped him to say, "I'm Moss Hart. I'm the man who wrote that book!"—and autographed it while the old man beamed. Moss's dream was to see *Act One* in The Modern Library series. We are going to put it there for him this year. I can hear him telling me, "You did it just in time to save me from Doubleday."

Disasters turned into joyrides under Moss's guidance. Bill Paley's pool in Jamaica was filled with sand instead of salt water because of faulty filtering one winter. Moss made it the subject of a hilarious calypso song. A terrible play opened on Broadway and the after-theater gathering at the St. Regis looked like a morgue. Moss organized an impromptu cheering section, and had even the stricken author and producer laughing at themselves before the gathering disbanded. A modest party planned to celebrate the success of *Act One* was taken over by Moss himself and turned, with the help of Harold Rome, Arthur Schwartz, Howard Dietz, Phil Silvers, and a host of other friends, into one of the most notable evenings in the life of everybody who came.

Most of those guests are here again today, not so much to mourn Moss, I think, as to agonize over the sheer joy and excitement that have gone out of their own lives with his passing.

What happiness he gave us all! Thank God we had the opportunity to know him!

Moss burst upon the scene in New York in the most incredible way. He was born in Brooklyn in absolute poverty; when he was very small his family moved up to the Bronx. His father, who was English and until the day of his death spoke with a slight accent, worked in a cigar factory. Moss had a maiden aunt who loved the theater passionately, and every Saturday afternoon she took her little nephew to a show. They would sit up in the galleries in twenty-five-cent seats, and Moss fell in love with the theater too. His devotion to it led him to get a job as office boy for a play producer, which turned out to be a great experience. For one thing, he could get free tickets to every play on Broadway, and he saw them all, good and bad. The job ended when his employer produced a play that Moss, not yet eighteen, had written—a flop, but an instructive one. By this time Moss had met Edward Chodorov, who introduced him to a little-theater group that included young unknowns like Dore Schary and other fledglings who later became famous, and he learned a lot that he would later put to use.

After a few years as a highly successful social director at summer camps—known as the Borscht Circuit—Moss wrote a comedy about Hollywood, a place he'd never been to. He managed after many difficulties to get George Kaufman to read the script, and George was so impressed that he agreed to collaborate with Moss in getting *Once in a Lifetime* ready for production. When the play opened on September 24, 1930, a month before Moss's twenty-sixth birthday, it was a smash. The audience howled with joy, and he became famous overnight.

I met Moss through the Kaufmans. Beatrice took Moss in hand right at the start and introduced him to all her famous friends, as she had done with me years earlier, and they all came to love him. Moss bought a great big place down in Bucks County, Pennsylvania, right near the Kaufmans'. He was always being hoodwinked because he thought people were doing him a favor by selling him things; he never bargained with them. Beatrice tried to take care of him; we *all* tried, but it didn't make any difference—he was making money so fast. He began planting new trees and shrubs and moving old ones to improve the scenery. That's when Alex Woollcott, by now a great friend, pulled his famous line. After he saw what Moss had done, he said, "Just what God would have done if He'd had the money."

All the rest of Moss's life he was prodigal. As one big hit followed another, he became one of the most popular, successful, famous people in the entire theatrical world. A high point was in 1941, when he did *Lady in the Dark* and discovered Danny Kaye. Another was when he directed the Broadway production of Alan J. Lerner and Frederick Loewe's *My Fair Lady*, which, of course, was one of the great triumphs of the modern theater. But Moss never tired of talking about the days when he was poor. We all kept begging him to put the stories he told us into a book, until finally he gave in and began work on *Act One*, which was to be the story of his early days before he had his first hit. He would read bits and pieces to us, and of course we loved them. I'll never forget the day, however, after he had written about four chapters, when he began to go into one of his sloughs of despond. He wanted to tear the whole thing up, and I almost physically had to keep him from doing so. Just before he reached the end of the book, we went through the same agonizing routine again.

But *Act One* did get finished—and it was enchanting, about as good a book on the theater as has ever been written. In the months between our receiving the manuscript and the actual publication of the book, Moss put on quite an act as the demanding and discontented author. He had made up some new words to the tune of "On the Road to Mandalay," and he would march into my office singing, "On the road to Doubleday, where they big advances pay"—or something like that—and he delighted in pretending to be critical of all of our editing and designing and promotion-planning. He wrote snide memos to me about Albert Erskine, who was his editor, and to Albert about me, and we wrote caustic answers back, always with carbons directed to all concerned. He was really quite pleased with what we were doing, of course, and we were all having a ball; back in those days we had time for such playing around. Moss was actually one of the most cooperative and helpful of authors, interesting himself in every stage of the process of getting the book out, making good suggestions but not interfering. I wrote out my idea of what should be on the jacket flap and sent it to Moss. He slaved over it and sent back his version, saying that writing jacket copy was harder than writing the book. What he had done was to rearrange part of what I had written and add some ideas of his own. Then Albert did

Moss Hart on trip to entertain servicemen in South Pacific during World War II

some revising, and then Moss and I did more, and we arrived at what was finally used—a joint production that satisfied us all.

When the first copies came from the printer, we all agreed that it was one of the most beautiful books Random House had ever produced. There

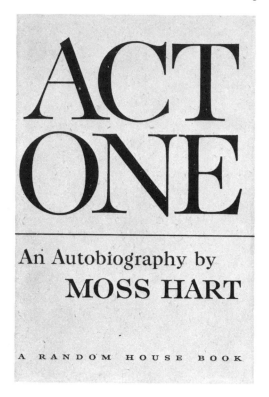

was only one snag: the proofreader, a really good one, had been so fascinated by the story that she let slip by her an incredible number of typographical errors, which had to be corrected before the next printing. Typically, Moss was less upset about a hundred typos than some authors are about three.

Just before *Act One* came out, Moss asked me how much money I thought he might make out of it. I told him that books about the theater had never been wildly successful, but I estimated he might earn as much as twenty-five thousand dollars. He thereupon decided to give the whole thing to his children, with all the royalties to be divided between Chris and Cathy Hart, who were very young at the time.

The book was an immediate sensation. It was number one on the nonfiction list for months on end. In addition to everything else, he got about two hundred fifty thousand dollars for the movie rights, and of course it all kept going to Chris and Cathy. Moss would carry on about

Moss Hart

this, although he really loved it. But it became one of his routines. He called them the Lear kids. He would complain, "The Lear kids are getting all of this dough," and then scream at me, "You dog! You told me it would never be a real best seller!"

On October 23, 1959, we gave the big party to celebrate *Act One* at Leone's restaurant, and Moss, being Moss, immediately took charge of this party in his honor and directed a big show. Those of us who performed were ordered by him to get costumes, and he made us rehearse until we had our parts down pat. The result was one of the greatest entertainments. Every star in New York was there—if something had happened to that restaurant that night, the theater would have ended in New York.

One hilarious number was a quartet in which Adolph Green, Martin Gabel, Moss and I were four cleaning women—and dressed as such—from Doubleday, Random House, Simon and Schuster and Little, Brown. We came out with our pails and mops and sang a song Moss had written for the occasion, with a chorus for each of us about what we found in the trash baskets at night—manuscripts and personal letters. It was screamingly funny. Then Arlene Francis, Florence Rome and Kitty and Phyllis came on and sang a song about Moss that he had also written. For this one he had done parody lyrics (something he did for practically every occasion) to the tune of Cole Porter's "You're the Top." I can remember only these lines: "He's the top! He's a Lindy waiter. He's the top! He's a borscht potato"— and on like that.

Moss Hart, Bennett, Adolph Green, Martin Gabel

Kitty Carlisle, Phyllis, Florence Rome, Arlene Francis

Betty Comden and Adolph Green wrote a number and so did Harold Rome. The highlight of the show was a little one-act musical, "The Story of *Act One*," by Howard Dietz and Arthur Schwartz. It was written just for that evening, but thank the Lord we made a record of it (I fear the other numbers are all lost). There's a lovely song in it, "It Happens Just Once in a Lifetime," which Kitty sang.

Moss teamed up again in 1960 with Lerner and Loewe to produce *Camelot*. When the show opened in Toronto, disaster struck—Moss had a heart attack. That was his first, and then later he had another. Although he had been warned by the doctor that he must be careful, he kept on going to parties, living his life the way he wanted to. In 1961 he and Kitty bought a house in Palm Springs. Phyllis and I were planning to visit them the following February, but a few days before Christmas, I picked up the phone and understood our switchboard operator to say, "Mr. Hart is calling." I expected the usual insult—that was the kind of relationship we had—but it was Kitty. She said, "Moss just dropped dead." I'll never forget that as long as I live. We were on a plane for California the next day.

Moss's death left a big hole in our lives. We had spent every holiday we could with Moss and Kitty—the Fourth of July, Labor Day, winter vacations—and just being with Moss would always make it wonderful. We were often joined on these occasions by Arthur and Leonora Hornblow, and since we were all terribly fond of each other, it was always just about perfect.

Leonora Hornblow is one of our great friends and is a writer herself, the author of two novels, both published by Random House—*Memory and Desire* and *The Love-Seekers*—and one of our Landmark Books. She has read practically everything and knows more about books than any other girl I've ever met. Many writers are her friends and turn to her instinctively—as I did when I decided to do a big anthology called *Take Along Treasury*. As the title implies, it was intended to be suitable for people to take with them on trips or vacations. I felt that her help would be invaluable to me, and indeed it was. We collaborated in selecting a great variety of first-rate pieces, some by well-known authors but many others by newcomers who were not yet established. Doubleday published our book in 1963, and I have always been proud of it.

Arthur Hornblow is a long-time close friend of mine, and when he was courting Leonora, Phyllis and I watched his progress with interest and concern. When he finally won out against considerable competition, they were married in our house. Arthur has had a long and distinguished career in Hollywood as the producer of many famous and successful movies, among which were *Gaslight*, *The Asphalt Jungle*, *Oklahoma!* and *Witness for the Prosecution*.

Leonora and Arthur Hornblow, Bennett and Phyllis, Kitty

In the 1960's after Arthur had more or less retired from movie-making the Hornblows found a wonderful new occupation that they could enjoy doing together—writing carefully researched children's books for Phyllis' Step-Up Books. Their first was *Animals Do the Strangest Things*, which they followed with similar books about birds, fish and reptiles.

Our friendship with Arthur and Leonora caused a slight inconvenience with one of our authors. Arthur had produced the film version of a

ss Hart caught "having wonderful time" at Round Hill, Jamaica.

novel we published—*Cass Timberlane* by Sinclair Lewis—in which Spencer Tracy starred. That project brought Arthur into conflict with John O'Hara. John had just turned forty—this was about a year before he came to Random House—when Arthur engaged him to work on the script of *Cass Timberlane*, and then, dissatisfied with John's work after a few months, dropped him. Needless to say, we had to be careful after that never to invite the Hornblows and the O'Haras to the same party.

It was a red-letter day in my life when I signed up John O'Hara. I had met him through Phyllis and occasionally saw him at parties, and we had many mutual friends—Harold Ross, Wolcott Gibbs and the whole *New Yorker* group. When he had a falling-out with his publisher—I don't remember just what it was about—he made it clear that he would come to Random House if we made the proper deal with him. He hadn't written a novel since 1938, he was drinking too much, and a lot of people were saying that he was through. He was very angry about this, but except for short-story collections, he just hadn't published a new book for years. He had been out in Hollywood, but he was restless there and his drinking was worse than in New York; he was a writer and he wanted to get back to serious work.

We made our deal in a place called the Tavern, which has since been torn down but was then a sort of Toots Shor bar and grill. In fact, Toots Shor was once the bouncer there. I remember saying, "John, this is a great day in my life, because I think you're one of the great authors of America." John said, "*One* of the great authors? Who else?" I said, "Well, Hemingway and Faulkner." He said, "Well, I'll buy Faulkner."

When John O'Hara came to Random House, he came to stay, and we were his publishers for the rest of his life—for twenty-three years, in the course of which he produced twenty-three books. The first, in 1947, was *Hellbox,* his fourth volume of short stories and, as it turned out, his last for some time to come. Nearly all of the stories in *Hellbox,* as in his earlier collections, had been first published in *The New Yorker.* By 1949 John had been for twenty years one of its most faithful and frequent contributors; but when in that year we published *A Rage to Live*—his first novel, incidentally, in eleven years—his relations with the magazine came to a grinding halt.

The huge success of *A Rage to Live* was not the result of the review received in *The New Yorker,* which was a savage attack. John was grievously hurt by this treatment. He couldn't understand why, in spite of his long association with them, the editors seemed so eager to attack his novels (this was the second time) in the pages that had been so hospitable to his stories. There had been other areas of friction, of course, but that review enraged him. He not only broke with *The New Yorker;* he even quit writing short stories.

In fact, for about five years he wrote very little of anything—except for *The Farmers Hotel,* which he had begun as a play and then rewritten as a short novel. We published it in the fall of 1951, and just before it was announced, something happened that showed how childish John could be on occasion. He came to see me one day and said he thought he'd like to call the book *A Small Hotel*, for one of Dick Rodgers' songs. He said, "Do you think Dick will mind?" Dick and John were great friends from *Pal Joey*, the musical they had written together, but I said that John should at least ask, so he went to see Dick. He came back about a half-hour later, black with rage, as only John O'Hara could get in those days. He said, "I'm calling it *The Farmers Hotel*," and stamped out. As soon as he was out of sight, I called Dick Rodgers at his office. Dick said, "He came in here and

John O'Hara

said he wanted to name his book *A Small Hotel,* after one of my songs. I said, 'That's great, John, but to be exact, the name of the song is "*There's a Small Hotel.*"' O'Hara said, 'When I need you to name my books, I'll tell you,' and left without another word."

When the time came to set the exact publication date of *The Farmers Hotel, The New Yorker's* review of *A Rage to Live* was not the only bad one John remembered; Orville Prescott in *The New York Times* had also been negative. So John wrote Donald and pointed out that by publishing on a Thursday, we could avoid Prescott (who reviewed on Mondays, Wednesdays and Fridays) and be reviewed instead by Charles Poore, who had shown himself to be more appreciative. So *The Farmers Hotel* was published on Thursday, November 8, beginning a custom which would be further refined when O'Hara's next big book, *Ten North Frederick,* came out in 1955 on Thanksgiving Day, which thereafter was established as John's own private publication day.

Authors will remember a bad review long after they've forgotten the good ones. They take the favorable ones for granted, as only their due. But when somebody knocks them—oh, how they remember. I'll never forget the night we invited Alicia Patterson and Sinclair Lewis to a dinner party at our house and placed Alicia and Red next to each other. When we sat down, she said, "You know, Mr. Lewis, I've been looking forward to meeting you for a long time." He said, "You have, have you? Then why did you write that terrible review of *It Can't Happen Here* in the *Daily News*?" The *News* was her father's newspaper, and for a while Alicia had done book notices for it. Alicia said, "I don't know what you're talking about." Doubleday had published the book years before. She had forgotten it entirely, but the author hadn't.

And not only authors! One night Phyllis and I were going to a dinner at John Mason Brown's in honor of Francis Taylor, head of the Metropolitan Museum of Art. It was quite a formal affair. About six o'clock Danny Kaye, who had just flown into town and didn't have anything to do that night, called us up. So I called John Brown and said, "Can we bring Danny Kaye with us?" He was entranced! Danny was at the top of his form. He's the greatest mimic in the world. He was imitating Taylor and everybody, and all the guests were howling. Danny, Phyllis and I were the last to leave. John, who was a very warm and endearing man, said, "What a thrill to have you in my house." Danny said, "It's too bad you didn't feel that way about me when I opened in *Lady in the Dark,*" and proceeded to reel off what John had said about him in his review. Brown said, "Ridiculous! From the moment I first saw you I've insisted that you're absolutely great!

As a matter of fact, I've got all of my reviews in scrapbooks. I'm going to show you how wrong you are."

He got a ladder and climbed up in his closet and pulled down the index of 1941, the year *Lady in the Dark* opened, and looked up the review. Danny was right. He had remembered it word for word eleven years later! John O'Hara could remember such things far longer than that!

In his work O'Hara was the true professional, always in complete control of what he was doing. Before he wrote anything, he had planned it and knew what he wanted to say; he could stop in the middle of a sentence and go to sleep, and the next day get up and finish the half-done sentence he'd left in the typewriter. He worked at least six hours a day, usually consecutive. He'd start in the night and work until two or three in the morning, when nobody was around to disturb him, then sleep until noon. (It was therefore practically impossible to get O'Hara on the phone in the morning.) He took great pride in delivering his manuscripts on the precise dates he had promised, sometimes months in advance. For example, he might tell me in April that on August first he would be bringing in the finished manuscript of so-and-so; then, just like clockwork, he'd phone in late July and make a date to come in on August first. It was very impressive, but I later learned that it wasn't always the feat it seemed to be. In the sixties he was writing books faster than we could publish them, and sometimes I think he'd already finished a book before he announced its future delivery date.

In the early fifties several things happened that had a profound effect on the life of John O'Hara and on his work as well. Right after *A Rage to Live* was published, John and his wife, Belle, decided to move to Princeton—partly because they thought it was a better place for their four-year-old daughter Wylie, whom John always worshipped, and partly to get away from the bars of New York. The move was a good idea, but it didn't stop his drinking, and in 1953 he was taken to the hospital with a bleeding stomach ulcer. The doctors gave him a choice: if he wanted to go on living, the drinking had to stop. So he went on the wagon. A few months later Belle, whom he deeply loved, died suddenly—the kind of shock that in the past would have caused him to run for the bottle, but he never took a drink for the rest of his life. The year after Belle's death, John married Katherine Barnes Bryan—"Sister," as everyone called her—and she was perfect for him.

In the fifteen years he had left, John did far more work than he had in the previous twenty or so, when he had been a big drinker. The first book to be published during that incredibly productive time was the major novel *Ten North Frederick*, which was followed, in rapid succession, by *From the*

Terrace, Ourselves to Know (always one of my favorites) and *Sermons and Soda-Water.* Then in the sixties came his most prodigious output; he had by now made peace with *The New Yorker,* and in addition to five novels, he produced six great collections of short stories.

During the time Cardinal Spellman was my neighbor, he complained to me several times about John O'Hara's books. John was really way out ahead in writing sex scenes and using four-letter words and whatnot. Now his books are mild in comparison with the stuff that's coming out, but then they were quite daring. *A Rage to Live* was considered very gamy because it had a detailed episode of a seduction, described rather graphically. Finally I said to Spellman, "He's one of your boys. Why don't you talk to him? I'd like to bring John to lunch. Would you like to have him?" The Cardinal said, "I'd love to meet him." I told this to John, wondering how he'd react. He was delighted. He drove up in his brand-new Rolls-Royce and parked it in the courtyard, where elaborate arrangements had been made to reserve a parking space for him—a ritual that was repeated many times over the years. I said, "Now, John, please don't go off the handle or something." I remember John's reply: "Which one of us is the Catholic? You don't have to tell me how to behave."

Usually, whenever I went over to the Cardinal's house, one of the maids would open the door and I'd wait for him to come downstairs to the

Rolls-Royce, Albert Erskine, John O'Hara, Bennett

Cardinal Spellman, John O'Hara, Bennett

little reception room. This time the Cardinal came to meet us in our courtyard. He was a little nervous about the meeting, too. I said, "Your Eminence, this is Mr. John O'Hara." John bent over and kissed the Cardinal's ring; then took an envelope out of his pocket and said, "My mother was always very much interested in your favorite charity, the Foundling Home, and I'd like to give you a donation for it." The Cardinal's face was a study—he hadn't expected this to happen at all, and neither did I. He was astounded.

The three of us walked over to lunch, and they took to each other at once. We had a wonderful time. They forgot I was there. After lunch the Cardinal insisted on showing us his coin collection in the Archbishopric. Since I had seen it about four times before, I broke in, "You two have nothing to do, obviously, but I have to get on with some publishing." So off I went, leaving them very happy together.

John set great store by trophies or tokens of esteem, especially those that were engraved to commemorate some occasion or triumph, and over the years his study became crowded with them. When our sales of *A Rage to Live* passed the hundred-thousand mark, we presented John with a silver cigarette box inscribed "From his grateful publishers and the first hundred thousand purchasers . . ." This gesture was to be repeated for *From the*

Terrace and several times when sales of his paperback editions reached a million. One of his most highly prized possessions was a cigarette case that he received from another author he loved—John Steinbeck. The inscription read: "The lonely mind of one man is the only creative organ in the world, and any force which interferes with its free function is the Enemy." John O'Hara never let anybody interfere with his lonely mind.

Another such treasure led one time to a rather embarrassing episode. In December, 1950, Bill Faulkner was passing through New York on his way to Stockholm to receive the Nobel Prize, so Phyllis and I gave a small dinner party for him the night before he left and invited Belle and John, who had never met Faulkner. The Nobel Prize was probably the one thing on earth that John yearned for most, and he was quite an authority on the subject; so within a few minutes of being introduced, he informed Bill that the Nobel money he was about to receive would be tax-free—a fact that none of the rest of us was aware of. Then after dinner when Bill needed a light, John leaned across the table and handed him a cigarette lighter that had been given to John, which had an inscription from his old friend, the playwright Philip Barry. When Bill admired it, John said he'd like Bill to keep it to mark the big event. Bill merely said thank you and put the lighter in his pocket, not rising to the occasion. It was easy to see that John was deeply offended, and since this took place when he was still a heavy and sometimes a belligerent drinker, I was terrified of what he might do; but fortunately, Belle saw the danger and arranged their departure before anything happened.

Of course, going on the wagon didn't eliminate the O'Hara temper altogether, but it did soften it. He still had many of those ridiculous little outbursts, which could be terribly funny when you got to know him, but not exactly pleasant if you were on the receiving end. He had supreme confidence in himself, and he was right. John O'Hara was grossly underestimated by many literary critics and academics. He got their goat by his sometimes insolent manner and the fact that he was an utter loner and nonconformist. He said what he thought and often blasted people—including me sometimes—but I think he and I understood each other. He called me "Cerfie," and I could tell immediately what mood he was in by his voice when he greeted me on the phone.

Phyllis and I were genuinely devoted to him. He was a loyal friend, and something very endearing to me is the fact that he was the one famous Random House author who made a point of following my personal activities. If I made a speech in Columbus, Ohio, John knew about it. If I didn't mention him, he seemed to know about that, too. It's incredible how he kept up with what I did. When I was on *What's My Line?* all those years, he never missed it, and he'd usually have some snide comment to make, kidding me. He'd call up and say, "Boy, were you terrible last night"—but he was always watching. One night when I was on *The Tonight Show*, I said, "John O'Hara's not only a great author but a wonderful man; and the fact that I know he's watching is not why I'm saying this." I looked right at him. John called me the next morning, obviously pleased, and said, "You were looking right at me." I said, "You're absolutely right." That's the rapport we had!

When we celebrated my seventieth birthday, we had a few friends—all neighbors of our Mount Kisco home—for dinner. John was deeply hurt that I had not invited him, but when I explained that I didn't want him to take the long trip from Princeton to Mount Kisco in hot summer Saturday afternoon traffic—particularly in light of the fact that his back was troubling him—John forgave me and the next day I received an incredible package of American Beauty roses: one for every year of my life. Occasional gestures like this made up for all the ludicrous explosions that might otherwise have marred our relationship.

In April, 1970, I acted as chairman of the Moss Hart Memorial Dinner, sponsored by the Friends of the University of Southern California Library. A few days later, while I was still out West giving lectures, I heard that John had died in his sleep, so I had barely finished honoring the memory of one dear friend when I lost another, and the following month I conducted a memorial service for John O'Hara at Random House.

Donald Klopfer, Bob Haas and I each owned one-third of Random House from 1936, when Haas joined us, until 1956, when Bob decided to retire and devote the rest of his life to philanthropic work. We bought back his stock. Donald's stepson, Tony Wimpfheimer, who later became our managing editor, took some of it, but Don and I kept complete control, and to all intents and purposes, owned the entire business.

One thing that we were always worried about was the value that would be put on the company if one of us died. In a privately owned business the inheritance-tax problem is often very difficult. If there is not some kind of stock on the market to establish the value of a business, you have to wait for the government to evaluate it, and heaven knows what price they may come up with. We had always put back into the company any profit we made. We took very low salaries right from the start, and years later, were still making less than some of our editors and salesmen, because we preferred to plow all the money back into the business to keep it growing.

At any rate, Donald and I knew that the real value of the company had increased each year, but nobody knew by how much. If its value was too high, how could the survivor afford to buy the other half, and how could the widow of the one who died raise enough cash to pay the estate tax? What if the government put a value on it of five times what it should be? Since we didn't know ourselves, we had a contract drawn up whereby the survivor would be able to buy the other one's half for five hundred thousand dollars, which would prevent, we hoped, the other partner's having to sell—a problem that plagues quite a lot of partnerships.

We also hoped that the price we had set would influence the government in determining what the value of the business was. Then, in 1957, we were having lunch one day with some members of a publishing house that was expanding. They didn't think too much of their own trade department, and they asked if we would be interested in discussing a possible merger. Donald and I were absolutely astounded by this, since nothing like it had ever entered our heads, but we investigated just to see what they thought our business was worth. It never got past that initial stage, but the negotiation was pleasant, and it turned out that they valued our business at something in the neighborhood of two million dollars. We had only one or two meetings, but they put ideas into our heads.

The next people who approached us were Holt, Rinehart. Although we never got down to discussing a definite figure, they said, "Tell us what you want. We'll give it to you." The plan was to buy Random House and have us come in and run their trade department (trade books are those sold in regular bookstores) which was not nearly as good as their textbook division.

Then came the splurge when every business under the sun began getting out stock issues. Here again is an example of how everything in my life seems to have been tied together, because Charles Allen—one of the boys who worked next door to me in the cashier's cage when I worked down in Wall Street—had by 1957 become one of the most successful men in the Street, head of the huge banking institution Allen & Company. He had real guts, and he still has; he invested in projects that the older banking houses thought were too speculative, and in a number of them, like Syntex, he made millions of dollars.

I consulted my old friend Charlie one day, and he said, "Sure. We'll get out a stock issue for you." Suddenly Random House embarked on its

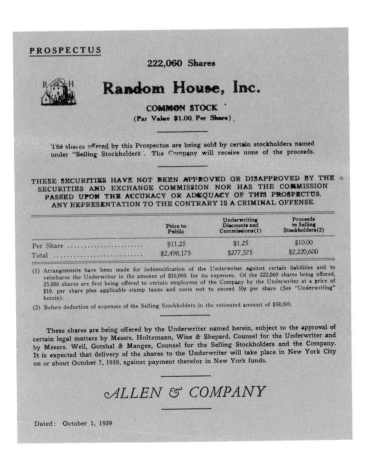

PROSPECTUS

222,060 Shares

Random House, Inc.

COMMON STOCK
(Par Value $1.00 Per Share)

The shares offered by this Prospectus are being sold by certain stockholders named under "Selling Stockholders". The Company will receive none of the proceeds.

THESE SECURITIES HAVE NOT BEEN APPROVED OR DISAPPROVED BY THE SECURITIES AND EXCHANGE COMMISSION NOR HAS THE COMMISSION PASSED UPON THE ACCURACY OR ADEQUACY OF THIS PROSPECTUS. ANY REPRESENTATION TO THE CONTRARY IS A CRIMINAL OFFENSE.

	Price to Public	Underwriting Discounts and Commissions(1)	Proceeds to Selling Stockholders(2)
Per Share	$11.25	$1.25	$10.00
Total	$2,498,175	$277,575	$2,220,600

(1) Arrangements have been made for indemnification of the Underwriter against certain liabilities and to reimburse the Underwriter in the amount of $10,000. for its expenses. Of the 222,060 shares being offered, 25,000 shares are first being offered to certain employees of the Company by the Underwriter at a price of $10. per share plus applicable stamp taxes and costs not to exceed 50¢ per share (See "Underwriting" herein).

(2) Before deduction of expenses of the Selling Stockholders in the estimated amount of $58,000.

These shares are being offered by the Underwriter named herein, subject to the approval of certain legal matters by Messrs. Holtzmann, Wise & Shepard, Counsel for the Underwriter and by Messrs. Weil, Gotshal & Manges, Counsel for the Selling Stockholders and the Company. It is expected that delivery of the shares to the Underwriter will take place in New York City on or about October 7, 1959, against payment therefor in New York funds.

ALLEN & COMPANY

Dated: October 1, 1959

financial career and expansion. This marked a big change, since the minute you go public, outsiders own some of your stock and you've got to make periodic reports to them. You owe your investors dividends and profits. Instead of working for yourself and doing what you damn please, willing to risk a loss on something you want to do, if you're any kind of honest man, you feel a real responsibility to your stockholders. It was a very important decision.

On October 2, 1959, Allen & Company sold thirty percent of our stock to the public, leaving us, of course, still in control of the business. I nearly fainted when I saw the check that I got—over a million dollars. Donald and I had always said that by going into the publishing business we had deliberately passed up real wealth for the joy of doing what we wanted, and suddenly we were rich in spite of ourselves!

Random House stock came out at $11.25 a share and began going up right away. It was $14 the next day. There was a big demand—for two reasons. For one thing, two of our books—James A. Michener's *Hawaii* in fiction; Moss Hart's *Act One* in nonfiction—rapidly went to the top of the best-seller lists and stayed there, and six or seven other Random House books were on the *Times* best-seller list for months on end in that fabulous year.

Furthermore, this was just the beginning of the wild speculation phase in all publishing stocks, and we issued ours just about the time it was starting. From then on, we were publishing with one eye and watching our stock with the other. Then several other firms went public, and suddenly the prices of all these unseasoned stocks began to escalate. It was frightening because they went up without rhyme or reason. In one week, for instance, Random House stock went up by more than the price at which we had issued it, and got up to $45 a share—the stock that had come out at $11.25. But it was also exhilarating, and within six months after our going public, we embarked on another adventure and achieved something of which I had always dreamed: a merger with Alfred A. Knopf.

When Atheneum Publishers was formed by Alfred A. (Pat) Knopf, Jr., Hiram Haydn and Simon Michael Bessie, the event turned out to be more important to Random House than was apparent at the time. Pat had been working at Knopf, and his departure left Alfred very much up in the air. Where was the business he had founded and developed going to end up? One day in the spring of 1960, when we were having lunch at the Stork Club, I suggested to Alfred that perhaps the time had come when Random House and Knopf, which had a great deal in common, might consider merging. I said, "Business details have always been a bore to you, anyway. Look at it this way. You'll keep absolute control of your company, and all the business worries will be over." To my astonishment, Alfred said he was interested. I said, "Donald and I will talk about it, and we'll come to you with some kind of proposition." So I went back to the office, wildly excited. Of all the publishing houses in the world, Knopf was the one I had always admired the most.

Donald and I worked out what we thought was a very fair proposal, involving an exchange of stock. An advantage of having stock is that a purchase can be made without using cash. When somebody sells a company for cash, he has to pay taxes immediately, but if he can exchange stock, the tax liability is postponed. So it's good to have negotiable stock to buy with, and it's even better for the seller. Ours was a generous, fair offer, but we were afraid Alfred might not think so.

I went with Donald to the Knopfs' office and proposed the terms to Alfred and Blanche. Alfred said, "Do you and Donald think that's a fair offer?" I said, "If we didn't, we wouldn't be making it." He said, "If you think it's fair, I'll take it." It was just like that! We shook hands.

The Knopfs got a large block of Random House stock, which they were free to sell when they wished. It made them rich overnight. Also, because we were by that time a public company, it was advisable for Alfred, Blanche and every key person at Knopf to have a contract that would spell out the terms of their employment in the new combination. We made certain that all of them would participate in the deal. They all got their share. We assured Alfred that we would have absolutely nothing to do with Knopf's editorial policy—a promise which we have scrupulously lived up to for two reasons. One, I'm a man of my word; and two, I'm scared to death of Alfred. If he starts roaring at me, I run!

Knopf, Random House in Publishing Merger

Bennett A. Cerf

Random House emblem

Deal Made on Handshake Over Luncheon —Cerf's Company to Buy Stock, but Knopf Will Stay on Job

By GAY TALESE

Alfred A. Knopf, for forty years a giant in American publishing whom H. L. Mencken called "the perfect publisher," will sell Alfred A. Knopf, Inc., to Random House, Inc., this week.

The move, unexpected in the publishing world, was confirmed yesterday by both Mr. Knopf and Random House's president, Bennett A. Cerf.

Random House will control all Knopf stock, but Mr. Knopf, and his wife, Blanche, with whom he founded the concern in 1915, will continue to run it under the Knopf name. They will retain their regular editors, writers and their long devotion to craftsmanship in printing and design.

The Knopfs will be paid in both Random House stock and cash, but the amounts will not be announced until later this week. Mr. and Mrs. Knopf will also serve on the Random House board of directors, but the two concerns will combine

their bookkeeping, shipping and selling activities.

The decision, which was decided over a luncheon last week, will unite two of the nation's most celebrated publishers of quality writing.

What prompted the decision is debatable, but the merger follows a trend in the publishing field, as well as outside of it. Book publishers, forced to economize, are joining forces.

Also, Mr. Knopf, now 68 years old, was said to be deeply disappointed when his only son, Alfred Jr., quit the family concern last year. He started his own company, Athenaeum, with two other editors, Simon Michael Bessie, formerly of Harper Brothers, and Hiram Haydn, formerly of Random House.

It was a "gentleman's agreement," a mere handshake, that completed the deal this week between the two publishing houses, Mr. Cerf said.

Present at the luncheon, in

Continued on Page 76, Column 6

Alfred A. Knopf

Knopf emblem

From front page of The New York Times, *April 17, 1960*

Celebrating merger at lunch: Alfred Knopf, Bennett, Blanche Knopf, Donald

I had always worshipped Alfred, of course, but I had also been very fond of Blanche. Before I married Phyllis, sometimes Blanche and I would read together. Alfred would go up to his place in Purchase, and since she disliked the country in the winter as much as I did, she would stay in her New York apartment and we'd often have dinner together. Then we'd read our manuscripts and stop every once in a while to have a drink and argue, and on one memorable occasion I was reading a manuscript and grumbling that it was boring me to death. About six months later—she had a memory like an elephant—Blanche was on the phone, innocence itself: "Dear Bennett, that book the Book-of-the-Month Club just picked—wasn't that the one you were reading and complaining about over at my house?" I said, "You know damn well it was, and I knew I'd hear from you about it." She giggled happily. It was that kind of a relationship. We were jealous, but also proud, of each other.

Blanche was in some ways the most gullible woman in the world, and I loved to kid her. I once told her that we were cutting our discount at Brentano's. I said, "They need our books. We're going to cut their discount to thirty percent, because they have to buy them anyway." Very shortly thereafter, Alfred was on the phone to me and said, "If you don't stop telling my wife these damned stories ... I'm the one who suffers." Of course I knew she would run back to Alfred with the story. It was obviously ridiculous, but Blanche took it all seriously. She was such fun to fight with.

When Blanche began to lose her health, she fought with all the strength she had. She was an amazing woman—very courageous, very gallant. She died in 1967, and Alfred later married Helen Hedrick, a very lovely woman who has been a godsend to him. Alfred comes to the office only one or two days a week, but he's still extremely interested in educational and historical books—his history list is the best in the country—and in books from and about South America, which he has published religiously, though very few of them ever showed a profit. Some of his excellent music books lose money, but they're all distinguished publishing.

The books that Alfred is most ashamed of are the ones that have made him the most money! At one time he had on his list both Irving Wallace and Harold Robbins, two of the great sellers today. He says in all sincerity, "Two of the things that I'm happiest about is that I'm rid of those two hacks. The stuff they're writing now I wouldn't publish." He means it, too, but despite his artistic leanings, Alfred has published some of the best-selling books of our time. *The Prophet,* by Kahlil Gibran, sells between a hundred and a hundred and fifty thousand copies every year. When someone mentions *The Prophet,* Alfred merely grumbles. *This Is My Beloved,* a book of poetry by Walter Benton, sells year after year—though Alfred

deplores it. He published long ago a book called *Sorrell and Son* by War-
wick Deeping, which he screams about, though it was a big success. He
published *The Snow Goose* by Paul Gallico and *The Human Body* by Logan
Clendening and, more recently, *Markings* by Dag Hammarskjöld. Besides
that, his list of important authors, many of whose books he has kept
continuously in print, would stagger anybody—Willa Cather, Thomas
Mann, Thomas Beer, Joseph Hergesheimer, John Hersey, John Updike,
Albert Camus, Jean-Paul Sartre, William Humphrey, Julia Child. The
minute the Random House sales department got hold of the Knopf back
list, we doubled their business in a single year.

The year after our merger with Knopf, we acquired Pantheon, which
had been started in 1942 by Kurt Wolff and his wife, Helen. Jacques
Schiffrin joined them the following year. Kurt Wolff, who had been a big
publisher in Berlin, had fled from the Nazis and come over here. His sales
manager, Kyrill Schabert, whose father was the head of the German department at Yale, soon became a partner.

They began building the Pantheon list, which at first was distin-
guished though not lucrative, but in the years just before the merger,
Pantheon had burst forth with such best sellers as *Dr. Zhivago* by Boris
Pasternak, *Gift from the Sea* by Anne Morrow Lindbergh, *Born Free* by Joy
Adamson, *The Leopard* by Giuseppe di Lampedusa, *The King Must Die* by
Mary Renault.

Success often breeds dissension. While it was a struggling little firm
and there was no money to fight over, peace reigned, but when Pantheon
suddenly found itself with some solid best sellers, the arguing began. Who
was going to get what? Who was in charge of what? Schabert and Wolff
began picking on each other. Wolff had been backed by the Rosenwalds,
whose fortune came from Sears, Roebuck, and their business representatives
became annoyed with all the dissension. They knew nothing about the
publishing business, so they decided to sell their stock. It was now worth
infinitely more than what they had paid for it. They had bought into
Pantheon only to help Kurt Wolff get started, and suddenly their stock was
worth a lot of money.

By June, 1961, certain members of the Rosenwald family had agreed
to take over Kurt Wolff's interest after he went to Switzerland in a huff.
Eventually Wolff made a deal with Harcourt, which still has a division
called Kurt and Helen Wolff Books. When he died, his widow, a very
brilliant woman, carried on. A number of important Pantheon authors left
to go with the Wolffs.

We bought Pantheon, and Schabert came along with Paula Van
Doren, Carl and Irita Van Doren's niece, and André Schiffrin, son of
Wolff's early partner. We set them up and they became part of Random

House, though remaining, as in the case of Knopf, entirely independent in their editorial decisions. But Schabert found it extremely difficult to keep authors who were dedicated to Kurt Wolff, and the business started wavering. One big author Schabert managed to keep was Mary Renault, who has had two Book-of-the-Month Club choices since we took over the business.

We selected the ideal man to run it, André Schiffrin. André had important connections abroad, and excellent judgment. Pantheon has been nursed by us to do fine books. We didn't expect them to produce best sellers, although every once in a while they have come across a big winner. They've done very well.

To show how lucky I am. It looked for some time as though we paid too high a price for Pantheon, but then *Dr. Zhivago* was made by MGM into one of the three or four most successful motion pictures in history, almost as big as *Quo Vadis?* and *Gone With the Wind* and *The Sound of Music*. The sales of The Modern Library Giant edition and the paperback of *Dr. Zhivago* have earned us over half of what we paid for the entire business.

From the moment that Random House stock was first sold to the public, my burning ambition was to be listed on the New York Stock Exchange. I wanted the firm that I had started, Random House, to be on that list with U.S. Steel and Du Pont. In order to qualify, we had to get more stock into the hands of the general public. So we had a stock split and gave four shares for three, reducing the cost of our original issue from $11.25 to about $8.50 a share. When we went on the Exchange on September 20, 1961, our stock opened the first day at 32¼. That was the equivalent of about 40 for the original shares because of the four-for-three split.

Later that fall came the dawn. There was a terrible break in the market. Our stock, along with every other publisher's stock and most other new stocks that had gone flying up, went flying down. Random House shares went all the way down to about $9 a share—in other words, down to just above what we had issued it at. That was fine at the time we brought it out; but after it had gone up so much, to see it back to 9 did fearful things

On floor of New York Stock Exchange (from left): Tony Wimpfheimer, Lewis Miller, Albert Erskine, Bennett, Keith Funston (president of the Exchange), Alfred Knopf, Horace Manges, Donald, Robert Haas

In front of Random House trading post: Alfred Knopf, Bennett and Donald

to my ego. I began to be afraid to go out at night. I'd think people were saying, "There's that incompetent Cerf, whose stock has gone to hell."

By 1965 the stock began creeping up and up and up and got back to about 17. It was then that our business was expanding to a point where big firms that were beginning to spread their wings became interested in us. Big computer houses and business-machine companies were going into education with their teaching machines and saw the potential value of having a publishing company in their fold—especially one with a list like ours, to say nothing of our Modern Library and Vintage Books and our part ownership in the highly successful Bantam paperbacks—so approaches began to be made by huge companies. Everybody was listening, and so were we.

Several people who approached us, we didn't even consider, but we discussed with Time-Life a possible merger which had a lot of things at that time to recommend it. In one way it looked like a glorious combination, since Time-Life had built up a superb mail-order department and we had, I think, the best juvenile list in the world and a potent back list. We had a couple of conversations and got along beautifully. The mail-order business we could have done together was fantastic. But we soon discovered that the government wouldn't stand for the merger. Our lawyers and the Time-Life lawyers sounded out the Department of Justice. They said, "Absolutely nothing doing," and our discussions ended.

When RCA showed an interest, we certainly responded, because it is one of the great corporations of the country. The two big bankers for RCA are Lazard Frères and Lehman Brothers. We have friends at both firms, and we heard from them that RCA was beginning to think they'd like to own a publishing business and were investigating various houses. Without our knowing it, they were going over our published figures very carefully and questioning people—the way big companies do. They were impressed with us, as well they should have been.

So we started talking. I already knew General David Sarnoff—a remarkable man. After very little talk, they made us an offer, which we refused out of hand. Their first offer was half a share of RCA for each share of Random House, and that wasn't enough for us, I thought. So after some more dickering—this was late in December, 1965—they raised the offer to three-fifths of a share of RCA for one of Random House, which was a considerable increase. It was sixty percent instead of fifty percent. Several of the people at Random House were for taking this, but I had made up my mind that we were going to get the equivalent of forty million dollars for our business—quite a jump from our old private plan for getting half of it for five hundred thousand! How quickly you change your sights. To give us what I wanted, at what RCA was selling for then, it meant sixty-two one-hundredths of a share instead of sixty one-hundredths—a difference of two one-hundredths of a share. That may sound like nothing, but it amounted to over a million dollars in all.

The bankers were very angry with me, and said I was destroying the deal. I was in the glorious position of not giving a damn whether they bought us or not. We didn't need them. I said, "If they want this deal, they're going to give us exactly what we want or—no soap!"

So they arranged a Sunday meeting between the General and me at his house on 71st Street, only a few blocks from my own home. It was a cold Sunday afternoon in December, and there was a championship football game on TV that day: the Colts and the Packers were playing. I was indignant that I had to leave for this all-important meeting when I was watching this game, which, incidentally, was on CBS, not NBC. I found the General waiting for me. Mrs. Sarnoff, who is a wonderful woman, was watching some unimportant American Football League game because it was on NBC. I said, "You're watching the wrong game." She said, "I don't watch CBS." She speaks with a great French accent. She added, "The only thing I watch on CBS is *What's My Line?*" So she was my ally all the way through.

After the General greeted me he said, "You're being very stubborn and stupid, demanding this extra two one-hundredths, which is just some whim of yours. I'm not going back to my directors. I've been back twice on account of you to say that you weren't satisfied. You are either going to take sixty one-hundredths or the deal is off." I said, "Fine with me, General. Let's watch the end of the game. We'll still be able to catch the last quarter." He said, "You mean you won't make the deal?" I said, "Of course not. I told you that I want sixty-two one-hundredths. Let's forget the whole thing." He said, "You know, we're very close to buying another business." I knew they were considering the American Book Company, so I said, "Well, General, if you would rather buy the American Book Company than Random House because of two one-hundredths of a share, good luck to you, and let's stay friends."

General Sarnoff angrily told me, "You may not realize it, Bennett, but you're dealing with a very arrogant and egotistical man." I said, "General, I'm just as arrogant and egotistical as you are. Let's watch the game. There's no sense going on with this." So grumpily he called in Bobby, his son, and one of the bankers. They were waiting in the wings and had champagne on ice, all ready for the conclusion of the deal.

The General was quite miffed. He said, "We had better talk some more about this tomorrow." I said, "That's impossible because tomorrow my wife and I are leaving for the Coast to spend the holidays with Frank Sinatra. We're going to collect his girl"—that was Mia Farrow, whom we had not yet met—"and we're going to fly out in his private jet. I wouldn't miss that for the world." The General said, "You mean to say that with this deal hanging fire, you're going to go off on vacation?" I said, "You're right, I am. I'll be away eleven days." He said, "When you come back my offer may be withdrawn." I said, "I've already turned down your offer. My proposition stands. When I come back I will still make the deal at sixty-two one-hundredths. You don't have to renew any offer at all. You have no obligation."

So I went home. I felt that I held all the aces. I knew that they wanted us very badly. I knew that two one-hundredths was not going to keep RCA from closing the deal. It meant little to them, but it meant a great deal to us. Donald was a little annoyed at me. He was all set for the sale by this time and so were our top editors. I knew we'd get exactly what we had demanded when one of the Lehman Brothers bankers called me up from White Sulphur Springs to tell me how unreasonable I was being. He had been kept aware of every step in the negotiations. They *wanted* us!

The next day we flew out to Palm Springs with Mia and stayed for ten days. The minute I came back our negotiating was resumed, and the General, rather huffily, said, "Well, we're not going to argue with you over that two one-hundredths of a share." So the deal was made, including one very important specification in the contract, spelled out clearly, that we kept absolute control of our business and that RCA had no right at all to interfere with what we published. We received sixty-two one-hundredths of a share of RCA for each share of Random House, which brought the value of Random House to just what I had dreamed it should be.

Since Blanche Knopf died right after the merger, and Alfred was becoming less and less active in the business, it was evident that we needed to plan the future of Knopf. The good editors who had helped add to the great Knopf list in recent years were still there but no longer young—Angus Cameron, Harold Strauss, Herbert Weinstock and Bill Koshland, who was now president. But there was a gap: the succession that every publisher needs was not there. Then came our miracle. We heard about the disaffection of three people at Simon and Schuster—Robert Gottlieb, Anthony Schulte and Nina Bourne—who were almost a publishing business in themselves. Nina had been the advertising manager at Simon and Schuster for twenty-eight years and is just about the best in the business.

For Knopf, these three were manna from heaven. A lot of other companies were after them, but we made an offer that was so attractive they couldn't turn it down. They came to Knopf on March 1, 1968, to be for a while a sort of separate unit. Bob Gottlieb is a very strong, attractive publisher and knows his business; Tony Schulte is a fine administrator; and there's nobody like Nina in the advertising business. To have gotten even one of them would have been a coup, but to have all three was a miracle. I was very happy because this assured the Knopf succession.

No such gap had developed in Random House itself, though a number of our former editors were no longer with us. Three that I've mentioned were still on hand—Albert Erskine, Robert Loomis and Jason Epstein—and we had added others as we needed them.

Joe Fox, who is meticulous in his work with authors, came to us from Harper. Besides taking care of Truman Capote's books, he has worked with Peter Matthiessen, Philip Roth, Renata Adler, Stanley Elkin, David Halberstam, Alison Lurie, Mavis Gallant and many others. Lee Wright, among her other accomplishments, was already an outstanding mystery editor when she moved to us from Simon and Schuster in 1958, bringing with her such top writers as Ellery Queen, Stanley Ellin, Alfred Hitchcock, Mildred Davis and Harold Masur. She is Ira Levin's editor and brought us *Rosemary's Baby*, a huge success in 1967 as a novel and then as a stunning movie.

The man who heads the editorial department is James Silberman, who joined us in 1963. As editor in chief, Jim has the complicated job of supervising the activities of the other editors and making budget decisions connected with the publication of every book on our adult trade list, but apart from all that, he has brought us some of our most important books in recent years: Adam Smith (*The Money Game,* 1968), Elie Wiesel (*Beggar in Jerusalem,* 1969), Alvin Toffler (*Future Shock,* 1970). All three of these were outstanding best sellers by authors who, I am happy to say, continue to add to the strength of our list. In 1971 Jim introduced a newcomer, E. L. Doctorow, whose novel *The Book of Daniel* was a great critical success. The sale was small, but Doctorow shows great promise.

I think we have the best editorial board in the United States of America today. We've got a wonderful list and wonderful salesmen to sell it. Lew Miller, who built our great sales department, is still on hand, though he and other veterans like Irving Mendelson, James Russell and Howard Treeger are approaching retirement; but we have bright younger men—Robert Bernstein, Richard Krinsley and Richard Liebermann—to take over when the time comes. The back list of Random House, Knopf and Pantheon put together is so good that I think if we closed up the whole business for the next twenty years or so, we might make more money than we're making now, because our back list is like reaching down and picking up gold from the sidewalk. There's nothing like it.

Lewis Miller, Donald, Robert Bernstein, Bennett

Just before we sold to RCA, I had decided it was time for me to step down from the presidency. I was getting older; I was sixty-seven and Donald was sixty-three. My sons wouldn't be ready for a long time—Chris was only twenty-three and Jon was eighteen. Our publishing house was getting very big, and we had to do something about the management succession. I believe you should pick your succession when you're still around and active. Many businesses go to pot because the owners think they're going to go on forever, and when they vanish from the scene, there's nobody ready to take over. Until they train or find somebody, they're in trouble.

I have always likened a business to a baseball team, using the New York Yankees as an example. The reason that team stayed champions year after year was that smart people there were building up the succession. While the championship team was playing magnificent ball on the field, replacements for the active players were already being picked, so that when the pitching staff declined, and Reynolds and Raschi and Lopat, the star pitchers of the Yanks, all seemed to lose their stuff at the same time, five new pitchers were ready—Ford and several others—to step right in.

We had somebody ready, the right man to step in. Robert Bernstein, who had come to us some years back from Simon and Schuster as sales manager, had proved he had everything he needed to be responsible for our combined operations. So we made Bob president and I continued as chairman of the board. Then, in 1970, I stepped down as chairman and Donald took over the post, and both Phyllis and our son Christopher resigned as Random House editors—Christopher to accept a key position with the triumphant television show *Sesame Street*, and Phyllis to work on book projects on a free-lance basis.

Nothing really changed at Random House for a while. I was still there and Donald was still there; we could give advice, take care of our big authors and keep things rolling.

Bob Bernstein is just as strong as I am, and gradually I found him taking over more and more, making decisions without consulting me. In a way, I was thankful for it. I could now laugh at all of the nuisance and all of the problems—and they were manifold—and say to Bob, "Well, you wanted to be president. Solve them," and go off on a vacation. That's the way it should be. But I've had to watch myself; every once in a while I realize I am actually resenting the fact that he is doing not only what he has every right to do, but what I *want* him to do.

Giving things up is very hard, especially while you still have all your faculties. When you get really old and start breaking down, you haven't got the energy any more, but I still have the energy I had as a boy. I don't like getting old, but growing old happens to everybody and you've got to be philosophical about it. I don't fear death. I don't believe in organized religion; I believe in being good. If there is a God, He'll approve of your being a decent fellow. You don't have to go through the formalities, which to me have always been artificial.

I've had a very happy life. I've been as lucky as can be—lucky to have Donald as my partner and Phyllis as my wife, and to have two sons of

Christopher, Bennett, Phyllis, Jonathan

whom I am very proud. My health has been fantastic. The only time I was ever in the hospital in my life was when I had a cataract operation in the summer of 1967. I was in for one week, and the doctor told me when I left that they were going to give me a diploma for being the worst patient in the history of St. Luke's Hospital. I've got to be up and doing!

I can't say this too often—that a little humor can make life worth living. That has always been my credo. Somebody once asked me, "What would you like your epitaph to be?" I've always said that I'd like it to be: "He left people a little happier than they were when he came into the room."

Shortly after Bennett's death, the *Saturday Review*, for which for fifteen years he had written the column "Trade Winds," printed an obituary which closed with these suitable words:

> He set out to be a book publisher, and he became one of the best. He gave full measure to his profession. Everyone connected with the world of books is in his debt.

INDEX